MY BETTER HALF

BY

RALPH HOMER

NEW MILLENNIUM
292 Kennington Road, London SE11 4LD

Copyright © 1999 Ralph Homer

All rights reserved. No part of this publication may be reproduced in any form, except for the purposes of review, without prior written permission from the copyright owner.

British Library Cataloguing in Publication Data.
A catalogue record for this book is available from the British Library.

Printed and bound by Watkiss Studios Ltd.
Biggleswade, Beds.
Issued by New Millennium*
ISBN 1 85845 269 4
*An imprint of The Professional Authors' & Publishers' Association

ACKNOWLEDGEMENTS

Without Mary Lomax suggesting that I put my Army experiences into some form of sequence that my family and friends could read, this book would not have been written. So I am grateful to her for that initial spark and my gratitude extends to all the kind souls who have given me encouragement along the way. The memory had faded in certain areas and I appreciate the jogging of it by Ron Ellis, Reg Abbott, Brother Vincent McCardle, S.J., my sister Betty and Bernard Wilkinson. To Bernard I must also add my thanks for typing the whole thing out.

DEDICATION

This book is dedicated to Celia and Andrew,
my loving children, and the memory of their
wonderful mum, Josie. Not forgetting
Baby Peter, who left us just before
qualifying for a second candle
on his birthday cake.

Contents

Foreword XI

Chapter One The Meeting 1

Chapter Two The Parting 17

Chapter Three The Journey 29

Chapter Four The Camp 43

Chapter Five The Move 77

Chapter Six The Posting 97

Chapter Seven The Discharge 169

Chapter Eight The Wedding 197

LIST OF ILLUSTRATIONS

Author at Monfalcone	28
Camp layout at Duino, Summer 1946	42
Latrines, various	51
Sick parade at Duino	52
First-aid post at Paese (Washing line not included)	76
With MT Wallah patient	82
With Kempie	82
Bice and Enrico (When I went to collect my washing)	96
O2E Battaglia Terme	99
'Out' drive at O2E (It's no different to the 'In' drive)	100
02E Dining room	101
Officers records department 02E (On the flat roof)	102
Aerial view of Lake Garda	137
Lake Garda	137
Gottfried and truck	138
Alfredo (They don't come any cuter!)	153
Aldina, Elisa and Anna Bar staff at Battaglia Terme	157
Wilf Sutton at 02E If only he could drive	158
Wilf Sutton and Author "It's a hold up"	158
On the Presbytery steps at Paese	167
In the Vendramin's garden saying goodbye to Bice and Enrico	168
Josie's Mum	196

George, my best man	229
Josie's dad and mum	230
Dad, Josie, Mum and author	231
Betty, Author, Josie, George and Margaret (Tom and Marie in the background)	235

Foreword

As a child and a youth I often heard my father or some other married man introduce his wife to someone with the phrase 'meet my better half'.

My little story is how I met my better half, Josie, and paid courtship to her mainly by steadfast use of the postal services.

I met Josie just about half way through my army service and I consider that the 'better half' of my life as a soldier was spent from the time that I met her until my discharge, not just because of my own 'raison d'être' but because I met with such a variety of incidents as you will see from my musings.

When my grandchildren ask me "What did you do during the war, Grandpa?" I can say without hesitation "The most important thing I did was meet your Grandma".

Chapter One
The Meeting

Throughout life we all constantly make decisions. The outcome of these decisions can be of no consequence or of great consequence. The initial decision does not, of itself, have to be of any great importance to have an incalculable result. Imagine a child being offered a chocolate from a box with a variety of fillings. He chooses the Turkish Delight upon which his sibling says that that was the very one that she was going to choose and why didn't he take the Coffee one, his favourite? Mum and Dad are drawn into the squabble that ensues and their unwitting remarks result in one child being admonished, who instantly accuses the other of being Mummy's Darling. Most children forget their differences before the sun goes down but with a few there is a tendency to revitalise enmities (with frequent cries of 'Mummy's Darling' for instance) and those feelings can run through the whole of their lives; and it all started with choosing a chocolate.

Choosing a new car, of course, is a big decision. Should it be a Ford or a Nissan? It depends on the image you wish to promote; but then again decisions are necessary. Which has the better layout of instruments? Which is the sharper away from the traffic lights? Which is the more economic? Here we have a case of one decision leading to many others. Who would have thought that the decision of one man to fire an assassin's bullet in Austria in 1914 would lead to the deaths of hundreds of thousands by the bullet in the Somme, Ypres and other French battlefields over the following four years?

I will tell you of one seemingly trivial decision that altered my whole life but before I do I will explain the surrounding circumstances.

It was Spring 1946. I had been posted to 114MCD (Military Convalescent Depot) following a few months in the Derwen Cripples Training College at Gobowen in Shropshire which was serving as a wartime emergency hospital.

The 114MCD was sited at Saighton Camp some two and a half miles south east of Chester in pleasant flat countryside and was a typical wartime barracks comprised of mainly spider huts in creosoted timber. It had, naturally, the obligatory square and a couple of drill sheds plus NAAFI and a number of various offices all built in timber. A dozen or so brick houses were on the Northern side of the camp and of these some were occupied by Officers and some used as married quarters. There didn't seem to be many Officers. Perhaps they don't get wounded or injured as frequently as Other Ranks. The ratio of Sergeant Majors to O.R's seemed a little excessive and I couldn't help but wonder if 'friendly fire' was in some way responsible for this. One of those Sergeant Majors was, I remember, a fellow named Merrick who had been goal keeper for Aston Villa prior to the onset of the war. He had hands like hams and could pick up a leather football in each hand.

To those readers not familiar with the phrase 'spider huts', I must explain that in a plan view of such a structure there was a close resemblance to a spider. The body of the spider is a communal block housing rows of wash basins, toilets, bathrooms and showers. Six legs radiate from the body and are furnished with beds, each leg having a small end room for the use of the NCO in charge of the room or billet. The beds at Saighton Camp were of the 'bunk' variety and were rather tall creating difficulties for some of the smaller chaps who had suffered leg injuries and were still a little weak after weeks or months in hospital. The lockers were of the open variety and were situated between each pair of bunk beds. They resemble the lockers seen in hospitals today except that they had no doors and were in timber bearing many cigarette burns and more injuries than many of their users. There were a few electric light bulbs, each having a Chinese 'coolie' hat shade. They were controlled from a switch within the NCO's room. So you see the furnishings were very basic and consequently so easy to keep clean and tidy. Whereas in basic training I had had to scrub (with a wire brush) my 'bed space' each morning before breakfast, here a quick brush over with a soft broom was quite acceptable.

Discipline was, as you can easily imagine with such a transient population, almost non-existent. There were no kit inspections, no room inspections and definitely no arms inspections as the only rifles around were the ones in the guard room adjacent to the main gate. We had all come from one hospital or another so we were 'unarmed'. Talking of which - it is said that once in the forces one never forgets one's service number! If any one reading this comes across a Lee-Enfield 303 bearing the number BF10104 then give it a 'pull through' for me!

Most of our days consisted of sessions of physical training and 'square bashing' in order to get us fit enough to return to our units, but, of course, there were one or two exceptions to this. One such exception was when a sergeant was instructed to take a party of us on a five mile 'run and walk'. This I did not relish, as I had not long before dispensed with my walking stick and wore an appliance in my boot to eliminate some of the pain I suffered when walking. My fears were unfounded because the sergeant was obviously a man of good sense - the typical backbone of the British Army- for when we had left the camp behind us he looked for a suitable field in which we could recline, smoking and swapping yarns, for the next hour. To give you some idea of the extent of our run I would point out that we didn't reach the village of Saighton which lies less than a mile south of the camp. The sergeant, bless him, instructed us to straggle back into camp and to complain loudly and bitterly about the treatment that was supposedly making us into fitter human beings.

On another occasion we had a most interesting day 'market gardening by numbers'. The war in Europe was over but rationing was still very much the order of the day. So many of our merchant ships lay at the bottom of the oceans that supplies from abroad were less than what we had pre-war deemed to be routine, so home production of all things possible was still promoted throughout the land. Many people turned their front gardens over from flowers to vegetable growing. Someone at Saighton Camp had the idea that the dormant space between the huts should be put to good use and so the work commenced in the style that only the British Army commands. Whether or not the Army has a manual on crop growing I do not know(it seems to have a manual on most things) but the ground seemed to be dug over to one and a half spades in depth in a very short space of time. Of course there were about twenty spades each with a digger available.

Then came the interesting bit (to me at least). A dozen or so of us were issued with a forged device the likes of which I had not seen before and, for that matter, I have not seen since. I will attempt to describe it although I would find it easier to sketch it. Imagine a pair of blacksmith's tongs, but very much larger. The reins, or handles, were some three quarters of an inch (or twenty millimetres today) in diameter and about two feet (sixty centimetres) long.; at the point at which they hinged the forging spread out, the sides and back face forming half of a box when the handles were spread wide apart. The nose portion of the device was wedge shaped forming, when the handles were once again spread apart, a shape like the bows of a ship some three inches (seven or eight centimetres) in length. A kind of stirrup was forged on one of the handles giving the opportunity to press the functional end of the gadget into the soil with, as you will have guessed, a seed potato in the box or pocket. The only other equipment necessary for the operation was a very long piece of string with an NCO at each end. The string was drawn taut and the row of gadget wielding soldiers plunged their agricultural tools into the ground at preordained intervals along the string. A second row of soldiers held the seed potatoes and they on the command (wait for it!) placed the potato in the box.. The next command 'squeeze' was the order to close the tongs which, for the want of a better word, caused the potato to be ejected into the space between the two wedge shaped extremities. The planter was then withdrawn leaving the potato to raise its family whilst the rows of soldiers repeated the process at each new positioning of the string. Supernumeraries were called upon to apply their boots to the loose soil above each potato without waiting for any word of command (such freedom!) Such paroxysms of laughter ensued from this exercise that I feel the whole of the camp wished to start gardening. Anyone who has had the smallest experience of arms drill will know the 'two, three' pause between movements, so just imagine the foregoing practice in command jargon. 'Position', two, three 'thrust', two, three, 'Place spud', two, three, 'Squeeze', two, three, 'Withdraw'. Then imagine some poor fellow on 'Thrust' fouls a rock or piece of builders rubble that the 'diggers' had failed to remove whilst everybody falls about laughing at his bad luck. As we were from all walks of Army life I wonder that the in depth planning that is the Army's forte didn't devise this exercise like a military operation with the Ordnance Corp detailing the measurements between rows, the REME handling the mechanical devices, the Service Corp inserting the spuds, the Catering Corp inspecting the spuds before planting and, of course, the PBI putting their boots all over the site to finish things off.

Occupying the next bed to mine was a guardsman Chadwick of the Coldstreams. He was a 'regular' and some ten years my senior. I must say here that the majority of 'patients' were of my age group - late teens and early twenties and ninety five percent were, like myself, conscripted.

Chadwick was a typical army wallah, a swashbuckling devil may care type with a touch of the Errol Flynn about him. He had twice been made up to sergeant and twice brought down to the ranks for fighting with people not classified as the enemy. It was entertaining to listen to his tales of his exploits in the North African and Italian campaigns. He was the recipient of three gongs (medals) for bravery, valour, whatever and he said that his proudest moment was when King George VI said to him, 'What, you again, Chadwick?'

The account of how he earned his third gong is worthy of putting on record so I will tell you without the usual embellishments you might expect in an old squaddies' story.

Early in the Italian campaign, long before our troops had engaged in the battle for Monte Casino, Chadwick had been taken prisoner by the Germans. He was, along with many others, put aboard a train for an unknown destination; a P.O.W. camp for sure but would it be Germany, Poland or elsewhere? All that Chadwick knew was that they were travelling north, not in cattle trucks as was often the case, but in coaches with compartments and corridors. Another Grenadier and he planned to escape and as the guards were few in number (their troops were needed at the front) they hatched their simple plot. They asked in sign language, one after the other, for permission to go along the corridor to the toilet. They believed that between the two of them they could remove the window frame and make a jump for it when the train wasn't travelling too fast. As it was at night they had to take a chance as to what sort of terrain they would land on. After successfully removing the window, Chadwick jumped first but searching through my memory I recall him saying that he never saw his fellow escapee again, so perhaps he did not jump or was caught about to jump or perhaps was injured having jumped. That may of course be another story.

However, our ex P.O.W. decided that there was nothing to be gained by travelling South as he would have to make his way through the German defences to get to the Allied Forces Front. He found that a peasant family he approached was friendly- they were not enamoured by the German occupation of their country, killing their livestock and eating their crops- and they willingly kitted him out with some old clothes. Dressed as an Italian peasant he found little difficulty in continuing his journey Northwards, begging his way from village to village, town to town with the majority of people of a friendly disposition. It appeared that the German army was anticipating a retreat because Chadwick came upon a strategic position heavily set up in defensive mode. He made a note of the position and the nature of the defences. With his knowledge of military tactics he rightly assumed that there would be an O.P. (Observation Post) connected to the heavy artillery and that other positions would be equipped in a similar style. At this point he had a change of mind, deciding that the information he now had would be a great advantage to the Allies and that it was his duty to get the details to them. The enemy defensive positions could be bombed by our planes long before the Army had advanced to that line of artillery. Making his way back would be much easier in peasant attire than attempting it in khaki. So with these thoughts in mind he did a comprehensive 'recce' of the territory and recorded the military details (not by map references as he had no map, but by the proximity to villages, mountains etc.), finding a line of defence running from East to West across the country. Armed with this information he travelled South avoiding any Germans like the plague because, had he been found possessing such information he certainly would not have lived to tell the tale. Crossing over from the enemy front line to the Allied one was not easy as the 'front' was not defined as it had been in the First World War with troops dug in facing each other for months, but was a more fluid one with positions changing daily. However he made it and approached a sentry at night calling out quietly that he was an English soldier who had been taken prisoner and had escaped his captors. Dressed as he was in ragged peasant attire he was treated with the utmost caution and was taken back to the Unit's H.Q. with a bayonet pointing at his ribs; after all, quite a number of Germans spoke very good English and you could never tell what tricks they might pull. At dawn he requested an interview with the unit's C.O and eventually convinced him that he had information of great importance to G.H.Q. and the War Office. He insisted that his findings were sent along the line with his name, rank and serial number and was then quite happy to rejoin his unit. Hence the third gong.

'Borrowing' in the Army has the same meaning as 'begging' in civvy street as there is rarely any intention of making repayment. Chadwick, like so many old soldiers, never had any boot polish, tooth paste or shaving soap and no doubt he would have had no blanco if that had been called for at

114MCD. It was never his 'round'. He must have been saving up for something big, like buying himself out. One evening when most of us were sitting around chatting he decided to polish his boots (they already shone as if he were on duty at Buckingham Palace) and wished to borrow some Cherry Blossom. No one answered his request for a loan of the stuff so he let us know in a loud voice that 'there is nothing so good to get a super shine as Guardsman's spit'!

He was proud of his regiment and its achievements and regaled us with many exciting stories of incidents that had taken place in North Africa. One such happening was when his battalion had taken a position from Rommel's men and having captured the vantage point handed it over to the adjoining American unit who immediately succumbed to a counter attack. The 'Coldies' were ordered to retake it, which they did and handed it over a second time to the 'Yanks' who repeated their former error. Having to capture the position a third time they had no intention of going over the same ground again so they hung onto it.

Another story I remember was when on one occasion he was taking out a renaissance party at night (he was a sergeant at this time) which included a young chinless wonder with a 'pip' direct from Sandhurst. As happened frequently in the North African campaign the enemy was quite close, so silence was essential. There was a full moon that night and intermittent cloud cover so the party crept quietly around the bases of the sand dunes looking and listening for 'Gerry'. Suddenly the young lieutenant was standing on top of a sand dune in the full glare of the moon and no doubt in full sight of the enemy shouting in his 'plum in the mouth' voice; 'Chadwick! Chadwick! Where are you?' The enemy never fired. They must have thought it a trick to get them to fire thereby giving away their position. The lieutenant was chastised by Sgt. Chadwick for his foolish behaviour on the party's safe return and I can well understand the officer's parentage being brought into doubt!

After a few weeks at Saighton Camp I was put in charge of my billet, my only additional duty being to call the roster each evening before 'lights out'. There was little point in this exercise as no one in the right mind would have wanted to go absent. It was the cushiest number I had had outside of hospital. On the plus side this meant that I now occupied that little room at the end of the billet which had a door that shut out all but the loudest of snores and a window with a blind. I could switch on and off my own private light! but there was a bigger plus than that. A tiny bit of the camp was occupied by a contingent of the Army Catering Corps who were training recruits in the culinary arts. A number of men in convalescence were assigned to help the A.C.C with their chores (washing the basins, pans, dishes etc.) each day and I saw to it that some of my billet got what the Yanks call K.P's (Kitchen Patrol). Remember, rationing was still the order of the day long after the war finished. The mouth watering pies and cakes those chaps brought back to my billet were out of this world in those days and we behaved like naughty school boys with our midnight feasts; with my blind drawn, of course. I must explain that the reason that I was put in charge of the billet was that I was the only N.C.O there. In my training with the South Staffs I had risen to the giddy heights of Lance Corporal, a rank I was later to find out I was not entitled to. No one had pointed out to me that this unpaid rank was relinquished automatically on being in hospital for three weeks or more. I continued wearing my stripe in ignorance until I was kitted out with khaki drill uniform in Austria some months later when I decided that it would be a little presumptive of me to lord it over battle weary privates when I had seen no active service, always assuming that my superiors didn't 'demote' me in any case. So I didn't transfer my stripes to my new shirts.

At Saighton Camp I only did one guard duty and managed to make somewhat of a hash of it. With my aforementioned stripe I was appointed second in command of the guard and the sergeant in charge and myself elected to share the duties with me taking to the bed until midnight and then taking over the early morning calls whilst he enjoyed the bed during the early hours of the morning. So, as the men signed themselves back into camp I got my head down on the bed in the ante room. Just before midnight I was given a shake by one of the guard and told that the Orderly Officer was here and wanted to inspect the guard. What a liberty!; I was just enjoying a good sound sleep. I stumbled outside and stood to attention, the men not actually on guard falling in line alongside me. The sergeant called them to attention and accompanied the Officer on his round on inspection. 'Do your collar up corporal' was his first command at which I took the customary pace forward, fastened the hooks and eyes in my battle dress collar feeling a little bit abashed at having let the side down and hoping that he wouldn't think it worth a mention in his report. However, worse was to follow. The early morning calls were my responsibility and I took it seriously. After all if you didn't get the cooks up in time there were hundreds of men angry with not having their bacon and eggs. One of the early calls was for a Major who had requested his call to be at 4.30a.m. I managed to find my way to his billet and gave him a good shake (as instructed) at 3.30 a.m. He didn't even make a fuss when I told him the time - merely saying 'My call was for 4.30- come back in an hour' I can only assume that he was leaving the camp and didn't want the aggravation of having to come back to give evidence against me if I was to be put on a 252 (charge). Lucky me!

One day I was in the guard room which was joined to the company office by a door. The orderly was busy out of sight bashing away at his typewriter when into the room came a sailor complete with kitbag and a hat at a jaunty angle. We hadn't seen a member of His Majesty's Navy here before. Now I'm inclined to think that what happened subsequently was by way of a joke - but you never can tell. A soldier, standing in the doorway, acted as go between for the orderly and the sailor and the conversation went something like this.

'What brings you here, sailor?'

'I've been posted here for convalescence'. (The typewriter is still being bashed). In a louder voice cast into the company office, 'A member of H.M. Navy here, corporal, wanting accommodation' Reply- 'Name, Rank and Serial Number?'

To the sailor: 'What's your name, rank and number?'

Answer to the soldier in the doorway 'A. Wren, able body, an eight figure number'. This message was relayed to the still busy typist. The message came back: 'Tell him to put his kit in Hut G7 and report to the quartermaster who will issue him with two blankets and then to come back here for documentation'. I was still in the guard room when the sailor came back a few minutes later. He was looking quite flustered, which surprised me, when I heard that Hut G7 was allotted to A.T.S. girls and he had gone boldly in and was surprised to find Army issue scanties hanging on a washing line across the hut. The typist came out to explain that he thought the newcomer was female when he was given the name 'A. Wren'. Had he given his full name of 'Albert Wren' then there would have been no embarrassment.

However, the young salt soon got the size of things and made himself at home and what is more he had his revenge on the Army if not on one particular corporal. Anyone who has been in the Army will know that the parade ground (the square) is holy ground as far as any sergeant major is concerned and to violate it by putting a foot on it except under orders is, to say the least, perilous if not bordering on the suicidal. To reach a point on the other side of the square one has to walk or trot around the perimeter. It seems that in naval barracks the square is classified as the quarter deck and has to be traversed at the double when crossing as an individual. Our tar was to be seen many times a day doing just that. Sergeant majors had apoplectic fits shouting 'Get off my bloody square' That is the funny thing about Sergeant Majors, they each lay claim to that piece of holy land. Mind you, there were so many of them there that had they shared it there wouldn't have been many square yards each.

One of the rules at Saighton Camp at that time was that in order to leave camp in leisure time ties must be worn. It was not permitted to leave with battle dress blouse collar fastened up. A young paratrooper recovering from a broken ankle sustained in training was short of a tie and like the rest of us on half pay was short of cash too with which to buy one. I felt that I was a competent seamster having recently spent a fair amount of time in hospital doing embroidery, tapestry and drawn thread work, so I offered my services. Using my own tie as a pattern I ascertained that the sleeves cut from a shirt would be enough material to do the job leaving enough of the sleeve to be acceptable as a short sleeved type. The first part of the job after making the first irreversible move- that of cutting off the sleeves-was to hem the remaining stubs. The next move was for the owner to go to the quartermaster and complain about the state of the shirt he had had back from the laundry and could he exchange it for a new one. He returned to tell us that the QM had given him a good telling off (he never guessed why the sleeves were missing) but I would rather classify it as a 'dressing down' The material was carefully cut out (on the bias) stitched into shape and turned right side out and as we had no smoothing iron it had to be made thoroughly damp and placed between two pieces of cardboard which in turn went beneath the mattress of the paratrooper for a couple of nights. I was very pleased with the result. I had the satisfaction of a quite acceptable job and he had a new shirt and tie and what is more the tie was a perfect match colour wise.

 During my stay in three hospitals prior to coming to Saighton I had come across soldiers from many different corners of Great Britain and I prided myself on being able to pick out the home ground of many from their accents. An accent that had me guessing I heard one day in the company office and curiosity compelled me to ask the bearer his origin. 'I'm a Dutchman' he said. His grammar was faultless and I complimented him on it. He told me without any trace of conceit that he was gifted with the ability to pick up languages easily and quickly and spoke both German and French fluently and had a smattering of other tongues. I remember him saying that the secret of learning a language was to throw yourself wholeheartedly into it and if you cannot think in that language in three months then give it up. I do not think that many could achieve that maxim. He had obviously mastered our language as he had earned a couple of stripes and was doing most of the typing in the office.

The weather was glorious and we were told we could go into town in shirt sleeve order. It was the first week in May and Chester Races (at this time there was only one race meeting held each year) were taking place for the first time since the war ended. The whole camp was given the day off except, of course, the guard, the cooks, janker wallahs and a skeleton staff. Early on Wednesday morning a chap came up to me in the billet and said; 'Are you going to the race meeting, Corp?' I replied that I thought I might do but I wasn't certain and why did he ask. He told me he had a brother who worked in stables and he had sent him some tips. With no further to do he gave me a list of the names of five horses all running at Chester on Cup Day which is always on a Wednesday. I thanked him and felt a little more inclined to savour a visit to witness the sport of kings, something I had never done before. I went and boarded the bus at the Rake and Pikel which is the pub next to the camp entrance and rode into town.

It was not difficult to find the race course, although it was the opposite end of the town to the camp, because it seemed that eighty per cent of the population was moving in that direction. The entrance fee was half a crown (twelve and a half pence in today's money) which was a princely sum considering that I was still on half pay (one and sixpence per day or seven and a half pence today). Having no previous experience of these matters; not only had I never been to a race meeting before I had never placed a bet on a horse or other animal or being for that matter, I thought it wise to observe the procedure. So I watched people approaching the bookies, exchanging money for tickets and I watched horses thundering round the course. I also noted that the first two names on my list had come in first! Now is the moment of truth I thought and went to one of the row of bookies and pressed into his hand my other half crown and gave him the name of the third horse on my list. 'Retsal' it was and it came in first at four to one. Five half crowns in pocket I couldn't bring myself to chance losing some of them by betting on the two remaining names given to me. That was a mistake because from those five horses listed there were four firsts and one second. When the meeting finished I crossed Grosvenor Street to the Little Roodee where Pat Collin's travelling fun fair was in full swing. I didn't spend any time or money on rides - it's not much fun on your own, but I did spend a little time gazing at the traction engines as they laboured away producing electricity to supply power to the dozens of roundabouts and thousands of light bulbs. As a child I had always been fascinated by these wonderful machines that used to draw two or three huge trailers along the High Street on their way to Porter's Field at Cradley Heath where the annual fair was held and once there sat throbbing and shuddering as that terrifying belt whipped round driving a mammoth generator mounted on a platform at the front of the machine. The shining brass knobs on the governor whizzing round at a terrific speed used to mesmerise me and I used to wonder how the occasional bucket of water and a few sacks of coal could produce such tremendous power. To me as a child I used to look on these machines with as much awe as I would look upon an elephant.

Half way along Foregate Street in Chester, opposite the top of Love Street, there is a shop that sells holidays. On this site in the days I am writing about there was a small amusement arcade. It housed twenty or so 'grab your penny' machines, a few chairs around three or four tables, a counter where you could change your silver into pennies with which to feed the machines and on the counter was a tea urn and tray that held a few buttered buns. This establishment was frequented by the lads in khaki; not just the ones from Saighton Camp; but others from the 'Cheshires' or perhaps others on leave. It was a well known and well used rendezvous. One Saturday, as I approached this arcade, contemplating having a cup of tea, an Army lorry came hurtling along and came to a screeching halt right outside. Smoke was pouring from the nearside rear axle. A squaddy jumped out of the passenger seat, sped across the pavement into the arcade and without so much as a 'by your leave' took the lid off the urn, picked up the urn, spun round returning to the lorry and poured the contents over the axle. The smoke was replaced by a cloud of steam. I often wonder who paid for all that tea! Mind you, there was no milk and sugar in it!

Reporting for sick parade was not a frequent happening during my Army career, in fact, after combing my memory rigorously, I can only remember one occasion when I did so and that was at Saighton Camp. I had had, for as long as I can remember, a little soft wart at the top of my left shoulder and when we had been doing long marches in full kit the chaffing caused by the shoulder straps of my webbing equipment used to make the area quite sore and red. I thought that if they are going to make a soldier out of me all over again and I am sent back for retraining, or worse still, send me to Burma, now was the ideal time to get this little matter put right. There were two M.O's. whose quarters doubled as a surgery and, on this particular morning, one doctor was seeing to the patients whilst the other relaxed in a chair - reading. I presumed that they probably took turns in attending to the sick. My problem was explained to the doctor who, quite naturally said, 'Right. Let's have a look at you. Off with your shirt and vest' I complied, he took one look and immediately called to his colleague; 'Bill; take a look at this. A wart. A perfect specimen of the pedunculated variety'.

Was I to be alarmed or relieved? I had never heard the word before! Bill came over, had a look at the offending wart, agreed with the diagnosis and went back to his book. 'We'll soon fix that for you', said the M.O. and proceeded to open his pen knife! My first thought was, 'Well, if he is going to cut it off, I would have thought he would have used his scalpel and, at the very least, have a plaster ready to stick on over the wound immediately afterwards'. My thoughts were wrong! He went over to his bed (it could have been his colleague's - I didn't ask who had the top bunk), stuck his knife into the side of the mattress! My next thought was; 'What sort of doctor do we have here? Is this some form of voodoo?. Where are the chicken entrails? He proceeded to insert his forefinger and thumb into the slit he had made, drew out a horse hair with which he made a little knot, placed it around my wart and then pulled it as tight as he could! There was no sensation of pain or discomfort so obviously there was no nerve there. He then snipped off the ends to within a quarter of an inch (six millimetres) of the knot and told me that as the wart was now deprived of blood it would wither and fall off in a couple of weeks. He was right; within two weeks it had gone and did not even leave any scar to show where it had been!

Three or four of us had decided to go to see a film at one of the cinemas in town but I cried off at the last minute because I had developed a rotten head cold and I thought that an evening in a smoky atmosphere would only make it worse. It was that decision that changed my whole life. Instead of going to the cinema I went to the Y.M.C.A. hut for a cup of tea and a couple of aspirin. The young lady who served me was one who, in those days, we would have described as 'a smashing bit of crumpet' and, because she wasn't too busy, we had a few moments of conversation. Today you would have said she was 'drop dead gorgeous'. I ascertained that she was not married and, surprisingly, unattached. I told her that I too had no commitments. When I asked her for a date she told me that her evenings were full with serving tea and buns etc. at another forces club and with housework and gardening, but if I cared to turn up at 23 Vicars Cross for a cup of tea and a chat I would be welcome on Sunday morning. You bet I turned up - not only that Sunday but every Sunday, helping her by mowing the lawn and weeding. I had fallen for her in a big way. She was beautiful and what she saw in me I do not know. I had a bit of a limp, a Black Country accent and I wasn't exactly Hollywood material when it came to looks, but she fell for me too.

Chapter Two
The Parting

After about five visits to Vicars Cross and a couple of weeks after Chester Races the unit was told that it was to move to Hereford and I was dismayed at the thought of no more Sunday trysts. I gave my word that I would write to let her know my new address so that we could communicate by post. We had both had doubts initially about the validity of each other's claims to being unattached. Many people were getting engaged and married at an early age during the war, grabbing a little happiness before being separated by great distances and long spells between leaves. Some time later I was to find out that Josie had been in love with a fellow whose mother didn't think that she was the one for him and made the relationship untenable. She had been caught on the rebound and, for my part, I had had my two year courtship ended abruptly by my girlfriend ditching me in favour of a married man who, I found, was in the regular practice of chatting up girls whose boyfriends were in the forces. So I too was rebounding.

An early reveille one Tuesday morning and we all packed our possessions into kitbags and valises (infantrymen have two webbing containers in which to carry their belongings apart from ammunition pouches and the larger of these is called a valise whilst the other is known as the side-pack). These we carried down to the parade ground and placed them in nice compact stacks awaiting the arrival of the vehicles which would take them and us to Chester railway station for our train journey to Hereford. A surprise awaited us. There were only three trucks (Austin three tonners) and they would only be making one journey and that was to Hereford. Our kit was to go by road and we by train, so had the army laid on some coaches to take us to the station? Not on your Nellie! We had to walk. You can imagine the size of the moan that went up from two to three hundred squaddies gathered in the square. We were told, however, that there would be a concession! We would be permitted to walk as opposed to marching as long as we stayed in columns of three. During our training we had been on long marches, perhaps twenty plus miles with full kit and we had lifted our spirits by singing songs from World War One (It's a long way to Tipperary, Keep the Home Fires Burning etc.), sung to the tempo of the march. Now, walking to Chester Railway station, it was just chatter as we strolled along as if it was a Sunday afternoon jaunt and the weather was superb. A pleasant break from the normal routine with wonderful views of the river Dee at the bottom of Sandy Lane and again at St. Paul's Church and then into the built up area of Boughton and finally into City Road, bringing us to the Great Western Railway station. We didn't have to wait long before our special train drew in and we all got aboard wondering what awaited us at Hereford. I had spent two days at Bradbury Lines, as the camp is named, fifteen months before when I had been recommended for a commission. The Infantry 'WOSBY' (War Office Selection Board) was situated there as well as being the H.Q. for the S.A.S.. Because I had sprained an ankle a few days before going to the Board I was unable to complete the assault course and so I was ruled out. Had I not sprained my ankle and if I had been successful in gaining a commission then I would never have met Josie and I wouldn't be writing all this about how I met her and fell for her, hook, line and sinker.

 We were met at Hereford station by a fleet of Austin three tonners with the conventional canvas roofs and slat seating which conveyed us to the camp. Entering the camp I shall never forget the anguished falsetto cry from one of the soldiers in our truck: 'Look at the size of that bloody square'. It was of magnificent proportions - truly the biggest I had ever seen and had a tarmac road running across it at the centre. As usual the organisation was flawless. We all had a meal, drew two blankets from the QM's stores, got to our allotted billets and selected our beds. Then we retrieved our kit from the stack that had, by now, been delivered by the trucks. Next morning you would have thought we had been there for years because we fell into the same routine that was the vogue at Saighton. The following weekend was a leave (Friday afternoon to Sunday midnight) or a forty eight hour pass as it was known and I naturally asked for a railway warrant to Chester.

Arriving at Chester I made my way to White Friars where Josie had told me I would find bed and breakfast accommodation. Having booked in for a couple of nights I went to the Gaumont theatre where I had noticed they were advertising a Richard Tauber concert. Josie and I had discussed our tastes in music, amongst other subjects, and I felt this would make suitable entertainment for a Saturday afternoon. I bought two balcony seats and proceeded to Josie's home. She was both pleased and surprised to see me; surprised because I had not had sufficient notice of my leave to let her know. I was dismayed to learn that she had received offers of Saturday entertainment at the cinema from two other admirers. It was foolish of me to feel dismayed because, if I found her company desirable, then obviously so would other people. I had bought the matinee concert seats with the object of giving Josie pleasure, so I offered her the tickets saying that she should choose whoever she favoured as her companion to accompany her. She thought this was a magnanimous gesture and has referred to it on occasions of nostalgia during our married life. I really believe that this quite spontaneous action on my part helped a great deal in cementing our relationship. We found the concert most enjoyable and I felt privileged to be her escort. 'You are my heart's desire and where you are I long to be' became 'our song'.

When I had met Josie to escort her to the concert the sky was blue and the sun was beating down. She was wearing a pale blue *crepe-de-chine* dress, a real summery affair with short sleeves and conforming to the current fashion in length. (Because of shortages in supplies to make clothing, dresses had become shorter and were mostly knee length). On leaving the theatre we found that the weather had changed somewhat and the sky, now grey, was threatening rain so we made good speed towards the bus stop. In those days the bus stop stood where the ring road now sweeps round to pass over the canal and past the building we had just left, which is now a Bingo Hall, and we had not made half of the distance before the heavens opened. It was not what could be called a deluge but in a summer dress and without an umbrella it was more than enough. The rain was no doubt cold on her arms but what she was most concerned about was the fact that her dress was visibly shortening in length. Tights had not, at that time, been invented and allowing a glimpse of stocking tops was unseemly. Whilst we waited for the bus she gave her dress a downward tug at intervals, all the time hoping that the shrinkage had reached its limit and also hoping that I would not be too embarrassed escorting a girl with such a short dress. It was an experience that we laughingly relived many times during our married life.

The accommodation at White Friars, long since demolished to make way for yet more offices, was in a little 'two up and two down' cottage with no bathroom and a toilet in the back yard. The little Irish lady who offered this service was advanced in years but quite active whilst her husband, of a similar age, was most definitely retired and sat or wandered round like a spare part. She was delighted when I volunteered to wash, shave and brush my teeth at the kitchen sink to save her carrying a jug of water upstairs for my ablutions. They were of Catholic persuasion and had a votive candle burning before a statue in a tiny shrine and other objects of piety dotted round the room. The dominant feature in the bedroom was a notice pinned to the wall, printed in a shaky hand which read. 'Please do not sit on the edge of the bed as it breaks the springs' It was not exactly the Ritz but, remembering that I was still on half pay, it was within my financial reach and, what's more, previous occupants had observed the notice and the bed was comfortable.

Sunday morning saw me at 23 Vicars Cross again. I helped in the garden, the weather having returned to sun shine and I was invited to stay for dinner; my first real meeting with Josie's mum. She was a little circumspect, I thought, in her approach to me, and, as Josie was to tell me much later, with due cause because so many men from the forces had been introduced to her with the assurance that ' this is the one' that she was naturally sceptical. Having doubts about how long I would be in favour did not deter her from producing an excellent dinner despite the restrictions imposed by rationing. She was a top class cook and I was later privileged to enjoy hundreds of meals prepared by her. Not only was she a top class cook but she was also a top class teacher as each of her three daughters turned out to be experts in the culinary arts. The afternoon brought the inevitable journey to the station where I caught my train for the return journey to Hereford.

After a few more days at Bradbury Lines I was declared fit enough to rejoin my unit and was again given a forty eight hour pass and railway warrants entitling me to travel home and then on to my unit at Pembroke Dock in South Wales. They were pleased to see me back home for this short break as I hadn't been there for quite a few months. In fact my last visit home was not a leave but I was escorting a hospital pal, Joe Sherman, to the limb fitting centre at Birmingham and the sergeant major in charge of the discipline in the hospital had said that as I was a 'Brummie' I could take Joe with me to my home for a couple of days. We slept one night at the Salvation Army hostel in the city as I thought it would deplete my family's rations somewhat if we descended on them for two days. Joe was one of the many unsung heroes. He had gone to fetch an injured comrade from a minefield in France and had, unfortunately, triggered off an anti personnel mine himself and, as he fell, he had fouled another which severed his leg above the knee. The mine which had exploded beneath his left foot had shattered the bone structure into small fragments which the X-ray showed had virtually fused together over the ensuing months. He had a steel calliper on this leg to reduce the amount of pain induced by walking. He had about nine inches of femur left in his right leg so was able to wear an artificial appliance. It was the trip to collect this 'tin' leg that gave me this mini leave. My Dad came with us to see off the two lads in hospital blue. He said it was the first time he had walked down High Street with a fellow's leg under his arm!

The trip to Pembroke Dock was uneventful but drawn out. G.W.R. had suffered, as had the other railways, from the bombing of the tracks by the Luftwaffe and by lack of maintenance to the railway stock and consequently the detours and delays caused by track repairs made the journey a tedious business. I arrived at the barracks at about seventeen thirty hours (half five p.m.) and was surprised to find no guard on duty at the main gate. Not only was there no guard but there was nobody. I wandered a few yards into the camp and couldn't see a soul anywhere. No sign of life. It was completely, and as far as I could see, absolutely deserted. It was like a ghost town.

I looked into a hut and it was bare apart from bunk beds. What a posting! I could set myself up as C.O.. There must be someone about, I thought. They wouldn't leave a camp entirely empty. I strolled along one of the company lines and eventually heard the sound of a radio. I made my way towards the sound and finally found half a dozen lads in a hut playing cards, smoking and generally enjoying themselves. 'Where is everybody?' was my obvious first question.

'They all went off to Worcester last week,' I was told. 'We're the rear party; the caretakers until the next unit takes over.'

Nothing was to be gained by going back to the station until the next morning so I joined my new companions in a snack and a stroll to the town. I should have said, 'A stroll down to the favourite bar' because that is all we saw that evening. A good night's sleep (with hundreds of beds to choose from) and I was up with the lark next morning. Ablutions performed and breakfast enjoyed, I took a little walk along the camp's perimeter spending a little time to enjoy watching the three or four Catalina flying boats riding gently at anchor across the bay. What beautiful lines they had, I thought, not knowing that I would spend the majority of my working years helping to produce flying machines. Flying machines with beautiful lines - I still maintain that for simplicity of contour and all round grace there is no jet plane to equal the De Havilland Comet with its engines faired into the wings instead of hanging on great ugly brackets as is the modern pattern. I'm proud to have had a hand in making them and the maritime successor the Nimrod which has been so fruitful in air sea rescue ventures.

Eventually I had to make my way to the railway station to find what time I could get a train that would get me to Worcester and then to Norton barracks where I had completed my infantry training. It turned out that there was a train scheduled to arrive at Worcester in the evening and that suited me fine because I knew that buses ran on a regular basis to and from the barracks and only the last one was 'full to busting' with well oiled soldiers. Arriving at camp my explanation for the full day's absence; backed up by R.T.O's (Railway Transport Officers) stamps was accepted and I was allotted a hut and drew the customary two blankets from stores. The strange thing is that when taking those blankets one never questioned whether they had been cleaned since the last recipient used them. I think I might be a bit more fussy these days.

I was still wearing my stripe (in ignorance) and this gave me a marginal advantage over the privates. Norton was now a holding battalion of the South Staffs and Worcs so the frantic square bashing and assault course activities, plus lectures and field exercises, the polishing of brass and blancoing all gave way to a lot of inactivity. We all paraded after breakfast and some were given duties. Others returned to their billets to play cards, write home or read a book or comic. With all the influence of my single stripe I was given the job of overseeing half a dozen men to clean the ablutions. This suited me fine because I could take a shower daily and the job was finished by midday. Then I could write to Josie and write home as often as I wished. This job lasted about ten days. I was summoned by our major and asked if I would like the job on a regular basis as barman in the sergeant's mess. I told him that I knew nothing about such duties as I was teetotaller and entirely without experience, but he said that he thought that I would enjoy the job and would be advised and trained by the civilian caterer who ran the establishment. So I became a bar-tender.

My new quarters were superb, the first surprise being sheets on the bed; a proper bed, not a two tier affair. A wash basin and wardrobe, bedside lamp on the locker - this was luxury. I was told that as I would be washing glasses and polishing tables till past midnight on a daily basis I should ignore the reveille bugle and could relax until about eleven hundred hours. I was never one for lying in bed but it was nice not to have to fight my way to the ablutions for that shave as soon as the bugle sounded.

One hundred and fourteen warrant officers and sergeants shared that mess so it is not difficult to imagine how busy we were. Fortunately there were only two varieties of beer, these being pumped up from wooden casks in the cellar and few of the drinkers went in for spirits so knowledge of cocktails and other many varieties of drinks available today did not present a problem. The prices were listed on a card stuck behind the bar. Also behind the bar were shelves holding a small selection of cigarettes and a few tablets of good quality soap. A tablet of top quality soap was indeed a luxury in those days and I was delighted when the caterer told me that I could buy some to send home.

The month was July and it was a sizzling summer so I found that my morning duties consisted mainly of reducing the temperature of the beer in the casks by playing the hose on them and on the walls of the cellar. My bedroom was above the cellar and adjacent to the Band Room. The regimental bandsmen spent their mornings polishing their instruments and playing scales and arpeggios. The afternoons I enjoyed because that was when they were put to task playing, not just marches, but waltzes, intermezzos, concertos in fact, whatever took the band master's fancy. Many of the warrant officers and sergeants were 'regulars' who had returned from abroad and were now living in married quarters on the camp site and a fair number of them brought their wives to the mess.

One evening the assembly of forty to fifty in the bar suddenly and of one accord jumped to their feet and fell perfectly silent. For a split second I could not account for this and then my eye fell on the RSM (Keebles) in the doorway. He stood stiffly to attention (as did everyone else in the room including the ladies!) and let his eyes slowly take in all that was happening in the room. In fact nothing was happening in the room. Everybody appeared frozen in time; men were afraid to swallow; wives dare not flinch for fear that it would reflect on their husbands. He walked with a slow and measured pace to the bar; ordered a pint of beer which the caterer drew after giving me the nod that he would attend to this one. On his taking his first sip the whole assembly resumed their chatter' perhaps a little more subdued than before. Veneration or fear? Whatever it was set him apart from, the rest and I was amazed that men who had seen the bloodiest of battles in North Africa and in Europe could be made so submissive by one rather portly individual; with such influence I believe he could have replaced the whole of the Eighth Army single handed.

I mustn't forget to tell you about the first pint I served. The caterer had demonstrated to me how to place the nozzle of the tube against the inside of the glass whilst gently and evenly pulling the handle downwards. This prevented the beer splashing on the bottom of the glass thereby causing the production of an excessive amount of froth. I satisfied him with a couple of attempts and it fell to my lot, after opening the bar, to serve a sergeant with a pint. Well, my mother had told me as a youngster that it was circumspect and good manners to fill a tumbler or glass to within a quarter of an inch (six millimetres) of the top so that none would be spilled on the table or the attire of the drinker. With my complete lack of experience in 'quaffing' I assumed that the same would apply in a bar. It didn't! The sergeant gently pushed the glass towards me and asked what he had done to offend me and pointed out that he had requested a pint and that is what he expected for his money. I considered myself somewhat fortunate to have had such a mild mannered first customer. It took almost fifty years for the glass manufacturers to come up with a glass that would satisfy the sergeant (and my mother) - an oversized glass with a line where the pint is achieved.

The caterer explained to me that on occasion a drinker would say 'And have one yourself' and, upon this show of affluence, it was customary to thank the customer and to take out of his change the price of a half, telling him that I would be drinking it later. There was no chance of retiring on the cost of the number of halves I received. After about a week or ten days the caterer said how pleased he was with me and told me that the till was showing a better daily total by about two pounds with the same amount of beer consumed. Also the cigarette stock was not getting depleted as quickly. It's no wonder they wanted a change of bar-tender!

Another change of bar man was soon to follow for my name was posted on Part 11 Orders for attendance at the medical centre to receive certain 'jabs' on Friday followed by seven days leave prior to posting overseas. A cocktail of injections was administered and listed in my little brown booklet, travel warrants collected and on Friday afternoon I was on my way home. What a good thing I had elected to spend the first half of my leave at home. My left arm felt as though it was filled with lead and I was feeling definitely unwell so, on reaching No. 33 Newtown Lane, I went to bed straight away. Within an hour I was having an awful bout of uncontrollable shivering which continued through until Saturday morning. The cause was obviously the injections and, as I was fairly fit, the ague left me as rapidly as it had arrived and I was my old self by Saturday evening. During the next three days I called on friends and relations to tell them that I would be going abroad, destination unknown. I presumed that I was only getting seven days leave because I had had the usual embarkation leave of three weeks just prior to my accident.

The remaining three days I spent at Chester and as Josie was working (at the Road Transport and General Insurance

Company) my day time was used watching the activity down by the river and watching the excavations going on for the pool in the park and with leisure activities in the evenings. Those days flew by and all too soon it was time for our goodbyes with promises to keep in touch by post.

Author at Monfalcone

Chapter Three
The Journey

Eight of us was the party sent by train to Dover. We didn't have any information concerning our destination. It all seemed 'cloak and dagger' stuff as we just had a document with a number on it which was to be shown at points along the journey. At Dover we found ourselves corralled in some cattle pens along with hundreds of other chaps in khaki and, as you can easily imagine, it didn't take long for one or two of them to start bleating like sheep. Soon the whole ensemble took up the chorus. I bet it could be heard in Calais.

We learned that about half of them had been in Dover the day before but the weather had been too rough for them to put to sea so they had had to 'doss' down in the barracks for the night. Filing up the gangway I wondered where the Plimsoll line would be with twice the expected cargo. Up on deck I made my way to the rail somewhere up the sharp end and took a look out to sea. It looked fairly calm but the clouds were moving in a manner that indicated a lively breeze.

In a remarkably short time we were all aboard, the gangplank slid aboard, the hawsers released and we were on our way. This was my first journey abroad and I couldn't help but think about so many who had gone this way before never to return. I was so lucky, the war in Europe having finished, I was looking on this as an adventure with very little risk attached.

The white cliffs of Dover receded. They were a brilliant white in the morning sun just as they are pictured on postcards and calendars. Somehow I hadn't expected such whiteness. Some eight or nine miles out to sea and the waves developed into sizes that were a little bit frightening. We were all ordered below decks and battened down. Down below it was dank and miserably dark, what little light there was coming from a few bulkhead lamps and there were no portholes.

The sea got rougher and the ship moved up and down like a lift out of control. I was surprised that there was so little rocking from side to side. It seemed to be all vertical movement as one moment we were riding high with the screws thrashing round in the air and the next we were at the bottom of a trough with the engine labouring in an attempt to get the ship to make headway.

Below decks there was nothing to indicate what progress we were making but a slackening of speed and a sensation of turning indicated that we were approaching our destination or, maybe, avoiding a collision with another vessel. Word was passed down that we would be sailing along the French coast for a little time as it was too rough to attempt to dock. It was therefore some two uncomfortable hours later that we put into Calais harbour and disembarked.

We were carrying our kit and there seemed little point in taking a look at the town thus laden and we had been advised that the troop train would be leaving in an hour or so. The eight of us stuck together and went to a little cafe within sight of the dock gates and enjoyed our first French coffee.

The French railway engine seemed much bigger than its English counterpart; whether this was an illusion caused by the fact that there were no raised platforms in the dock area, I do not know. It appeared so big and masculine that I was amazed when, a little later, I heard its whistle. It was shrill and effeminate and entirely out of keeping with the engine's presence.

We still had no knowledge of our destination but we hoped that it wasn't too far away as the accommodation was definitely not the Orient Express. The train had nine or ten coaches with a refreshment coach positioned fairly centrally. The coaches were built after the fashion of the English ones of those days except that the seats were made of varnished wooden slats rather like park benches. There were no photographs or mirrors as in the English coaches. The luggage racks were of mesh supported by cast iron brackets. Entraining was not easy with full kit and kitbags, especially as we had to make our way from ground level.

As we climbed aboard we were each given a pack of 'haversack rations' comprising a little parcel of sandwiches, a slice of fruit cake and an apple. It was reminiscent of the Sunday

School treats of the nineteen twenties and thirties. We were advised that six personnel per compartment would give adequate space for each person. It was just about enough considering we each had a kitbag and all our webbing equipment. Two of our number had to go to the next compartment and share with unknown others.

I took it upon myself to organise the sleeping arrangements (always supposing that we would get some sleep) and two tickets went into a hat for those fortunate ones who would get the seats, two others the spaces under the seats and the other two on the racks. It fell to me to occupy the space under one of the seats. Sleep didn't claim many hours because of the discomfort. It would be naughty of me to suggest that the coaches had square wheels but it did feel as though the rails had many knots in them. When the train negotiated any curve it felt and sounded as though the track was a series of straight lines, the wheels grumbling as they changed direction at each rail joint. I honestly believe that the R.A.F. had so consistently and regularly bombed the railway tracks that the maintenance men responsible for the condition of the track were hard put to keep it in any sort of order.

The train pulled into a station at about nine o'clock. There was no station name visible and I presumed that, as in Britain, all signs had been removed to confuse any enemy that might find his way there. Two things I remember about that stop. The first was a young French mother standing with her little baby girl in her arms with a number of 'squaddies' giving her their chocolate ration. Perhaps I was somewhat cynical but I thought it highly possible that this was a routine visit which would be repeated on the arrival of the next train so I decided I would save my chocolate for some other poor mite further along the track where gifts of chocolate would be fewer. (This was always supposing that by that time I had not already consumed my chocolate)

The second memory I have is the sight of a somewhat coarse looking soldier leaning out of his compartment window shouting to a pair of well dressed business men. His cry was 'Dellow'. My French is very poor but I thought 'surely I should be able to translate a single word'? The cry went up again in a more demanding tone; 'Hey, Dellow' and this time I caught on because he was waving his water bottle. 'De l'eau' was what he was demanding and, what is more, he got it. One of those bank managers or whatever went to a tap on the wall to fill his bottle. Whether he did it out of fear, embarrassment, kindness or, indeed, was he just grateful for being released from Nazi oppression?

Travelling on through lush countryside we came to a large camp straddling the railway track. Alongside the track at intervals of about a coach length was a pole surmounted by a loud speaker. Instructions were given to us through this system. 'Do not de-train before you are told. You will be able to have a shave and a shower after you have had your breakfast. After having your shower do not forget to collect your haversack rations and return to the train'. A couple of minutes later; 'Number one coach. Parade with your knife, fork spoon and pot and proceed to the dining room'. Above the doorway to the dining room was a sign in letters of white on a black background which read; 'Marnjay Toot Sweet'. The organisation here was fantastic. On entering this long hut each soldier picked up a metal tray with indentations in it and progressed at a fair pace past a line of cooks who dished up fried egg, bacon, beans, tomato, fried bread like an automated line of robots. I've heard it said that they could serve two thousand meals in an hour and I would lay a wager on it. So, back to the coach to park the knife, fork, spoon and pot and collect soap, razor, towel etc. for the equally well organised ablutions.

Off we went on our journey again; the terrain now changing to hilly with mountains visible in the far distance. It was time to write to tell Josie about the changing scenery. I had already written to describe the Channel crossing. It seemed that the only way to have Josie for my own was to keep in constant touch. Our relationship was based on such a tenuous foundation. We had only met for a few Sunday mornings, a weekend away from Hereford and a half week of embarkation leave, yet I felt that she was the one I wanted for my soul mate and I hoped that she had the same feelings about me. I vowed to myself that I would write each day unless duties prevented it and this I managed to do and, on the odd occasion, I wrote two letters. For me it was easy to keep Josie in mind but I thought how tempted she must have been with her frequent contact with many soldiers and airmen to 'go to the flicks', as we called the cinema in those days, or to a dance. She was in no way obliged to refuse any offers - we were not engaged - in fact, it would even be difficult to class it as courtship. However, she remained faithful to our unspoken promises.

Soon we were approaching mountains. I had done my advanced infantry training on the Black Mountains of South Wales and it dawned upon me that they were mere pimples compared to what lay just ahead. At one point the train stopped for a minute or two and then advanced at a very slow pace. Curiosity compelled us to go to the windows to look out and the sight made ones flesh creep. We were crossing a chasm of immense depth. A small river ran along the base and visible were people who looked the size of ants. The terrifying aspect was that the train appeared to be crossing as if by magic because there was no sign of parapets of any kind, no sign of sleepers for the rails to rest on, but even more terrifying was the creaking of the timbers from which the bridge was made, one that was put up to replace the one the Germans had destroyed in their retreat. Even the 'Bloody Hells' were spoken quietly for fear a loud voice might throw the train off balance. One soldier said; 'If we come back this route I hope at will be at night. I don't want to see this again'. The word was passed along the train that the refreshment department was now serving tea. One of the chaps in our compartment volunteered to get a mugful for me. I was still wearing my stripe and maybe he thought he would keep the right side of me, or, then again, perhaps he was just naturally kind. Army mugs, at least the ones I was used to were, to my mind, of a very poor design. They were enamelled steel and prone to chip easily, the shape was poor being twice as much in diameter as they were high and held about half a pint. The handle was circular so had to be held tightly to prevent rotation and consequent loss of the beverage. Heat from the contents quickly travelled to the handle so to hold onto a mug of hot anything became a juggling act, trying to transfer the mug from one hand, holding the handle, to the other hand, holding the rim by finger tips. That was difficult when you only have one mug. It is well nigh impossible with two mugs. Unfortunately the volunteer returned with two mugs, half full of tea, the top half having been lost due to the motion of the train and, worse still, he had two badly scalded fore fingers. I saw these fingers a month later and they still bore the scars.

Our next stop was a transit camp situated just outside the Austrian town of Villach. Many thousands of British Army soldiers know this camp which was the Eastern limit of Medloc 'C' railway route along which we had unknowingly just travelled. I say unknowingly because we were still showing our 'number' whenever we stopped and we were still mystified as to where we would end up. The camp had previously been owned by the German Army and they had provided a unique feature. As the camp was situated in a bowl designed by nature it caught the sun practically all day long and in August, as it was, the sun can be fierce. The Germans occupying the camp no doubt for three or four summers had experienced the heat and, as a result, had put their engineers to work. What was then called the 'Wind Tunnel'(I'm told that it no longer exists) was a huge Nissen-like structure made from corrugated iron. It was circular and about twelve feet (4 metres) in diameter. Imagine if you can from my poor description a length of this structure bent to form a circle with the interior space about the area of half a football pitch. Inserted in this tunnel was a huge fan the blades of which almost touched the walls and which, driven by an electric motor, slowly rotated. This caused a gently breeze to be wafted continually through the whole building. The air movement had to be gentle to avoid blowing all the paperwork as the entire centre circular room was given to office work. There were several access points where the circular section was interrupted to make way to conventional flat doors, which, for obvious reasons, were always closed except when entering or exiting.

It was in this building that the eight of us presented ourselves and showed our 'number', asking once more if we could be informed about our destination. We were told that we were to go to a unit in Italy. Outside the hut we put our heads together and decided to protest; in the nicest possible way of course because we did not want to be arrested for defying orders. A couple of us went back into the office as spokesmen and explained that we knew that there was no South Staffs battalion in Italy and we would like to join our comrades in BAOR where we knew there was a contingent. The BAOR (British Army of the Rhine) was made up of representatives of many regiments and corps including some of the airborne troops who had battled at Arnhem and with some of whom we had trained at Worcester.) Amazingly we were listened to and the Captain in charge promised to signal the War Office with our request.

Thank goodness the Q.M. stores was well supplied for the next day we were measured up for and kitted out with khaki drill trousers, shorts and shirts. It was very hot and we had been wearing full uniform up to that point. Other parties of men had been sent out as reinforcements and were kitted out likewise, so our legs were not the only lily-white ones on camp.

Was it Napoleon that is credited with the saying that 'an Army marches on its stomach'? How someone at that camp worked out how many stomachs would require filling was beyond my comprehension. Allowing that a train load was about six hundred bodies and trains were arriving and departing daily, some soldiers leaving by truck for their local destinations, some staying overnight and some staying several days, it all seemed to me to be an impossible equation. It was said that dozens if not hundreds of deserters were living quite comfortably in such camps.

It was at the dining room in this camp that I saw the biggest woman I have ever seen. She was one of the local people employed to perform the more mundane tasks. (I think it wouldn't be a practical proposition to have a regular squad of janker-wallahs to carry out such duties in a transit camp). Her job was wheeling the dirty dinner plates to the scullery on the longest wheelbarrow imaginable. She stood about six foot two inches tall and was one hundred per cent Amazon having the shoulders of a weightlifter and biceps like a blacksmith. Meeting her on the proverbial dark night would not be pleasurable.

Just outside the dining room were two or three huge oil drums that had been thoroughly cleaned and painted with gloss paint both inside and out and were there for the express purpose of depositing any excess food that had been left on the plates. This waste, we understood, was to be used as pig swill at the nearby farms. However, before anyone had the chance of scraping his remaining mashed potatoes or his half round of bread or whatever into the drums a number of children would appear, armed with a tin with a string handle, or a saucepan and assailed them with 'Please mister'? The oil drums did not get much waste. I knew that some of the children were painfully thin but it eased my conscience to think that maybe they had a pig in their back garden.

During the afternoon of our first full day at Villach, now attired in our new shirts and shorts, our little party of eight were chatting together when we were approached by a Major. He was, and others agreed with me, the antithesis of a military bearing. His lack of height was no fault of his but he didn't hold himself like a soldier but drooped as though, in civilian life, he had constantly leaned over a Dickensian desk and had been unable to straighten up afterwards. The Q.M's department had not been over kind when kitting him out, his shorts were much too large and, together with his pronounced stoop, made him look quite ridiculous. West Bromwich Albion football team of the thirties sprung to mind as they were known locally as 'The Baggies' because of the size of their shorts.

The Major informed us, in the tones of an aged maiden aunt, that there was a shortage of clerks, butchers and Military Police and he would be pleased to accept volunteers for any of the vacancies with a strong possibility of early promotion for those who volunteered immediately.

One of our eight volunteered, to the disgust of the remaining seven, to transfer to the Military Police. The remaining seven were to report to a certain hut at fifteen hundred hours. We paraded as instructed and found ourselves in a hut furnished with a dozen or more tables and chairs. It looked remarkably like a school room. Printed forms were distributed and we were put to task. The forms had a series of squares with a different pattern in each. We were asked to record, in the appropriate space, whether a, b or c would be the next pattern. This got progressively more difficult as we went down the page. There is, I know, a name for this sort of exercise, but it escapes me at the moment, but which presumes that from the answers to our questions some trick-cyclist can deduce to what job you are best suited. At other tables we were given more practical tasks, working against the clock, of assembling a bicycle pump and a bayonet type electric bulb holder, both of which had been stripped down to its component parts.

I had twice gone through these sort of tests before and can only assume that the Army was satisfied with what they had originally chosen as my lot; that of an infantryman because I hadn't been transferred to any other department.

Following 'tiffin' we decided to go for a walk into the town which was only a mile away to see what it had to offer in the way of entertainment. The inevitable happened- we ended up in a bar! Our currency had been changed at each frontier as we had passed through, firstly into francs at Calais, then into marks when we crossed from France into Austria so here we were with our pfennigs and schillings without a clue as to what they were worth. Drinks, however, were not expensive but the measure was disputed. My earlier experience regarding my first pint would have been just a mere giggle here because the amount of froth that appeared permissible was completely beyond reason. One fellow had his tankard about ninety per cent full of beer and topped up with froth whilst another had less than half his tankard with beer and the remainder froth. When he protested, admittedly in English, the barmaid just laughed and replied in German. It seemed that this practice was acceptable as we noticed that the locals were being treated (if that is the right word) in exactly the same manner.

An Austrian man aged about thirty to thirty five asked me in excellent English if I minded if he sat at our table. He was on his way back to his living accommodation, he explained, and had called in at the bar for a meal as he had had a hard day's work and didn't feel like preparing a meal for himself. The serving wench, dressed in typical Tyrolean attire, came to him bearing a large bowl of mushroom soup and a plate with two great slices of bread; he had obviously ordered before coming over to our table. He told me that mushroom soup was the most common dish available at eating houses and it was also the cheapest, but despite this, he still had to hand over his ration book so that the girl, armed with scissors for the job, cut out a docket. Rationing was even more stringent here than in the U.K.

Next morning we called at the office to see whether the War Office had replied to the signal sent on our behalf. It hadn't, so we busied ourselves keeping out of sight just in case we might be called upon to volunteer for something.

However, the following morning a message had arrived for us. It read quite simply 'Compulsory transfer to North Staffs Regiment'. Whilst this was not the reply we wanted we felt that at least we would be with chaps from the same county with accents not unlike our own. Strange that my own father in World War 1 had been transferred from South Staffs to North Staffs Regiment. The Q.M. could not be expected to carry a supply of cap badges and shoulder flashes for all the different regiments so we were told to get them changed on reaching our ultimate destination; somewhere in Italy.

That somewhere in Italy turned out to be a village on the Northern Adriatic coast called Duino. We travelled by train as far as the city of Udine and then on again to Treviso. At Treviso we stayed overnight at an Italian barracks and I was very impressed with what Mussolini had provided for his troops. The quarters were palatial with vast amounts of marble in the interior. Each bed, built hospital style of white enamelled tubular steel, had a mosquito net suspended above it on a metal frame. The ablution centre was clinically clean - it sparkled - and looked as if it had been prepared for an exhibition. I'm sure that, without any further preparation, it could have been used as a hospital operating theatre.

Little did I realise, during my bed and breakfast stay at Treviso, that the next ablution centre was to be the opposite in the extreme, but more of that later.

On the journey from Villach to Treviso we obviously crossed the frontier between Austria and Italy and in doing so we found ourselves changing our currency to suit our new circumstances. The lira was, at that time, rated at nine hundred to the pound and, as a result, I suddenly found myself rich beyond measure, at least it seemed that way. Five pounds immediately became four and a half thousand lira! At that time there were no Italian coins, all the money being paper money in a large array of denominations starting with one lira, which was worth about one nine hundredth of a pound or one farthing in our currency at that time. What a good thing that the Army uniform is well endowed with pockets.

At midday an Austin three tonner, the work horse of our Army, turned up at the barracks and the driver asked for the eight men designated to join the Seventh North Staffs Battalion. We explained that we were now seven as one had volunteered to join the Military Police.

Our kitbags and webbing equipment were tossed into the truck and we climbed aboard. We were now on the last leg of our journey and I couldn't help but wonder what the future held. After travelling some ten miles south the driver turned east and we went quietly along - no songs, no banter until some one and a half hours later we pulled up in a town called Monfalcone where the driver told us we could get a nice cup of tea at the Salvation Army centre. The drink was really welcome as it was the hottest time of the year and the hottest time of day.

All the shops around had their doors and window shutters closed and I wondered if it was early closing day. There was little sign of life - not even children playing. This was my first experience of the siesta.

After the quenching and refreshing drink of tea we continued our journey and found that our destination was only about three miles away. At last I could write home and to Josie with an address they could use to reply to my letters. I had accomplished my self appointed task of writing to Josie on a daily basis even though two of the letters had been despatched on the same day as catching the post collection was not always easy. Postage stamps were not required as the caption 'Forces Mail' written at the top of the envelope was enough to ensure its delivery to any address in the U.K. Writing paper and ink were the only costs in keeping in touch. The ball point pen had only recently been invented so a fountain pen was a necessary piece of equipment.

This reminds me of an incident which occurred when I was working in the bar at the sergeant's mess at Norton Barracks. Early one evening a smartly dressed man, a civilian, came into the mess and asked the caterer if it was permissible to offer his product for sale to the members of the mess. Following a few questions and satisfactory answers he was given the all clear and proceeded to demonstrate the features of the newly invented biro. The main gist of his selling spiel was the comparison of this new device with the fountain pen and listed its many advantages and capabilities. I have already mentioned that it was early evening and only a few of the sergeants and warrant officers were present; only about eight or ten were in attendance. He was explaining how useful this new pen could be. You could put it in your pocket whilst in an aeroplane without the fear that the ink would flood out, as it would with a fountain pen, in an unpressurised plane; you could write about eight thousand words without resorting to your ink bottle for a refill; you could even write under water which is absolutely impossible with a fountain pen.

At this point a sergeant interrupted; 'Who the bloody hell wants to write under water?'. To the best of my knowledge, he only sold one pen and the cost, I remember, was, compared to today's prices, absolutely phenomenal. It cost thirty seven shillings and sixpence which was, at least, one and a half weeks wages to me.

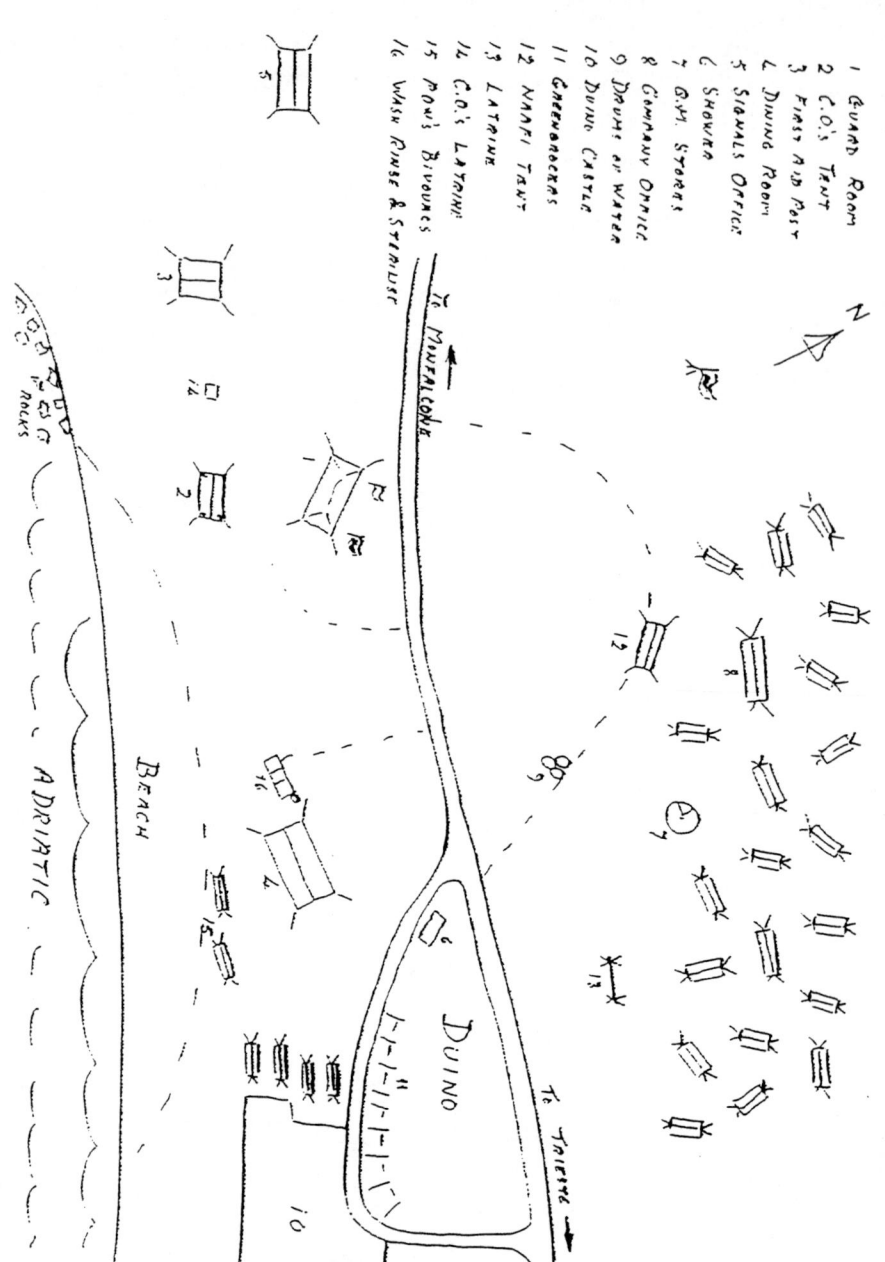

Camp layout at Duino, Summer 1946

Chapter Four
The Camp

Duino was a village some twelve miles west of Trieste and within yards of the Adriatic.

I say 'was' a village because looking at a most recent map I see that a motor way now runs through it and it has motel accommodation so things have changed somewhat. The walls of the castle which were then, and possibly still are now, in good repair and were lapped by the sea water. The castle was commandeered and occupied by General Sir John Harding, C.I.G.S. (Chief of the Imperial General Staff). I understand that this is the site where the Duino Agreement was drawn up by Sir John and his advisers which defined the location of what is now the border line between Italy and Yugoslavia. Both of these countries were desperate to have the ownership of Trieste which is important, both strategically and politically, and the squabble continued until the Duino Agreement was drawn up and signed some two years after the war in Europe had ended.

The road from Monfalcone to Duino and on again to Trieste ran in a south easterly direction and it was most definitely not made by the Romans because it followed the contours of the land about forty feet above the sea which was visible intermittently. It did not meander much because, if you look at the map, the upper reaches of the Bay of Trieste (Golfo di Trieste) you will see that Monfalcone to Trieste is almost a straight line. Arriving at Duino the road divides, the right fork being a narrow road that leads to the village and, about a mile on, rejoins the main road at a T junction, the main road forking to the left to avoid a large outcrop of rock and then proceeding, on a slightly higher elevation, skirting the coast line. The drop from the road was some fifty to sixty feet and the rock face was sheer.

In the interests of safety small concrete post had been erected along the parts of the road that had been made with the sheer drop to the sea.

A hundred yards or so before reaching the fork in the road our driver turned off on to an area of land that was of the same height and sloping slightly upwards. This area was surrounded on three sides by a natural and very rugged amphitheatre, mostly rock (possibly limestone) with a light covering of soil. There were no trees, shrubs or bushes and what little grass there was grew between the rocks and was parched and brown. This place was obviously the terminus so we let down the tailgate and proceeded to unload our kit. Whilst we were unloading four or five men approached and, as they got near, we could see that they were senior N.C.O's. They were, in fact, the R.S.M., the Q.M and the rest were company sergeant majors.

They greeted us, for the Army, very civilly and seemed particularly interested in how things were in Blighty. It did not dawn on me that these men had not seen the U.K. for upwards of three years and contact with people who had left there since the cessation of hostilities with Germany was something very special. We told them of the spirit of the survivors, of rationing still continuing, of the plans for rebuilding and so on. How pleasant it was to be approached by such high ranking N.C.O's who did not bark orders and verbally abuse everyone. I had heard that life abroad when in the Army was a 'doddle' compared to life in the U.K., and here I had the proof.

We were allocated to the four rifle companies, my company being 'D'. I don't know whether the reader would be aware but I will explain anyway. When using a field telephone, especially in a battle, the A,B,C and D letters which, apart from A, are phonetically similar, companies are given a name beginning with that letter. The four rifle companies are therefore called Able, Baker, Charley and Dog and the other two companies, being quite definitive in their sound, retain their titles of H.Q. (Headquarters) and Support.

Looking around the amphitheatre I could see a motley assortment of tents scattered around. There were large and small ridge poles, bivouacs, bell tents and a small marquee. It had been impossible, it was very easy to see, to erect the tents in any semblance of order because of the nature of the terrain. Rocks, both large and small, pointed to the skies at all sorts of different angles. Not one of the tents was erected according to the book as it was impossible to place tent pegs in the correct position. It was more a case of there being sufficient depth of soil somewhere in the vicinity of where they should be.

I was directed to one of the small ridge - pole tents, told to place my kit inside and report to the Q.M. stores to collect my conventional two blankets. The stores were but a few yards away and were housed in a rather larger than standard bell tent. Next morning, I was told, I should present myself for documentation and instruction to the company office which was situated in the small marquee.

The ridge - tent in which I was billeted had six beds, the design of which I hope to convey to you. Four of the beds were occupied by four privates leaving me with a choice of the other two. I dumped my kitbag and webbing in the space next to the centre bed on the right hand side and went through the introduction. Not one of them came from anywhere near my home town but at least we acknowledged that we all came from the same county of Staffordshire.

Now to the beds. This really deserves a chapter on its own. The frames were made from timber and designed for ease of assembly and dismantling. The timber was of the same section, four by two throughout. The head and the foot were identical in as much as they were about two and a half feet long, had two notches cut in about two inches wide by two inches deep and about two inches from the ends. Two rails fitted into the notches thereby forming a rectangle of about twenty two inches by six feet. Stretched across the rails was a piece of hessian which sufficed as a mattress. When it was new the hessian was certainly stretched across the rails but with the passage of time and having being used by others of indefinite weight, when I had to use it it sagged to the floor which I have already described as rocks with a modicum of soil around. It was a case of shuffling around to find a suitable indentation for the hip bone to rest in.

Surprisingly, I didn't sleep too badly considering the primitive couch and I was awakened at five thirty by the bugler sounding 'Reveille'.

Having read most of Percival Christopher Wren's stories - Beau Geste, Beau Sabreur, Beau Ideal etc- I felt a boyish thrill at answering the bugle. I thought, 'I'm going to enjoy this as much as I can'. It wasn't exactly the French Foreign Legion but it was a close cousin to it

Washing and shaving in cold water was no hardship as I had experienced plenty of that during my training, even using the dew from the grass on several occasions, but the amount of water allowed was extremely small as the camp did not have running water. All of the battalion's water was delivered by bowser and pumped into three huge steel drums. Not only was the amount of water small but there was none left with which to rinse out the bowl after the last chap had used it and the allocation of bowls was one to three. The bowls were of a fairly heavy gauge steel, galvanised and shaped like a wok.

Having partaken next morning of a bacon and egg breakfast I presented myself, as instructed, at the company office. I completed my documentation pointing out that they had perhaps drawn the short straw in accepting me as their newest recruit. I was physically down - graded to 'C2' and had to wear an appliance in my shoe. I therefore could not be expected to soldier on in the same way as the fit men I was amongst.

My next port of call I was told would be the Q.M's stores in order to collect my new cap badge and shoulder flashes. In addition I was issued with insignia to be sewn on to the upper sleeves which showed a black cat on a red shield which was the crest of Thirteen Corps, Fifth Army.

The Q.M. supervised the issue of these goods and my signature as a receipt for same. I was surprised when he told me to 'hang on a minute' and, turning to his storesman instructed him 'Give him one of those' pointing to a dozen Lee Enfield rifles secured by chain and padlock to the tent pole. The storesman unlocked the padlock and removed the chain and took one of the rifles from the bunch. He threw it at me and I caught it but immediately threw it back saying; 'I won't be needing that. I'm excused such things as I have been down graded' The Q.M's retort was; 'Give it back to him.

Somebody's got to keep the bloody thing clean'. The bonhomie of the previous evening had evaporated!

Long before I had unpicked all the stitches retaining my South Staffs flashes on two sets of khaki uniforms the bugle called 'Cookhouse' for the second time that day, the first being at breakfast. So it was time to join the queue with all the others carrying mess tins, knife, fork spoon and pot to see what treat was in store. I never found out which was supposed to be the main meal, whether it was the one served at about midday or the one dished out at six o'clock, because they were about the same size and, quite often, virtually identical in content.

Rations were not getting through as happily as we would have liked due, I imagine, to the tremendous loss of shipping in the Atlantic and the Mediterranean. Ships were unloading the food cargoes at Mestre, adjoining Venice, and from the stores there units throughout the North of Italy and Southern Austria were sending in trucks to collect their quotas. Sometimes we would be inundated with tins of sardines or tons of pickled beetroot. I like pickled beetroot but twice a day for a week was a bit much.

The locals were always ready to oblige with 'swops' and many tins of sardines were exchanged for locally grown tomatoes. Our bacon came in large tins which were labelled 'Canadian' and we never appeared to be short of bacon and always started our day with a proper English breakfast.

When I told you about our arrival at the camp and gave you my first impressions of its layout I only told you half the story because looking down from my elevated position on the hillside I could see that the camp extended over the other side of the road. There the land ran level for thirty yards towards the sea and then gently sloped down to the shore, this extent being some fifty yards wide. From this area the land, still rocky but not quite so unfriendly, inclined upward on the Western side and downward on the Eastern side. This meant that the road was some ten feet higher than the land as it curved towards the fork that led to the village and was supported by a wall built from the local rock.

On the relatively level stretch of this area were two marquees, one being the dining room furnished with trestle tables and slat benches, the other being the guardroom. The guardroom had the Union flag and the Regimental colours flying. Alongside the dining room was a row of three half oil drums (cut vertically) elevated two feet from the floor by bricks. The drums contained boiling water which had been heated by open fires placed between the brick piers. As at Villach soldiers scraped any unwanted or excess food into another cleaned up oil drum and then proceeded to wash their mess tins etc in the first two tanks and rinsed them in the third.

Inside the guardroom was a trestle table and two chairs alongside at the entrance flap whilst the far side had half a dozen camp beds. Two light chains hung from the centre line of the roof on which were hung two hurricane lamps.

On the eastern side of this plateau, where the ground sloped gently down, were two bivouacs, the sleeping quarters of four German P.O.W's. They were easily identifiable by the big square of yellow material that had been sewn into their grey battledress blouses. Whether it was conditional that they always wore their uniform when on duty or whether it was their own choice I do not know but the only time I saw them without their uniform was at siesta time on the beach. Their job was to do the cleaning of pots and pans for the cooks and to help in the preparation of our meals.

Just beyond the two bivouacs were several ridge pole tents which I was never privileged to see at close quarters which housed the officers with the exception of the Commanding Officer.

The first tent on the rising western side was obviously that of the C.O., Colonel Bird (referred to as Dickie) for it had a classical look about it with corner poles surmounted by finials. I never saw my C.O.. All the business was, I understand, conducted by the Adjutant, a Major of some thirty five to forty years of age who, from time to time, would disappear into this rather fine looking tent no doubt to get a signature or two.

It was said that Dickie was drinking himself silly every night and was never available for anyone, including the Adjutant, before noon. I was to avail myself of this knowledge as I shall report later.

If the C.O. was drinking to excess because it was so readily available and so cheap then he was a fool, but I am always inclined to look for the best in people and I couldn't help but speculate that he might have feelings of guilt or remorse at losing so many men at Salerno. The Germans had been well prepared to rebuff the invaders and had taken a heavy toll of 13 Corp's infantry to such an extent that the battalion had been reduced to half strength. The loss of three hundred or so killed and wounded is a big responsibility and this must have weighed heavily on his shoulders.

A few yards further on was the F.A.P. (First Aid Post) with the Red Cross insignia emblazoned on the wall. This was a ridge pole tent of fair proportions with a trestle table and chair for the M.O., a chair for the patient and a table that was occupied with the usual paraphernalia of a surgery, i.e. splints, bandages, slings sterilizer etc.. There was also a lockable wooden cupboard housing a variety of medicines and tablets.

Further on again on a level plateau that stood some fifty feet above the sea was the Signals office where six men had their quarters in yet another ridge pole tent. There were always two on duty right round the clock and they seemed to organise their own shifts.

Midway between the C.O's tent and the F.A.P. was something special. It was the C.O.'s toilet. It comprised a wooden structure about the size of a tea chest, having no base but having the necessary hole in the top. This was placed over a hole that had been dug into the ground. Four poles had then been driven into the ground (I do not know how with all the rocks in abundance) and hessian to about five feet in height nailed to three sides. The fourth side was a hinged frame of wood with hessian covering this time to about four feet in height.

The distinct advantage of this structure was that the C.O. could keep an eye on the far side of the camp and watch the traffic on its way to and from Trieste whilst he was doing something else.

Still on the subject of toilets I feel that I must describe the one that we shared on the other side of the camp. First of all there was a trench, no doubt dug by some poor so-and-so on jankers. This trench was some seven or eight feet long, two feet wide and about four feet deep. At each end was a roughly made wooden cross tipped on its side like the cross of St. Andrew. Resting on these two crosses was a pole secured by ropes. The practice in using this device was to drop ones shorts to the ankles and lean back with forearms resting on the pole, meanwhile holding a meaningful conversation with the other two or three who might be alongside you. I never saw a sergeant major there! Perhaps they don't like to be seen with their trousers down or maybe they don't enjoy good conversation!

At the fork in the road that I have described was a small rectangular brick building with the words 'Hocemo Tito' emblazoned on the side - not very well written because the Yugs sneaked around doing their graffiti in the hours of darkness. This, the only substantial building we hired, or rented, or leased, or commandeered, was, I found out, the shower. It was so tiny that only one person at a time could use it, undressing in one half and showering in the other. Because the water had to be brought in by bowser and pumped up to the roof tank the time permitted for each person was limited and supervised by a senior N.C.O.

When the word went round that the water was being pumped into the shower tank and that men of whatever company were due for shower parade it was customary to clothe as lightly as possible, wearing just shorts and sand shoes, so that maximum time could be spent actually under the shower. It was gravity fed and operated by pulling a chain with a stirrup handle. You only got water as long as you held onto the chain. The initial shock when you pulled that chain after being in the blazing sun was like being stabbed with a thousand icy needles. You would just be getting used to it when the cry would go up, 'Times up' and you would have to come out, the sun now feeling hotter than before, there was no need to bring a towel - you were dry in minutes.

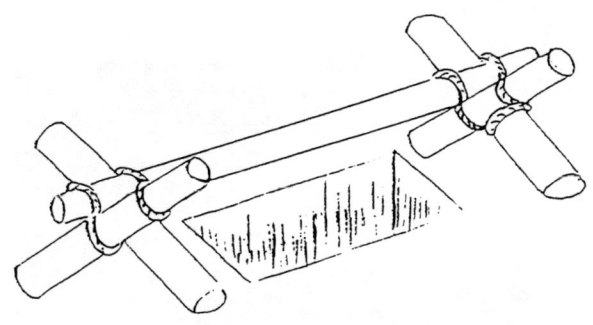

LATRINE AT DUINO

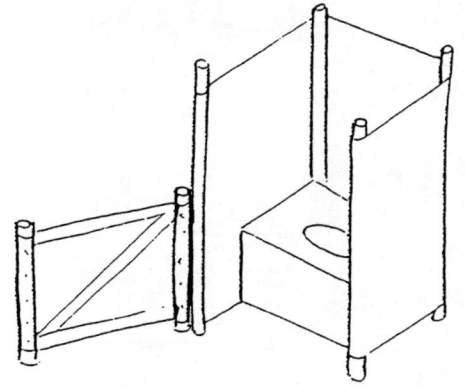

COLONEL'S TOILET AT DUINO

"INTERNATIONAL" TOILET AT O2E BATTAGLIA TERME

Latrines, various

Sick parade at Duino

As far as I could ascertain the role of the battalion was threefold. Firstly we were an extended bodyguard to Sir John who had his own personal bodyguard comprising of a small contingent of Military Police. Secondly, we supplied guards on a rota basis for places like the food store at Mestre, the road block at Trieste and our own twenty-four hour Regimental guard. Thirdly, we upheld a presence in the area which was considered to be very politically unstable.

Added to the above duties was a picket whose task it was to keep a watchful eye around the camp during the hours of darkness

I understood the need for this picket when my tent companions advised me to sleep with my rifle inside my blankets because there had been incidents of the Jugs (Yugoslavs) creeping down the hillside and thieving, with rifles and ammunition being top of their shopping list. The inconvenience of having a rifle in bed didn't seem to add much to the discomfort as it seemed to be all hard corners whichever way one turned.

One small advantage of sharing my bed with my rifle was that the cold night air didn't condense on the steel work so there was no chance of it getting rusty.

My medical classification excused me being involved in any of the guard duties so I had to be made useful in other ways. I became the Gunga Din of 'D' company, fetching and carrying as required. One of my regular tasks was to remove all the soot from the glasses of the hurricane lamps, of which there was a fair number, replenish the oil and adjust the wicks.

Another menial task was cleaning the tea canisters which resembled and performed the same job as a vacuum flask, except that they were about two feet long and about eight inches in diameter. Instead of glass these vessels had a lining of aluminium which had lost its polish at the open end somewhere in North Africa. The tea stains were almost impossible to remove so I asked if there was any abrasive powder available such as 'Vim'. The Q.M. explained that the usual practice was to make your own by rubbing two small pieces of rock together and catching the resultant grit on a copy of the 'Beano' or some such publication. I tried it and it worked.

Because of the nature of my work I was issued with a denim boiler suit which had seen better days but saved getting my khaki drill shirts and shorts dirty. It had no buttons so to preserve my dignity I gleaned a spare kitbag rope from the stores to use as a belt. My usual daily attire was a pair of underpants under my scruffy boiler suit and a pair of sand shoes.

When my work was done I changed into my proper uniform and looked like a soldier once more. At sun down it was compulsory to change into long trousers in order to minimise the number of mosquito bites.

We had no mosquito nets in the tents as it was impossible to hang them in the type of tents we inhabited so we did get a fair share of bites. Not as many as there could have been thanks to our 'Malarial Squad' - a party of men who toured around our area and, using back packs and syringes, sprayed any stagnant water with a fluid that prevented the little beggars' eggs hatching.

One night of my first week at Duino I had an unpleasant experience. I was awakened in the night feeling a light pressure on my chest. I am the type of person who on waking is immediately fully conscious. There is no drowsy half asleep period. My first thought was 'Jugs' and, not wanting to be knifed or dealt with in any other nasty manner, I kept perfectly still except for my eyelids. Opening my eyes, I could see by virtue of the fact that the moon was shining into the tent and we never bothered shutting the flap, that there was a snake lying across my chest. It was about one and a half inches in diameter and was draped with its head and tail on either side of my bed so must have been at least a yard in length. Whether or not it was poisonous I have no idea and I couldn't describe its markings to my pals next morning. I wondered, for a second or two, whether it was finding my body heat a comfort and whether it was likely to stay awhile but it soon made its way silently across me and slid under the wall of the tent.

Early one day I was told that I was to join a party that was destined to go on a foray into the mountainous area South East of Trieste. We were to go armed, not wearing our battle bowlers but cap comforters (a knitted woollen hat somewhat resembling the American doughboy's hat). My lot was to help out in the cookhouse in any way the cook could use me. The purpose of the trip was not announced but it was fairly obvious that it was to give the Chetniks the knowledge that the British Army was still policing the area and was still a presence to be respected.

The extremists from the Chetniks actually had little respect for anyone and frequently rode in a truck on to our little flat plateau. Their trespassing so flagrantly was exasperating because, not only was their truck an Austin three tonner (doubtless one that our boys had been forced to abandon in the Yugoslav conflict), but the rifles they brandished were Lee Enfields.

Our little party, about ten in number, set off in a jeep and a thirty hundredweight truck with food for the day. I was a passenger in the jeep which was the leading vehicle, the sergeant in charge obviously knowing the route either from previous experience or from having studied his map well the day before.

Having left the built up area far behind we found that we were gaining height rapidly as we progressed up a mountain track that had many tortuous turns and was not much wider than our vehicles. Inevitably we met traffic coming down. It was an old farmer with his donkey pulling a small dray. On meeting our jeep the donkey stopped in his tracks. The track here was, fortunately, a little wider and we thought that if the dray had two of its wheels hard against the mountainside we could just about get our vehicles past without losing two wheels over the edge.

None of us spoke the lingo but in very loud English it was explained to the old man what was wanted. He understood but, I'm afraid, his donkey did not and wouldn't budge. No amount of cajoling or beating could get him to move.

'Out of the trucks, lads' the sergeant shouted, 'We'll give him some help'. We placed ourselves around the dray and lifting it bodily moved it to the side of the track dragging the donkey's rear end along with it.

What a decent minded fellow that sergeant was. Another less thoughtful person might have moved the dray in the opposite direction with the risk of a frightened donkey and vehicle going over the edge and cascading down the mountain. We continued on our way and came to a halt in a bit of a clearing in a sparsely wooded area where we proceeded to go about our respective duties. The infantrymen disappeared with the sergeant in charge. I stayed with the cook and worked to his instructions. My first task was to unload about two dozen house bricks from the truck. These were set up in three rows as a basis for our barbecue. My next job was to collect a good supply of brush wood for the fires which were to blaze and smoulder between the bricks.

Some timetable must have been arranged between the sergeant and the cook because the squad appeared just as the chops and potatoes were ready for serving. Just a few minutes prior to this the cook had said to me, 'Will you make some gravy to go with these chops?' To which I replied, 'What do I use?' 'There is a bag of sugar somewhere ' he said, 'you know where the water tins are'. 'Just burn the sugar on that baking tray and add a little water at the right time'.

I hadn't a clue when the right time would be, so I confessed to my complete ignorance in such matters and left the job to him whilst I added wood to the fire, trying to look fully occupied. That gravy was probably the nicest I had tasted in the Army.

Stomachs replenished, the squad moved off again. 'Tiffin' was to be fried egg butties the cook told me and my job was to slice the bread. There was also butties to be made up with strawberry jam filling. The men would come back hungry so I was advised to slice the bread 'doorstep' thick. The example given was at least twice as thick as a thin slice of today's sliced loaf.

I sliced away at loaf after loaf through this crusty white bread with a knife that hadn't been sharpened since it left Sheffield and found that I had developed a blister with my efforts. The butter and jam were in seven pound tins which had to be opened with a can opener.

Estimating that each soldier would eat two jam butties following his fried egg sandwich I spread away noting that the stores had been generous in their allocation of all the varieties of food.

The men returned both weary and hungry. They had walked through the heat of the day and were more than ready to tuck into their repast. How the cook managed to satisfy each one as to how he wanted his egg fried I shall never know. He had half a dozen eggs on a baking tray greased with some butter and as each soldier presented his bottom round of bread for an egg to be deposited on it he would ask; 'Hard or soft?' 'Do you want it sunny side up?' He was a wizard with that spatula. Everyone had his egg butty and then the cry went up: 'Anyone for seconds before the strawberry jam?'

I had to set to slicing more bread for the several who wanted seconds. We ran out of eggs but no one seemed terribly disappointed as there was a stack of my strawberry jam butties and plenty of tea in the canister to wash them down.

Some hundred yards away in the wooded area we could hear some children laughing and shouting and the cook suggested that we should offer them a strawberry jam butty as we had plenty left over. So I and a couple of squaddies went towards the sound of their merriment. Having located them we beckoned to them to come and join us. They went silent and approached nervously, not knowing our intentions and no doubt afraid to disobey. We were unaware of what terrors they might have endured at the hands of strangers before and, not speaking their language, we couldn't allay their fears. There were five or six of them dressed in rags and not a pair of shoes or socks between them. They were dirty not having seen water for many a day and their poor legs were bearing cuts and scars, bruises and running sores. We instructed them in English and by signs that they should follow us and this they did for about half of the distance back when they halted and shouted out to us and at the same time pointed to the ground. Going back to them a little puzzled we found that they were pointing to a carpet of thorns that they couldn't traverse in their bare feet. We, of course, had Army boots and gaiters so had not noticed this hazard on our way to meet them. The answer was piggy-backs which seemed to relax the atmosphere for them and the journey through the thorns (the carpet was only three or four yards wide) saw them safely approaching our party. They sat obediently in a little arc and applied themselves to the sandwiches as though they hadn't eaten for days. There was no need to ask if they wanted 'seconds'. Ignoring my blister I happily sliced some more bread and spread it generously with butter and strawberry jam.

Now, more than fifty years later, I look upon this day as one of the happiest of my life. To see those happy faces partaking of a feast the like of which they had most likely never seen before was a glimpse of heaven. Those sparkling eyes and little words of appreciative chatter between bites was something I shall never forget.

To round off this happy incident we carried them back over the carpet of thorns each with a prize to carry home. A loaf for four of them and a half tin of butter for one, and a half tin of jam for the other. Instructions were given in a language that is almost universally known - 'A Mama' - and they disappeared laughing and shouting.

A few days after my excursion into Yugoslavia I was sitting in the tent writing to Josie. News from the U.K. took about five days to arrive, so by this time I had received my first letter from Josie, mine having taken the same amount of time informing her of my address. As I wrote I was trying to detach myself from two others who were in the tent and arguing loudly. They were each trying to persuade the other that they were right about some medical matter. It was impossible to gather my thoughts and apply myself to writing whilst they carried on so I put my pennyworth in by telling them which one was right. 'How the so-and-so do you know?' was the question from the loser. I explained that I had a certificate qualifying me as a competent first-aider and that I had served two years as a part-time member of a rescue team in the Civil Defence. My role as referee in the matter was not further disputed so I got back to my letter.

One of the highlights of each day occurred about eleven o'clock when the NAAFI truck used to pull up on our little plateau. On its arrival a shout would ring out 'NAAFI up' and everyone ,not on duty, would grab his pot and hurtle down the hillside to the truck and form a queue. The truck had a big panel in its side that was hinged and retained by chains which served as a counter. From this counter was issued mugs of tea and 'wads'. I soon learned that if you weren't in your tent or very near to it so that you could get your pot, then the rush down the hillside was not worth the effort because only the first forty or so got a mug of tea and only the first two dozen got a bun.

Being a little slack one day in getting to the NAAFI queue I was two or three places away from the counter when the word was shouted out 'Sorry, that's the lot, lads'. It was a particularly hot day and I was desperate for a drink so looking around to see that I was not observed I went to the water drums. I gave the dust and the dead flies a quick stir round and dipped in my mug. It was warm but it was wet. My luck was in - I didn't get an attack of dysentery or any other medical trouble that I had risked, as all water had to be boiled.

My only contact with the native population apart from the incident with the Yugoslav boys was when the lads in my tent introduced me to the woman from the village who did their washing and ironing. It was the strangest of introductions as we didn't speak each others language. The lads spoke in English and indicated by signs that I was a new customer for her and to me they said it would cost me two hundred lira a week. The amazing thing to me was how she and her four or five companions managed to remember what clothing belonged to which soldier especially as we were five or six to a tent and the tents themselves were scattered in a disorderly manner on the mountainside. There was never an error with my laundry and it was pressed and folded as neatly as if it had come right out of Burton's. Later on I saw the type of iron that they used and it was something new to me. The base was the same shape as today's electric iron but the body was some three inches deep and was hollow with a little hinged lid. Little bits of burning wood or charcoal supplied the heat.

The washer woman was about thirty five years of age and seemed to be of a serious disposition. It could easily be that her husband was a P.O.W or poorly paid and she was supplementing the family income by her labours. The nearest I got to a smile from her was a nod of appreciation when I paid her. It was about a day's pay to me but then there was little else to spend my money on as I didn't frequent the village bar but spent my evenings writing to Josie and my family.

Early one evening I was galloping down the mountainside on my way to the tent in order to change into trousers instead of shorts when the first notes of the bugle fanfare rang out. It was time to lower the flag and , as we all know that as the flag is being lowered, whatever a soldier is doing, he stops and stands to attention until the last note sounds. Racing pell mell, as I was, it took me several paces before I could come to a halt. A voice boomed out, 'Stand still, that man.' I came to a halt about six feet away from the owner of the voice, a sergeant major of another company. When the last note of the bugle had died he looked scathingly at me and asked, 'When did you last shave, soldier?' 'Last night, sir' I lied. It was actually the night before as I thought shaving daily was a waste of time with me being occupied in drudgery and not liable for parades. He grunted and gave me the benefit of the doubt. I was lucky.

A couple of days later I was busy with my daily task of cleaning the hurricane lamps when a soldier came rushing up to me and told me I was wanted at the guard room right away. I couldn't think what I could be wanted for but hastened over the road to find out. The guard had just been inspected. Two men stood on duty, brasses shining in the sun and blanco immaculate, outside the marquee entrance and the rest of them had filed inside to while away the time until their turn for guard duty came along. The guard commander, a sergeant (probably two years younger than myself) the C.S.M. and the inspecting officer stood outside chatting. What a comparison - the guard in their best KD nicely pressed, boots shiny, brasses glistening - and me in my ragged denim boiler suit (without a single button and held together with a kitbag rope) and a pair of sand shoes (pumps).

It was usual for the guard to be mounted with one man too many; that is to say nine men and the guard commander. The nine men would draw lots to see who was going to be 'stick man' The 'stick man's' duty was not to take a turn on guard duty but to be available to tend to the needs of the guards who were not on sentry or on patrol, collecting their food and drinks from the cook house etc.

As I approached the party of three, the C.S.M. turned to me and explained that one of the guard had suddenly reported sick and that I was to be stick man, foregoing the usual method of election. He then turned to the sergeant and said 'And put this man on a charge when your turn of duty is over. Charge him with not shaving'. I had thirty six hours of stubble on my chin. Some people never learn!

When the C.S.M. and Inspecting Officer had left the scene the sergeant said to me, 'I wont put you on a charge. If the C.S.M. should ask you, tell him that I gave you some extra duties instead. I'll back up that statement'. I thanked him and asked him what the extra duties would be. He explained where his tent was in relationship to the company office and said that under his pillow (the lucky blighter had a pillow) was a book. I was to go and collect it. It was a Western novel. Collecting that book turned out to be the full extent of my extra duties. I was lucky again!

From that day I never missed a morning shave. It might have been third time unlucky!

Exactly a week to the day after interrupting my two pals argument on a medical matter they told me that the M.O. wanted to see me and would I go along to the sick parade next morning. The M.O. had been holding first aid classes for a few weeks for anyone interested and they had told him about my interjection in their argument. I hadn't seen the M.O. and wondered if I was in for a roasting for giving my opinion. Was I treading on his corns?.

He had requested the pleasure of my company so there was little that I could do except accept his invitation to join the sick parade. There were about eight reporting sick and when he had seen to all of those I presented myself, telling him that I was not sick but he had wished to see me. He was sitting at his table when I went in but he rose when he realised that the parade was over and I could see that he stood about five feet eight, was well proportioned, had a shock of almost black hair, was in his late twenties and, as the conversation ensued, I found him friendly with no air of superiority as so many young commissioned officers I had met.

He questioned me about my first aid knowledge, how I had acquired it and to what extent I used it. To all of which I explained that I had taken my first year's exam in the Boys Brigade as a young teenager followed by gaining my badge in the second year's studies. Late in 1941 I had volunteered to join the local Civil Defence group as a member of the Light Rescue Team. I was accepted immediately in view of my qualifications, especially as the team leader turned out to be the very person who had lectured me over my two years studies when in the Boys Brigade. I signed on for a twelve hour shift every Sunday night. Most of these nights were occupied by lectures from doctors who could spare a few hours and by practising our skills on pseudo injuries and labelling them so that hospitals could appreciate the extent and nature of the damages. Luckily our area did not suffer much bombing on Sunday nights and my practical application of the skills learned was very little.

Did I mind if he tested me with a few questions he asked? To which I replied that I wouldn't mind in the least. A number of questions followed; on anatomy, physiology, the application of triangular bandages etc, all answered, I was proud to feel, to his satisfaction.

His next question both surprised and delighted me. 'Would I like to join his staff?' Not only would it mean doing something I was interested in but it would mean no more hurricane lamps and tea canisters. (and making my own Vim). 'Yes please' I said. He said he would arrange the transfer explaining that it would of necessity be an informal one meaning that I would remain on the strength of 'D' company but be attached to H.Q. company. I didn't mind how he arranged it and was over the moon when I became 'attached' a couple of days later.

My new colleagues were three in number, the senior member being Corporal Waterhouse. One of the first words I learnt in the Italian language was the direct translation of his name 'Waterhouse' to Aquacasa and this was what he was called by everyone. Next was 'Kemp' (his surname) and he was addressed universally as 'Kempie'. Then there was Albert, who was the M.O's batman, and not accomplished in any way with regards to first aid.

My new boss, the M.O., seemed pleased with my enthusiasm for the new job and I found myself present at sick parade most mornings.

The general health of the battalion was not good due mostly I believe for two reasons. Firstly, the diet was poor and in no way balanced. This was no fault of the cooks who were doing a remarkable job with the facilities and ingredients to hand. Secondly, the unsatisfactory sanitary arrangements

On most mornings the majority of patients were complaining of boils the majority of which were located on the back of the neck. I believed that the reason for all these painful swellings being located in this area was the neck was the favourite area for the mosquito to bite and having bitten the patient would scratch the area of the bite leaving a minute area open for infection. Trousers were worn and shirt sleeves rolled down and fastened during the hours after dusk when the insects were most active so there wasn't much opportunity for them to bite elsewhere. I spent many hours, I might say many happy hours because I was attempting to relieve their pain, preparing and applying hot poultices. Many necks got very sore from the daily applications of sticking plaster which held the dressings in situ and they often broke out into further boils.

It seemed that as the number of boils diminished the number of impetigo cases increased. The M.O. was well aware of how infectious this ailment was and advised each patient to get a biscuit tin from the NAAFI (or elsewhere) and use it exclusively for himself to wash in as the trouble was being passed from one to another via the washing bowls. There was no facility for sterilising or disinfecting them. The NAAFI did not sell so many biscuits and therefore it was difficult to make any headway with regard to the disease. We therefore resorted to painting each patient's affected area with Gentian Violet. Had this happened a few months earlier the Germans would have thought they were fighting the ancient Britons as there were so many purple stained faces throughout the battalion.

As I now had more or less fixed hours of duty and could not be called upon to perform unexpected tasks (such as stick man), I thought I would acquaint myself with the town of Monfalcone where we had stopped to enjoy a refreshing cup of tea on our way to Duino. Setting off along the road, when I felt that the entire camp was indulging in siesta with the exception of the two guards outside the guard room, I had only progressed half a mile or so when a staff car with pennant flying came along. It drew to a halt beside me and the occupant got out to address me. I knew that it was frowned upon to leave the camp during siesta time and I could feel myself preparing some excuses for being on my own in the heat of the day. In the second that it took this officer to reach me I had decided that my best excuse was that I'd only been in the country three weeks (true) and that I was ignorant on siesta rules (almost true).

The officer was dripping with gold braid and I could see from his insignia that he was a General. He was in fact Sir John and I gave him my very best salute which he returned. Why he wanted to stop and have a word with an ordinary soldier I have never been able to fathom for he hadn't stopped to chastise me but seemed genuinely interested in where I came from and was I enjoying life with the North Staffs. In the brief time that we conversed he came across as a very nice fellow and I felt sorry (but didn't tell him so) that he had to wear all that heavy garb and Sam Browne belt and gold tasselled epaulettes and ridiculous hat whilst I was in cool khaki drill.

I strode out and within an hour I was in the approaches to the town. I passed the Salvation Army outpost which was one of the first buildings I came to, thinking I'll have another cup of tea there on my way back. As I walked on I thought; ' Why have I come here at siesta time?' The place was lifeless with all the shops closed and houses all shuttered up.

At a photographer's shop I stopped to look in his window and thought; 'Yes, that's an idea. A photo in my new uniform to send to Josie and to home'. Whether he was normally open for business in the afternoon I don't know but I saw movement in the shop so I tried the door and lo and behold it was open.

Down to business right away. He spoke no English and in the three weeks I'd been in the country the only natives I'd had contact with was my laundry lady and her little girl so my Italian extended to Good Morning, Good Evening, Good Night and a fair grasp that I'd gained of numbers from my tent pals.

I indicated by signs that I would like to be photographed and he showed me some of his work asking whether I wanted a portrait in full length standing by his obligatory aspidistra plant on a bamboo table or did I want a head and shoulders job. 'Be a devil', I thought, and go for both.

We went into his studio at the back of the shop and he proceeded to stand me in the correct stance for the full length portrait, tilting my chin to the correct angle, positioning my hand on the back of the chair, flicking the dust of the road off my boots and so on until he was satisfied. He used an old mahogany plate camera so with that and the set up in the studio it felt as though I had stepped back in time a generation or two.

For the head and shoulders job he sat me down in the chair and viewed me from my left side, my right side and the centre. Assuming that he judged my profile showed too much nose, he set my facial position and told me to look at a certain object on the wall. (I forget what it was). He then adjusted the height of the tripod and brought it and the camera much nearer to me, looking through the lens from time to time as he determined its final position. Satisfied with the position he put his face right in front of mine and said 'Fare Cose' (pronounced 'faree cosy') and licked his lips. I didn't understand so he repeated it and made a great show of licking his lips and pointing to the fact that he was doing this and that I should do likewise. He smiled his appreciation that he had got through to me - the first time he had smiled. He took his job very seriously.

The shutter clicked as the magnesium flared and the ordeal was over. It would be five days, he explained, using his fingers to count slowly in front of me, before the finished article would be ready for collection and I settled for three prints of each postcard size.

When I came to the building with the Salvation Army sign over its doorway I went in as I had promised myself and found that I was the only 'customer'. A cheery round-faced man of about forty five years of age greeted me and told me that he was a Major in the S.A. and gave me his name which I have long ago forgotten. When I said I would enjoy a cup of tea he immediately offered an alternative. 'How would you like some tinned fruit?' he asked. That was a luxury that I hadn't tasted for years and I jumped at the chance. Opening a tin he poured the whole lot into a bowl and put it before me on a little cafe style table. I don't think I ever enjoyed tinned fruit more. It was icy cold, having come straight from the fridge, and in such direct contrast to my normal diet.

He chatted to me as I delighted my taste buds and, when I had finished, he asked me if he could show me the hall at the rear of the building. I could not think what reason he could have but I naturally acceded to his suggestion. It was a rectangular room of about fifty feet by twenty five feet and had a number of doors leading off to ante-rooms which, I presumed, would be kitchen, cloakroom and toilets etc.. He told me that the building had been the Northern Headquarters of Tito's army and that this was the room which had served them as a banqueting hall. The floor was the part of which he was most proud and he explained to me that on taking over the building that floor was covered inches deep in chicken bones and skin, crusts of bread and general food refuse. My mind went back to films of Henry VIII throwing his bones over his shoulder (not his bones but the bones of his food). He had personally, on his own hands and knees, scraped the whole place clean and restored the parquet floor to its original state. It glowed with a high polish and he was, justifiably, proud of it.

The medicines in our F.A.P. were naturally very basic. The most frequently dispensed medicine which was prescribed for coughs, colds, headaches and hangovers (the local wine, I was told, was rather rough) was one codeine, one Dover and one aspirin. These tablets were taken on the spot with instructions to return for a repeat dose at six o'clock.

Of the liquid medicines Mist Tressilicate for tummy upsets was the one we had to replenish most frequently, followed by quinine (given for high temperatures), Mist Expect Sed for persistent coughs, Lotio Plumbi for bruises and, of course, Gentian Violet for those who succumbed to impetigo. I actually developed quite a taste for quinine and I used to treat myself most afternoons to a little 'nip'. There was also surgical spirit to clean wounds and a salve (which, I think, was called acraflavin and had a strong orange colour) and, lastly, there was a plentiful supply of methylated spirit with which we heated our steriliser, this also doubling up as our source of heat for the poultices I have mentioned.

As with all things there are exceptions to the rules and one morning there were, in fact, two exceptions at sick parade. 'Homer, will you patch up these two men?' was the request. It was difficult to know where to start, so many patches were required, and most of the areas were not very suitable for bandaging, Everywhere a bone came near to the skin - the ankles, the knees, the hips, the shoulders, the elbows, the wrists, even the shoulder blades - there were nasty abrasions. First I had to clean the wounds which must have been quite painful and then apply dressings of gauze and lint, bandaging where I could or fixing with plaster where I couldn't. As I worked on the first one with his pal sitting on the ground nearby I asked how they had come to get such injuries and so identical.

'We were in a bar in Yugoslav territory' he started (we were only a stones throw from Chetnik country) 'and having a nice drink of the local plonk' 'That silly bugger gives the glad eye to a tart on the other side of the room, the only trouble being that she wasn't a tart, she was the wife of a bloke in the same bar'

It ensued that a fight developed and the local police were called in resulting in our two squaddies being banged up for the night. They were released next morning but the local population were not happy with the lack of punishment and decided to mete out some summary justice. This took the form of securing them both in chains and dragging them round the village behind an ox cart.

I won't say they both became teetotal! However, they were charged with being absent without leave but I never learned the outcome of their case.

Now that I was attached to H.Q. company I found myself amongst a different crowd of lads and one that I came across was one from my own home town. Wilf Dovey was about three years my junior and, in the Boys Brigade, had been a private when I had attained the dizzy height of warrant officer. Now it was I who was the private whilst he wore three stripes. The old adage came to mind about being nice to people when you're on the way up because you may meet them on the way down. He had always been a well behaved lad and a credit to the Company (1st. Cradley Heath Company, South Staffs and North Worcs Battalion). Could it be that the discipline and training in the B.B. had helped him achieve his auspicious rank? It hadn't done much for me rank wise!

I have previously detailed the location of the C.O's 'bog' and I have stated that he never rose until noon (or so it was reported). Putting these facts together it is not difficult to see that there was a great temptation to put the contrivance to greater use. It's not that I suffered from delusions of grandeur or that I felt superior to my colleagues in any way, but I did relish the idea of sitting, almost majestically, instead of leaning against that common pole.

Giving way to my temptation I tried it out. It was definitely a far greater pleasure attending to my needs in this respect and the morning visit became a habit. I honestly believe that, apart from the rightful owner, I was the only person to use it. There is mention, especially amongst forces personnel, of catching diseases from lavatory seats but I felt confident that I wouldn't catch drunkenness. One morning, as I sat there watching the traffic and musing and generally feeling at peace with the world I was suddenly assailed from beneath. The pain was not to be compared to the kick of a mule. That would have been a small ache in comparison. It was as if a stiletto had pierced me and a red hot stiletto at that. I feel it only reasonable to assume that a cry of anguish left me but I do not recall whether I had enough presence of mind to stifle it; particularly in view of where I was located. I do remember, however, leaping up and grabbing the parts that I would have hesitated showing my mum. My hand came away with the biggest red ant I have ever seen.!

I continued to favour the contrivance after that but only after a very careful examination of the seating arrangements.

A week had passed since I took my walk to Monfalcone and had had my session in the photographer's studio so I made my way there again in the company of two other squaddies but this time in the evening. After collecting my photographs with which I was rather pleased, apart from the full length one which seemed to give me the appearance of superiority more becoming to a young subaltern, we retired to a bar to spend a lazy evening. We had the best part of an hours walk back to camp so we left the bar at about ten o'clock bearing in mind that reveille was at five thirty.

We hadn't walked more than two hundred yards before a jeep came to a halt alongside us and a voice in very good English, 'Are you going to Duino?' When we replied in the affirmative we were invited to jump aboard which we did with smiles all round.

Leaving the town in an Easterly direction the road at some time ran beneath a bridge that carried a railway track from inland to the docks. The bridge had been destroyed and the remnants of the archway hung threateningly over part of the road with the ends of the rails projecting out into fresh air. As we approached this ruin which stood some fifty feet high the driver put his foot down so viciously on the accelerator that we almost fell out of the jeep as we were sitting on the tailboard. The driver explained that on occasions the 'Jugs' came along the old railway track and hurled rocks on to any passing Army vehicles and as he was driving a jeep he was playing safe by giving them as little time as possible to do their dirty work. Having passed this spot he moderated his speed and dropped down to about 70 m.p.h. Sitting on the tailboard in the cold night air at that speed it felt as though my hair was being pulled out by the roots and my scalp tingled for hours afterwards.

As I was now accepted as a medical orderly I automatically was assigned my position on the duty roster and consequently spent one night in three on the premises. We didn't stay up all night but slept in a camp bed in the F.A.P. and to the best of my memory that sleep was never interrupted by any emergency. Likewise one of us was always on duty just in case treatment was required at some time other than the official sick parade.

During one such spell of duty in the afternoon I was busy writing my daily missive to Josie when someone appeared at the tent flap. Silhouetted against the sky it was impossible to see who it was but the outline of the cap assured me that he was an officer. I stood up smartly to attention as I couldn't salute being attired only in shorts and sand shoes. He said, 'Good afternoon, soldier'. My rank was an unknown quantity so he played it safe. As he stepped into the tent I thought, 'Oh, no, not Sir John' because here was someone festooned with gold braid. It was not Sir John, he introduced himself as the ADMS (Assistant Director of Medical Services) and, I discovered later, he was the chief medical man in the whole of the theatre. I had found Sir John to be smallish in stature whilst this man was slightly above average height, of a good build and about forty five years of age.

He asked me of the whereabouts of the M.O. and fortunately I was in a position to tell him. The M.O. was an excellent swimmer and he had told me that he was going for a dip in the Adriatic. Maybe because ninety nine per cent of our battalion came from the midlands with no access to the sea and few swimming baths there weren't many swimmers although a fair number splashed about in the shallow water of the bay when they weren't on duty.

We went round to the rear of the tent to see whether the M.O. was within hailing distance but found that he was a good mile out to sea on his own. As the ADMS said it was important that he saw him I said that I would ask someone to go out there to give him the message. I picked up the field telephone hoping that 'Kingie' would be in the signals office and not on duty. Kingie was the best swimmer in the battalion and it was my lucky day.

Kingie came at the double clad in swimming trunks as he usually was and I explained the situation to him, pointing out the swimmer I felt sure was the M.O. With no more to-do he took a run and launched himself in a swallow dive off our escarpment. The little plateau we were living on was about fifty feet above the sea and from months of experience he knew the disposition of the rocks at the foot of our little cliff. As he emulated Tarzan on his way to reach the M.O. the ADMS entered into a conversation resembling that of Sir John. (Something they teach at Sandhurst?)

He asked me how I liked living under canvas and I replied that in this climate it suited me fine except on the odd occasion that it rained when you might as well stand outside in it as it came right through the canvas. He could well understand it he said because he remembered condemning this canvas in North Africa two years before! I was pleased that he didn't question me on the health of the battalion in case the M.O. had been cooking the books for some reason and my opinion might have clashed with his records. We filled up the time it took for the M.O. to appear (in trunks) with small talk.

On another occasion that I was on duty in the afternoon I witnessed an accident in the road. It is very rare that a person actually sees an accident. In the majority of incidents it is a case of a sound attracting attention followed by the witness turning to see the results of the accident. Stood as I was outside the F.A.P. I was in an ideal position to see, not only the accident, but all the circumstances leading up to it and to play an important part in its sequel.

Where the coastal road passed the area that we occupied it was wide enough for two vehicles to pass comfortably but wouldn't allow the width of three and, of course, was unmarked. Coming from the direction of Trieste the road made a long right hand curve as it passed the village and dipped slightly as it progressed.

As I gazed I saw a truck coming from the direction of Trieste. It had three short trailers each one with a huge cask that are used for treading grapes. Full or empty I do not know but I thought he was making good headway considering his load. No sooner had I fixed my gaze on him than a jeep appeared travelling in the same direction. The driver of the jeep swung out and proceeded to overtake. I noticed that he had no passengers. He accelerated and was advancing along the side of the trailers when, out of the corner of my eye, I saw a car approaching from the opposite direction which he, because of the bend in the road, could not see. I estimate that the jeep was in alignment with the first trailer (nearest the truck) when the driver spotted the car approaching at a good speed. The driver of the jeep realised he hadn't enough speed to overtake the truck before the car would be upon him so he braked fiercely. Turning to get behind the last trailer, with the car almost upon him, he mis-judged it and caught his wing on the trailer. The jeep bounced across the road and went over the edge falling some seven or eight feet and landing almost upside down.

Anticipating injury to the driver I dashed into the tent, grabbed the field telephone and asked the Signals duty man if he had any pals in their tent and if so would he ask two or three of them to come at the double to collect a stretcher. I briefly explained the situation and the site of the accident and asked them to go with the stretcher, gather up the patient (I felt sure there would be one) and bring him along to me. The M.O. had told me that he was going to the opera in Trieste and would be taking the ambulance as his transport so there was no point in me sending a runner to gain his services.

My next move was to put a light to the steriliser as I could foresee the need to use sterilised surgical tools. Many thoughts whizzed through my brain as I checked on splints, bandages, field dressings and so on. If it was a head injury could I still apply a capeline bandage as I used to be able to do? I mustn't forget to put a label with the time on it if I fitted a tourniquet. Could there even be a case for amputation? My mind oscillated from trepidation to exhilaration. On the one hand I had no help and feared what complications there might be. On the other hand I looked forward to a challenge the results of which would transcend all the glory I had achieved by applying hot poultices.

Still busy with my preparations, the two signals men appeared with the stretcher but no one on it. They explained that the M.O. had been delayed and was just about to leave for Trieste when the accident happened so he had decided to take the injured driver to hospital in Trieste. My moment of glory was not to be.

I learned that the injury was indeed a nasty one. The driver's foot had been caught between the pedals and as he had been twisted round in the fall his knee joint had given way resulting in his foot facing in the wrong direction. He was not from our unit so we never heard anything about his recovery or progress.

I now had plenty of time to write to Josie and there always seemed to be things happening to write about. For Josie it must have been harder with her job, the housework, the shopping and two voluntary evening jobs but she never failed to send me at least one letter each week. Then suddenly there was no mail from her. Three weeks and no letter. I could only fear the worst. She had found someone she liked better.

At the end of the third week without a letter from Josie I received one addressed to me in a hand I didn't recognise. On opening it I found it to be from her mother and it explained briefly the cause of the absence of any letters from her daughter. She had had an accident, I was informed, and would be writing to me in the course of the next few days.

My worries changed from being about whether or not I had been abandoned to worries about the nature and extent of her injuries and how she came by them. I could only imagine that the injuries were of a serious nature as an inability to write for such a period implied, unless it was a case of a broken wrist or damage to the hand.

The very next day I received a letter from Josie detailing the cause of the absence of letters. Leaving the office one lunchtime, she explained, she had slipped on the concrete steps (she worked in a first floor office) and had fallen, striking her head and had been rendered unconscious. She had been unconscious for some little time but on coming round had been helped back to the office where she sat for some time to gather her composure. Instead of sending her off to the hospital to be examined and X-rayed in case of a fractured skull the callous chief clerk told her to get the bus home and rest for the remainder of the day. He didn't even send a junior to accompany her safely to her home.

On arriving home her mother promptly phoned for the doctor. She came and gave vent to her feelings about the lack of common sense of the chief clerk, but more importantly, ordered complete quiet for the patient who she said was suffering from concussion and may drift in and out of consciousness. Each of the next few days she paid a visit and when the considerable swelling had subsided she expressed her opinion that if there was a fracture it was only a hairline one and posed no threat.

Some part of my three weeks of anxiety was due, I found out, to a delay in delivery of the post. Whether this was a fault on the part of the G.P.O. or whether the Army postal authorities had misdirected some of their mail I don't know, but I felt that if they must have weaknesses in their system they should arrange them at a more convenient time.

From our slightly elevated position it was easy to see what was going on at the beach, at the cookhouse and dining room areas. One day I noticed that the two bivouacs that housed the POW's were missing and enquired about it at the dining room asking one of the cooks what had happened to his helpers. They had lost their privileged position (nearest accommodation to the Adriatic) by virtue of the fact that one of them had enquired of two passing ladies attired for a dip; what their charges were. How were they to know that it was the wife of Sir John and her companion? Late September was approaching and with it a change in the weather. It was a shade cooler in the evenings and we were getting more showers. One change in the weather that appealed to me was the increase in electrical storms at night. I spent many happy hours watching the lightening playing amongst the mountain peaks during the hours of darkness. The lightening was so different from any I had seen in England. Flashes would last many seconds and would light up the entire countryside, showing everything in colour not just the black and white with silhouettes that I was used to seeing. I never heard of any damage caused by the lightening and can only guess that if there was any it was confined to the uninhabited tops of the mountains.

The word went around that we were about to move. We all hoped that our new home would be more substantial than the condemned canvas that we were now under and that there might even be some kind of improvement to our sleeping arrangements.

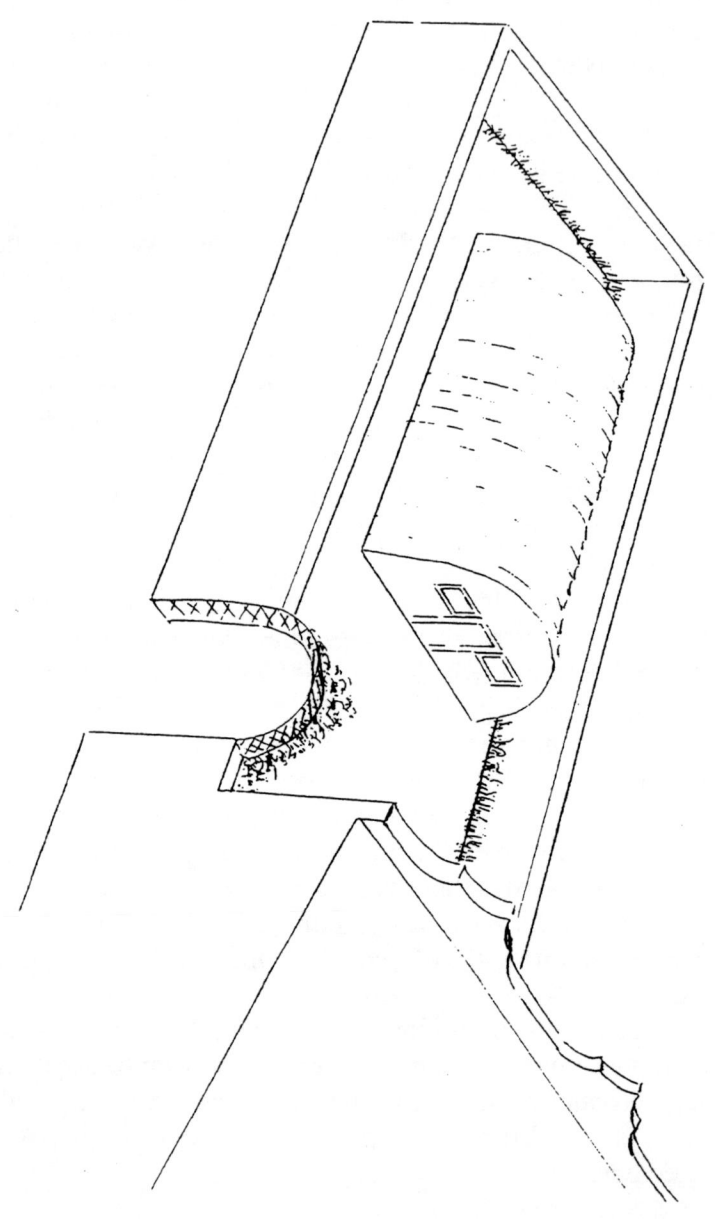

First-aid post at Paese
(Washing line not included)

Chapter Five
The Move

Orders were issued to the effect that we would be striking camp on such and such a day. I didn't keep a diary during my service life and so I am relying on my memory and all I can say is that it would be a day in late September or early October. (Shortly after our marriage Josie and I agreed to burn all our letters to each other although we had kept them all. We had each other and the hundreds of letters had served their purpose. Had we kept the letters I could have given a precise date to the move.. But it is of no great consequence).

An advance party went ahead a couple of days before the main body in order to set up the cookhouse which would have a meal ready for them on arrival.

On the appointed day we washed, shaved and breakfasted as usual and then set to stow everything aboard a thirty hundred weight truck that was assigned to us. When I say 'we' I refer to Aquacasa, Kempie and myself as Albert had been detailed to stay behind with the rear party, the M.O. being one of the officers left behind and he felt that he couldn't manage without his batman.

We loaded the medicine cabinet, the table, the bottles of medicine, the steriliser and the whole contents of the tent with the exception of the two chairs which, we thought, we might as well put on last as Kempie and I would be riding 'shotgun' on top of all the gear, with Aquacasa sharing the cab with the driver. Then we took up the tent pegs and folded the tent into a compact shape. As I have said before, the canvas was old, so with having lost its proofing by virtue of all the sunlight and constant attention of the coastal winds, it was quite easy to fold and drape over the complete load. The top of the load we found was higher than the cab so the prospect of putting the two chairs on top of that was a bit daunting. We placed the chairs beneath the canvas and elected to sit at the forward end of the load with our feet on top of the cab. As the saying goes we would be like 'two tits on a hayrick' and we were hoping that the speed of the convoy would not exceed the 25 m.p.h. recommended and that the journey would not be along a mountainous terrain.

Queuing for our haversack rations there was, as you can imagine, a lot of chatter. There was a buzz of excitement running through the battalion with thoughts and hopes being expressed about our future accommodation and duties. Some were saying that it couldn't get worse (they were averaging three guard duties each week not counting the picket duty to ward off the attentions of the Jugs). Some were going to miss their frequent splash in the sea unless by some chance we were going to another sea side venue. Generally there was a kind of happy excitement. Perhaps the fact that we would be moving Westerly (since we were about as far East as we could go) meant we would geographically be so much nearer home.

On collecting our rations we were told that the convoy would stop on route to our destination and that rations should be saved until then as tea would be available (from those aforementioned canisters) to wash them down.

At eleven o'clock the convoy began to build up on the road with our truck being about fourth in line Kempie and I were wishing things would get a move on. We were perched way up there in the blistering sunshine and we were looking forward to the breeze that our movement would bring about.

One of the squaddies in the truck ahead had befriended a dog and the dog was anxiously trying to get to his temporary master who was a passenger. He was an Alsatian and had been well fed and looked in good condition but he wasn't into jumping aboard a three tonner with the tail board up. As we set off at a leisurely pace to give the drivers a chance to adjust to the approved convoy spacing the dog ran behind the truck and as the pace increased so did his. Poor dog. He gave up after about two miles when he could no longer keep up with the speed of the truck. I wonder what happened to him. If he went back to the village I doubt whether any villager would take him in (Italians generally are not fond of pets). They could barely afford to feed themselves never mind a huge dog.

After about two hours driving at a steady pace we came to a piece of unfenced barren land alongside a river and the convoy was shepherded by a couple of Military Policemen into a circle on this land. This was our picnic area. My mind went back to those captivating films of my childhood when in those early Westerns the settlers always made a circle of their wagons when the Indians attacked.

Tea was dispensed and we tucked into our sandwiches.

For some reason, which I was unable to comprehend, we had to make a detour which incorporated fording the river at this point, which was about forty foot wide at the spot which lay opposite the inferior road we were about to take. Engineers had laid a concrete causeway wide enough for vehicles to pass over with three or four feet to spare each side for safety. The river flowed over this causeway at a good speed at about axle height. The water was crystal clear and was about four feet deep where there was no concrete, shelving gradually to the river's edges.

The two M.Ps took up positions ready for the convoy to move on, the guide fording the river on his motor cycle and waiting for the first truck to follow. The second M.P., a haughty obnoxious character, drove to the centre of the river and sitting astride his bike beckoned the first truck on to the causeway the vehicle being about two feet from the downstream edge of the concrete. He had to keep his engine running at a fair speed as the exhaust was in the water. It was a possibility, I suppose, that due to the river surface reflecting the sky it could have been difficult for the truck driver to see the causeway clearly and that a marker of some kind was necessary, but judging from the attitude of the conceited fellow it was more a case of showing off before the battalion.

Two or three trucks had made it to the other side of the river and were forming up in line awaiting the remainder; the M.P. still astride his bike making a great show of urging on the drivers. The temptation to deride this individual was too great and a large number were shouting unflattering remarks and suggestions to him which he never acknowledged.

Kempie and I were ideally situated, sitting on the top of our load, to witness what happened next. As I said previously the driver had to keep up a fair number of revs of his engine and he had failed to notice that, no doubt because of the vibration set up, the river was taking advantage of the situation and was very slowly edging him towards the limit of the concrete. His left foot went over the edge. He wobbled. There was not enough time to let out the clutch and rev up to get clear before the pressure of the water swept him over. A tremendous cheer went up. I'm sure it wouldn't have been bettered if the King had suddenly appeared. He was not hurt physically apart from being plunged into the icy cold mountain water but I'd like to bet that his pride took a knock when trying to explain how his machine ended up at the bottom of the river.

After a brief spell on the third class road, during which time Kempie and I tried to emulate limpets by hanging desperately on to the canvas beneath us, we came to a first class road once more and then proceeded uneventfully.

It was dusk when our driver pulled up two feet behind the preceding truck with a sigh of relief and the remark 'This must be it'. Two and a half minutes later, the truck that was following us did not pull up behind us but rammed us fair and square in the rear,. Kempie and I almost shot off the back on to the truck's bonnet. That wasn't the end of it. Our driver had not applied his hand brake when coming to a halt with the result that our truck shot forward colliding with the rear of the one in front. Kempie and I almost shot over our cab on to our bonnet. I hadn't had so much fun since I was on the dodgems at Pat Collin's Fun Fair.

Three damaged trucks. Three irate and weary drivers all cursing and blaming each other. Our truck, the filling in the sandwich, came off worst with a ruptured radiator. What a good thing that it happened at the end of the journey.

The cooks had done a good job and we did their work justice. When we were shown over our new quarters we must have presumed that we had been killed in that crash. We were most definitely in heaven. Our new home was a Nissen hut with electric light and running water. After tucking into that very welcome meal the three of us got down to unloading our gear and placing it in the appropriate compartments, the hut having been divided into three equal compartments. The centre third we assigned as our sleeping quarters and the third nearest the entrance to the compound over which we presided was to be the surgery.

Over the course of the next few days we got acquainted with our circumstances. We were occupying three Nissen huts apart from the one I have already described in the grounds of a moderately sized villa. You may wonder as I did 'how do you get a battalion into four Nissen huts'? The answer is that the battalion had actually been split and what happened to the remainder after leaving two rifle companies and three M.T. blokes with us I do not know. What I do know is that we never saw the M.O. again and guess that he must have recruited a new staff from the companies with which he was now stationed. We in the meantime had to fend for ourselves when it came to sick parades.

The officers occupied the villa. It would have been interesting to see what comforts they had there but I never found the opportunity to cross the threshold. The two officers that had been my patients at Duino never showed up so I presumed that they were with the other portion of the battalion. One of them had endured a particularly long session of boils whilst the other, a Major, had found my massage beneficial with regards to his lumbago.

It is interesting to note that about this time the battalion was re-designated. For some obscure reason we suddenly became the 107th North Staffs.

Our Nissen hut, the new F.A.P., was built in what in better times had been the stable yard and was surrounded on three sides by a rendered wall of about six feet in height and on the fourth side by the stables. Whoever had occupied this site before had the time and equipment to convert these stables into a smashing shower unit. All of the timber work had been removed

With MT Wallah patient

With Kempie

leaving a bare rectangular room the walls of which had been whitened just as the Army knows how. The water was fed through a single pipe to a row of sprinklers and it had the added pleasure of being lukewarm. Now we could soap each other's backs, something it was impossible to do in the solitary confinement job at Duino

Between our F.A.P. compound and the officers' quarters stretched a spinney of deciduous trees the canopy of which gave complete shade for the two hundred yards between. In the centre of this little bit of woodland was the latrine - much after the fashion of the one at Duino but not in the blazing sun and considerably more private.

Having familiarised myself with the geography of the camp I went on a tour of the village in which we found ourselves. Italians have a penchant for giving places lovely flowery names and I found that this village was no exception to the practice. It was called Paese (pronounced Payeasy) and means countryside. Apart from the ones engaged in field work I would imagine the population would be mainly employed in the town of Treviso only a few miles distant easily reached on a bicycle as the area is in no way mountainous.

The village consisted of simple cottages, a church, a bar, a barber's shop and a little school. It only took half an evening to cover the whole territory.

A few days after our arrival news reached us of a tragic and very sad event.

The corporal who ran the NAAFI at Duino was one of the rear party left behind to tidy up the site and to leave it as though we had never been there. He and a pal had decided to have a bit of fun one evening before joining us on completion of their task. They had made up their minds, for devilment more than larceny, to climb over the gate or wall to the greengrocer's premises in the village and pinch a few apples. The shop and adjoining yard was only fifty to sixty yards from the entrance to the castle and when the owner, hearing the thieves, shouted that he was being robbed the two guards on duty at the castle gate were alerted. The two lads were back over the gate and setting off down the road when one of the guards called out; 'Halt. Who goes there?' There was no reply - just scampering feet. The next statement; 'Halt or I fire' was shouted but ignored. The guards were quite right in challenging and taking action as the incident could quite easily have been a diversion created by the 'Jugs' to create havoc in the castle. The guard fired and although it was dark his aim at the direction of the sound of retreating footsteps was good. His bullet hit the corporal in the back.

Unfortunately the M.O. had joined fellow officers of the rear party in a visit to Trieste so the onus of looking after the injured corporal fell upon Albert, who was listed as a medical orderly but had no medical knowledge. The patient was lifted into the ambulance and was accompanied by Albert whilst the driver went hell for leather to the hospital at Trieste. Whether the corporal's life could have been saved if one of our first-aiders had been there we will never know. He died next day, leaving a widow and two young children.

Religion was a subject on which Josie and I had only lightly touched. She was of the Roman Catholic persuasion and I was a staunch Methodist. In one of her letters she had suggested that there was no better place than Italy to find out more about her faith. I could hardly dispute that so I set to in the most obvious way - I went to the church in the village. The church was empty and I assumed that the house next door was the presbytery as it stood out from the rest of the houses in regard to its architecture, so I presented myself there and rang the bell.

A little elderly lady dressed in black came to the door and, since I didn't speak Italian, I asked in English if she spoke my language, thinking that there was little chance of a reply in the affirmative. I was right. She murmured 'Momento', turned on her heels and sped back along the hall.

A slim, lovely-looking priest about thirty years of age came to the door and, I presume, asked me what I wanted or how he could help me. I said; 'Do you speak English?' He understood but replied; 'Non'. Then I asked him; 'Parlez vous Français?'. 'Ah, mais oui' he said, to which I said I only spoke a few words. At school I had given up languages in favour of handicrafts so my knowledge in that sphere was minimal. His French, although he claimed not to be very good at it, was understandable although having a strong Italian flavour.

He invited me into a fair-sized room that sported a nice big table and half a dozen chairs. It could well have been a committee room. There was no upholstery in sight and the walls had many shelves full of books.. It was, without doubt, his workplace.

His name, he told me, was Don Vittorio Freschi and he was the parish priest and also the village teacher. I answered with my name only. After asking me to sit down and occupying a seat opposite he got down to the nitty-gritty, asking the purpose of my visit. I told him that I would like to learn about his religion but in order to do that, as he was also a teacher, could he first of all teach me some basic Italian?

Excusing himself he quickly left the room and was back again before I could have a good look round, carrying a tiny book. Opening it at the first pages of text he showed me the present tense of the verb 'to be' and asked me if I had learned the equivalent in French. 'Yes, I have,' I replied.

As he was explaining that the book was also a vocabulary, the very one he used in the school, another priest came into the room and I was introduced to Don Luigi Morreto. Don Luigi was a sturdier man about five years older than DonVittorio. (aren't they lovely sounding names?). I was told that I could borrow the book and although it did not have an English translation of the words I found that as they were in related groups there was quite a bit I could pick up in the way of nouns. For example, I remember a group of words relating to the human body and ' occhio' can easily be recognised as something to do with the oculist. 'naso' couldn't be anything else but nose, 'denti' are without doubt teeth, 'visagio' must be face and so on. Any spare time I had after completing my duties and my daily letter to Josie I spent studying this little book.

DonVittorio was accommodating and offered to spend an hour or two each week discussing, as far as possible, the difference between our two religions. I remember on one occasion he reached for one of the many tomes on a bookshelf, opened it, searching for the name of Martin Luther and he passed the remark 'There are three hundred and thirty three religions in England' to which I strongly objected saying that the writer had got it wrong. He apologised profusely for not putting it in simple language and explained that it is an 'idiomatico' expression and not to be taken seriously - it merely means that there are a lot of religions in England.

Whenever I saw him in the village he was on his bike, a ladies bike, because like all rural priests he wore his cassock all the time. In fact he showed me some photographs of himself mountaineering in his cassock and dog collar. It was his hobby but in no way would he compromise his vocation.

Word was put out in the village that female labour was required at the camp and that applicants should present themselves at ten o'clock on such a day. That day it was my turn to take the sick that we could not diagnose to Treviso where we had located a Polish doctor who spoke a little English. I had three patients who were quickly dealt with and I was issued with the medication and instructions as to its administration. On arriving back at camp I was met by Kempie who could hardly tell me for laughing that I had missed all the fun.

I do not know how many females had applied for employment and what qualifications they had to possess to become employed but I learned that about eight had been approved, all but one being in their late teens or early twenties. The one exception was a widow of forty five to fifty probably elected to be chaperone to the rest. During my absence, Aquacasa had submitted all the girls to a medical, keeping a straight face the whole time. Kempie said that he had them in a line in the sun like a row of topless chorus girls.

Two of these girls later asked permission to hang a clothes line across our compound as one of their jobs was washing the tablecloths and napkins from the officers' mess. What a change it was from Duino!

Most of the girls came to us from time to time complaining of a 'male testa' (a bad head) and asking for aspirin tablets. It soon became apparent that these tablets were fetching a good price on the market and Aquacasa said the next one that comes with a 'male testa' will get a dose of cascara. The unfortunate one was the eldest and she must have passed the word on about the new cure because the epidemic of 'male testa' died down.

One of the girls was very attractive with a very lively character, a great sense of fun and an infectious laugh. Her name was Bice Vendramin (pronounced 'Beachy') and she told me that the girls had nicknames for all of us. I must have been favoured because I had two. Josie had sent out, by post, a briar pipe and some Four Square pipe tobacco and I enjoyed this more than cigarettes, hence one of my names was 'Pipa'. The other one was 'Fiocco' which translates as 'Tuft' as I had short cropped hair. Bice took on the task of doing my washing but whether she attended to it personally or whether it was her mother I don't know, but just like at Duino, it came back immaculately pressed.

Coming out of the hut one afternoon we found a snake sunning itself on the concrete of our compound. Not knowing whether it was poisonous we saw no alternative but to kill it as we felt that, even if we could chase it from the compound, the only way out was into the spinney where it would be a danger to everyone. We couldn't shoot it - we had no ammunition- we had no sticks to beat it to death and then someone came up with the idea of burning it when it, having seen us, retired to the dense patch of weeds along the base of the wall. We therefore poured methylated spirits along the weeds and dried out grass and put a match to it. It did not come shooting out as we half expected it to and we could not see it among the ashes, so we guessed or presumed it had wriggled along the wall to more weeds. Armed with a first aid splint each we gingerly poked around trying to find the blighter, all the time hoping that we were not going to get bitten. Going back to the spot where we had originally set fire to the grass and weeds we made a closer search, always ready for a lightening retreat, and found that the snake had discovered and occupied a cavity in the wall where the mortar and stone had broken away. I cannot remember which one of us summoned enough courage to root out this despoiler of our tranquillity. It had died from the intense heat but did not appear to have been damaged and we wondered for a little while if it was feigning death and might still lash out at us. We hung all four feet of it (I didn't think snakes had feet!) - we hung all one and a half metres of it on one of the washing lines. (Come to think of it; I didn't know snakes had metres either!).

Next morning two of the girls could be heard calling from the arched gateway to the compound. I went out to see what they wanted - they were usually not shy to approach us. They chattered away pointing to the snake and nothing would convince them that it was safe to hang out their washing until we had lifted the snake from the washing line.

Sounds of hilarity were coming from the shower room and I thought I would join the party as it was Kempie's turn on duty. The door was only eight or ten paces away from our hut and so I stripped off and, draping a towel round my waist, just in case the girls came along to hang out some washing, I don't remember whose suggestion it was, but I found myself fashioning the upper part of a bikini from a triangular bandage using a couple of handfuls of cotton wool to create curves in the right places. Just as I stepped out intending to display my newly acquired figure in the doorway of the showers and hear the comments that might ensue, a member of our M.T. crew arrived. He was coming for treatment but what it was seemed to slip his memory when he saw me and was easily persuaded to pose with his arm around my waist as Kempie took a snap shot. The camera changed hands and it was Kempie's turn to put his arm round my waist. Whilst the camera changed hands I had not heard Kempie say, 'Press the button as I whip the towel off'. I managed to maintain my dignity by grimly holding onto his wrist. I ran off the remainder of the film in the shower (with blackmail in mind?) but when I went to collect the prints from the old chap in the village who did the developing and printing he explained that, ethically, he could not print them and neither could he feel happy about giving me the negatives, so I ended up with just two shots of me with two different partners.

Early one evening I went into the village and entered the barber's shop. There were three or four men waiting their turn who were engaged in lively conversation about all sorts of things; not that I could fully understand, but the odd word here and there gave me a clue. Whilst I waited I saw an aspect of village life in Italy that might have existed in Britain a hundred years ago. A man came in dressed in dusty workman's attire and, pointing to the shaving gear, asked permission to use it. I got the impression that he was too poor to pay the barber for his time and too poor to afford to buy the tackle. Having got the 'O.K, Joe' from the barber he lathered up and, using the cut-throat razor, proceeded to shave. He put a sum of money down on the shelf with the tools he had used and with 'Thank you Luigi' and a 'Good evening' he went on his way. He obviously had an arrangement.

The F.A.P. was situated as far from the camp entrance as you could get within the grounds of the villa and was therefore somewhat isolated. Apart from mealtimes and shower days we did not see a lot of the lads, except the few who came on sick parade. However, one afternoon one kind soul came along to tell us that there was a fellow at the camp entrance who was selling watches and jewellery, if we were interested. I went along to have a look. He had a small attaché case holding a variety of watches in which I showed no interest as my existing watch was keeping good time, and a few pieces of cheap, but interesting, jewellery. There was a little cardboard box containing a necklace, a bracelet and a matching broach. They comprised fine filigree work in a silvery metal interspersed with semi-transparent pieces of coloured glass that were cut with many facets giving them a sparkle in the bright sun. I thought that I would buy a set for Josie but wasn't really sold on the colour, which was a pale pink, so I asked if he had a set in blue. He was sorry he said but promised that he would be there at eleven o'clock the next day with a set and I didn't have to buy them unless I really liked them. He was obviously one of the old school, he wouldn't have lasted long with today's pressurising street traders. I had asked the price, of course, and, when he returned next day, it was a case of deciding whether to pay in currency or cigarettes. I forget how many lira he wanted but I opted for forty cigarettes. There was no argument despite the fact that he had walked all the way from Treviso to deliver my goods!

They were wrapped and despatched the same day under cover of 'Forces Mail'. Some two weeks later I received a letter from Josie saying how delighted she was and how unusual the jewellery was. Such articles crept into the shops a few years later but you couldn't have got them for the price of forty cigarettes - nearer to forty pounds.

Kempie had consumed a considerable amount of beer. He was not drunk but he was happy. He was not always happy because he knew that somewhere in King's Regulations it said that once wounded a man would not be posted to an active unit again. Kempie had been wounded at Arnhem and felt aggrieved that he was having to rough it once more. No one else knew of this particular regulation but Kempie maintained it existed and frequently referred to it without, I might say, much sympathy. Our RSM didn't want to know about it. He was scarred all over with shrapnel wounds and, I understand, had been wounded eight times.

With the concrete and the metal of the hut retaining the heat we usually slept wearing just our cellular underpants but on this night following a large intake of liquid Kempie decided that even that one garment was one too many. At about midnight he felt that he needed to relieve himself and so he tripped out of the hut, through the archway entrance and on to the latrine in the spinney. He was spotted by the RSM and QM who were having a quiet chat and a fag. On spotting him they made it quickly to the area near the archway awaiting his return. Drawing hard on their cigarettes so that Kempie would spot them they stood there a little while and then made a slow saunter towards the villa. Kempie saw his opportunity to dash from behind the tree against which he was hiding to another one a bit nearer the archway but, of course, the wily RSM and QM felt that they had to return to the archway to continue their conversation. Kempie was forced to transfer his body to the shelter of another tree. In fact Kempie was forced to take advantage of many trees as the two of them casually strolled towards him always keeping between him and the archway entrance to our compound. I wasn't a witness to Kempie flitting from tree to tree in his birthday suit and he didn't say anything about it the following morning. The RSM and QM had of course eventually allowed him to make an undignified dash for the billet after they had ascertained who it was and it was one of these two who had related the incident to other senior NCO's and so the story found its way all round the camp.

Poor Kempie was the butt of many jokes over the next couple of days - remarks such as; 'They wouldn't have known who it was if you'd kept your underpants on' and other remarks too extreme to put on paper, Kempie, of course, cast doubts on the parentage of Regimental Sergeant Majors.

A German prisoner came along carrying a glass jar and wished to show me the contents. It looked like a grey almost flattish worm that half filled the jar. It was a horrible looking thing and what was more horrible was that it had hitherto been living within him. It was a tapeworm. He had not reported sick as he felt he could treat himself. Having passed several segments in his faeces he had guessed what it was and deduced that if he didn't eat then the worm would have nothing to live on and would be easy to eject. I explained that these worms are segmented and if just the one segment with the head was left then it would grow again so we examined it and found that it was complete with head. He was happy that he could start eating again.

Fame of a kind descended on our FAP. We learned that we had the only ear syringe in the North of Italy and so we got sporadic visits from soldiers in other regiments requiring treatment. I think some just wanted a half holiday.

One evening, just after sun down, the sergeant cook came rushing up to the hut in a right old state. He blurted out that his dog, a lovely golden Labrador that he had befriended long ago and had kept well nourished, was hurt. Would I go and have a look at him by the entrance gate?. I was alone and on duty and therefore unable to leave my post and so I enquired about the nature of the injury. The dog had run across the entrance of the camp just as a truck was being driven in and unfortunately he had been hit by one of the front wheels and couldn't get to his feet. His story was interspersed with threats of how he was going to get his cook's knives and carve up the driver to feed to his dog and also floods of tears but I couldn't help but wonder what his reactions were when a few months before his comrades had been dying alongside him at the landings at Salerno. Had he bottled up his feelings then and this was an occasion when he could 'let go'?. Today he would be a case for counselling but such service did not exist in those days.

I gave him a stretcher and told him to get a pal to help him load the dog gently and bring him back to me explaining that I was not a Vet and could not give any guarantee. The stretcher party arrived some fifteen minutes later and it only took a few minutes to ascertain that the humerus (if it is the same name for a dog's upper fore leg) was broken and, unluckily, right at the top against the joint. There was no wound to dress as the skin had not been broken and there was no way a splint could be applied. All I could do was advise him to search the town of Treviso for a vet the following morning and tried to convey to him my thoughts, in my best bedside manner, that I feared it would be a case of having the dog put down. My conjecture was right, I believe, because I did not see the dog around the camp again.

When I was a boy I saw a lot of poverty as did so many during the twenty's and thirty's. I was brought up in a loving, caring working class family in a working class area in the Black Country, the home of chains and shackles, anchors and all things made of iron. There were families in the street where I lived whose children had no shoes or socks until they started school and even then they were second hand or from jumble sales as were the rest of their clothes. During my tenderest years, fortunately beyond my memory, my father was without work for about two years and, at that time, was not entitled to any state benefits. During this period we were entirely dependant on the generosity of my paternal grandfather, my mother's parents having emigrated to the U.S.A with the unmarried half of their family, going like so many others to make their fortune in the land of golden opportunities. One of my earliest memories is of my aunt Hilda dressed just as you see young girls depicted on Christmas cards coming to say her good byes before setting off on that six day journey to New York. Most days, on going to school, my mum put an apple in my pocket when they were in season and I remember the clamour of five or six classmates begging me for the core. That would probably be the only fruit they tasted. Today I would see to it that they had my core in turns, in those days I doubt I was so caring. A lot of the poverty was self inflicted by virtue of the fact that so many men, working before furnaces for long hours, created huge thirsts which they assuaged with the local brewed ale. Many therefore had little money left to give to their wives after paying for the drinks that they had consumed and had entered on the slate. My father drank cold tea and gallons of the really tasty pop that mother used to make. With a background like that it is no small wonder that I and so many others who lived through those times and the stringent rationing hated to see waste of any kind. I saw an incident one evening that involved such a small amount of waste that I'm amazed that it has stuck in my mind all these years but

I felt really incensed at the time and, uncharacteristically, challenged the perpetrator.

With winter round the corner the QM, from somewhere, got a supply of coke for the cast iron stoves that were in the centre of each of the Nissen huts. We in the FAP did not have a stove so when not on duty we would go round to one of the rifle company huts and share their heat in the evening. Joining the lads toasting their knees we were in conversation when one of the chaps came along taking all of his money out of his pockets. He proceeded to sort out all of the small denomination notes, the ones, twos, fives and tens and threw them into the stove. I and one or two of the others protested at the waste and he replied that these notes occupied so much space and had such little value that they weren't worth keeping. After all a ten lira note was only worth about two and a half pence old money. My argument was that he could, with no effort, have given that money to the girls who did our laundry and it would have meant much more to them. They had had years of German occupation with all its privations and could have put the few shillings worth of lira to good use. Waste not, want not.

One evening a squaddie said to me, 'Have you read part 11 orders today?', to which I replied that I had not read them for ages as I was never referred to, having the quiet little job of medical orderly. He said, 'Well, you'd better read them today. You've got a mention'. I wondered what could be coming my way. I hadn't had a personal mention for many months so I went to find out what was on the cards. There, nailed to the usual tree, was the document with three or four people reading it. When I got near enough to read it I almost went into panic. I was to be posted and would depart the next morning along with five others. Packing your kit in the Army is no problem. It is not like going on holiday and selecting what to take, you just pack the lot but the trouble was I hadn't got the lot. Somewhere in the village was a set of khaki drill uniform with underwear and socks and I'd got to get them back, clean or dirty.

What a good thing it was that I had found out what the name of my laundry girl was. In the village I was soon to learn the location of the Vendramin family and Bice was very surprised to see me. She told me that my laundry was ready and as I didn't know what the future held for me where I was going, that was very handy. I was introduced to her sister in law who was in their back garden nursing a new born baby. The baby was only three or four days old but had a shock of black hair. Whilst we talked, Bice's fiancé arrived and I was introduced to him. His name was Enrico and he had recently been repatriated, having been taken prisoner in North Africa.

Enrico told me an amusing story of an incident that happened when he was a prisoner. He had been given the job of tending the petrol pump at the vehicle depot. One day, as he was topping up a truck's tank, the driver thought that he wasn't holding the 'gun' at the correct angle and therefore was not filling up as quickly as was possible, so he took over. He depressed the trigger and continued to fill the tank (no quicker than Enrico had been doing) . Meanwhile an NCO came up to him and held him in conversation. There was no automatic cut-out in those days and the inevitable happened. The tank's neck filled up and then the petrol proceeded to flood onto the floor. Enrico grabbed the driver's arm shouting 'Basta, Basta' which in Italian means 'enough', but which the driver interpreted differently. Enrico said that with one blow he was flat on his back looking at the sky.

I paid Bice her dues for attending to my laundry and took my leave after taking a snapshot of her with Enrico and one of her sister in law with the baby. She was sorry to see me go not just because of her little weekly income but we had had many laborious conversations and had formed a friendly relationship. I too was sorry to part company because it was having chats with her that was enhancing my knowledge of the language. There was no time left for me to take my leave of Don Vittorio and Don Luigi so I promised myself that I would write to them (in pigeon Italian) when I had settled in my new posting.

Bice and Enrico
When I went to collect my washing

Chapter Six
The Posting

After breakfast it was a case of saying goodbye to my comrades Kempie and Aquacasa and humping my kitbag etc. to the departure point near the entrance gate. We were not given any haversack rations so I presumed that the journey would not be a long one. We arrived in a little over two hours and having consumed too much tea at breakfast I found I was bursting. I launched myself over the tail board of the three tonner and sped up the imposing flight of steps to the front entrance doors of this magnificent building. I was met at the doors by an Italian who excitedly told me that I couldn't use this entrance but I ignored that and asked him where the toilets were. He pointed along the corridor and I hurried there. Having got that off my mind I made my way quickly back in case the truck had to be moved to another entrance but not before I noticed something new about the toilet arrangements. No more deep trenches and poles to lean against but modern Western type flush toilets modified to suit the rural Italians by having a block of concrete each side of the seat so that they could squat in their usual position.

If this was to be my new home then I was impressed. The front facade was, as I have said, not only imposing with a wide flight of steps and huge doors but the inside, what little I had seen of it, was impressive, all the walls and floors being of marble. When shown to our quarters I was even more impressed. Moving, as I had done, from 'shot at' tents at Duino to a Nissen hut with running water and electric lights, which I have already described as heaven; this must be seventh heaven because we had hospital beds with mattresses, pillows and mosquito nets. There were bedside lockers and large wardrobes which, admittedly, had to be shared. A couple of hand basins plumbed in with hot and cold water and a mirror behind. What more could a man want?.

I will attempt to describe my new home. It is a hollow pentagon three stories high with a flat roof. There are no lifts but wide pentagonal staircases at each corner. The banisters are of simple round tubing, not decorative in any way as the building was originally designed and built as a hospital. The windows are wooden framed, beginning at a height of three quarters of a metre and being some two metres in height opening inwards with louvred shutters to keep out the sun hinged outwards. Austere flush double doors all opened on to a corridor of three metres width which ran right round each floor. Adequate bathroom facilities are available on each floor, only one room having the special concrete blocks I have already mentioned, this being obviously set aside for the Italian personnel. A short corridor leads from the main corridor to a single storey building, once again with a flat roof, which is mainly used as a dining room but which also serves, as required, as a dance hall, concert hall or for meetings where the total staff have to be addressed together.

A very interesting feature lies alongside the hall and still within the hollow pentagon. It is a continuous bubbling up of boiling water. It is, as the village name; Battaglia Terme implies, a spa. Do not ask me how, but by some means someone had encapsulated this into a rectangular concrete basin. When the water bubbles up it flows, or rather, it overflows over the lowest side of the basin into another of equal size, about two metres by one metre, cascading from this basin into another, a total of six, before finally being drained off presumably into the sewerage system. There is a smell of sulphur around, not enough to be oppressive, but strong enough to deter anyone having a picnic on the spot.

After I had been allocated a bed and advised as to which department I would be working, I set to to write to Josie telling her of my good fortune and, obviously, of my new address. I was now a member of Officers Records 02E GHQ CMF, the other lads having been distributed amongst other departments. There was not much to do for the first few days except arranging desks and chairs for we found ourselves to be part of the advanced party.

O2E Battaglia Terme

'Out' drive at O2E
It's no different to the 'In' drive

02E Dining room

Officers records department O2E (On the flat roof)

The winter came suddenly upon us and we asked if we could possibly have the central heating on as we were working with our full uniforms on together with our greatcoats We were told that the building had been occupied by the German Army previously and, because of the shortage of fuel, they had diverted the boiling spa water into the heating system with the result that the pipes were now clogged with sulphur deposits. The Royal Engineers were trying to get the system working again.

If we were freezing cold during the daytime working hours some of us felt that at least in the evening we could take advantage of the spa waters so after the evening meal we retired to the cascade of hot water and, checking which basin held water at or slightly higher than body temperature, we stripped off and stepped in. The water was shoulder high and was, of course, in constant supply of new water at the same temperature. We stayed in night after night until about ten o'clock and came out looking like so many stewed prunes. It appeared that with the warm air rising above these basins there was fresh cool air being drawn in from the sides so the sulphuric vapours did not bother us primarily because our noses were only inches away from the water level.

There was, as with all things, a down side to this change of fortune. The rations were not getting through as we thought they should. In the first place, the bread, of which we were entitled to two slices each for tiffin, was infested with weevils. It was customary to search each slice on both sides for the little beggars and to flick them out with your knife but the braver ones did not bother and insisted that they were harmless having been baked and were therefore added protein! Then there was the bulk of the food which we were just not getting anyway.

Three of us decided that, instead of having a hot bath for three hour or four hours, we would see whether we could find somewhere in the village where we could have a good meal. I cannot remember the place as it had no sign whatever to denote that it was an eating establishment, but, having confirmed that the good lady did supply meals for hungry British soldiers (she had probably done the same for the Germans in the past) we asked what she could supply. There wasn't a terrific choice but, at least, it was more than we had been receiving. We started with a heaped plateful of spaghetti followed by a beef steak topped with a poached egg. It was superb and, after a short conflab, we said, 'Ancora per favore' and we all repeated the dose. It was nice to feel full again and it had only cost us about one pound each.

The main body joined us after about ten or twelve days and, hooray, they brought with them a lot of Valor paraffin heaters. Whether they used them in Maddaloni, which is a good deal further South near Naples, I do not know, but they were most welcome. We were still obliged to work in our greatcoats because of the bitter cold and used to take it in turns to stand astride the stove (one per office) with the greatcoat draped around like a mini bell-tent. I can recommend it as a superior way of warming the very cockles of one's heart.

The arrival of the main body caused a completely different way of Army life. Officers would not be saluted on the premises but would be shown the respect that their uniforms demanded. NCO's were addressed as Joe, Fred, Johnny or whatever they were known as and this included warrant officers (sergeant majors) with one exception. He was our chief clerk. He was a regular soldier and was from the Hussars and held the rank of sub-conductor, the equivalent of sergeant major, and was known, only out of earshot, as the bus conductor. 'A fine figure of a man' applied to him and I was told that, in his younger days, he had been a good rugby player and all round athlete. In his dress uniform of bright blue trousers with a broad yellow stripe down the seams, worn only on important occasions of course, he looked fit for a Gainsborough portrait. His one, very outstanding feature, was his bristling moustache which stood out sideways and which he frequently stroked to keep it growing in the right direction. It was said that there was only one moustache in the whole theatre with a greater span, but I never saw it. It seemed quite appropriate that he had a double-barrelled name - Garth-Atkins.

The function of 02E (Second Echelon) was to keep an accurate record of every soldier in the theatre and to liaise with the War Office in this respect. I was given a few files full of Officers' records, all names beginning with D,E and F, and given guidance by a very congenial bunch of fellows as to how I was to deal with them. I got to know these fellows very well because I shared their company for a year- the longest stay I had had with any unit.

Within days of settling in, 02E started to introduce its welfare programme for its staff. Recce transport was laid on for trips to Venice and Padua on Saturdays and Sundays, the journey to Venice taking about an hour and to Padua a little more than half an hour. Later on there was to be a photographic club, skiing facilities in Southern Austria, horse riding, a class where soldiers could be taught to drive and learn all about vehicle maintenance and a little chapel in the grounds where an interdenominational group, known as 02E Fellowship, met on Sunday mornings.

I soon took advantage of the opportunity to see Venice, a magical city, and, on my second trip there, I witnessed a scene that very few holiday makers have ever seen. It was the hardest winter that Italy had known for twenty eight years and was so cold that the sea froze. All the gondolas and barges were locked in the ice and, as a result, goods and provisions were having to be carried on foot over dozens of bridges. People were walking along the canals and I was told that some residents had actually cycled across the lagoon to Mestre where they worked.

During the ensuing months I visited Venice many times and always found it an exciting place to visit, there was so much to see. St. Mark's Cathedral is wonderful with all its biblical scenes portrayed by mosaics which can be seen close up by walking round the gallery, so popular in Italian churches. I had the pleasure of climbing the stairway inside that leads out onto the front facade and actually touching those life size bronze horses. The floor is undulating owing to its age, the millions of feet that have trodden over it, but what makes it so amazing is the fact that it was originally built on boggy ground at least six hundred years ago. Only the Italians would have the courage to build its campanile so big and heavy a few yards away.

Now I had something of real interest and excitement to write to tell Josie, hoping to convey to her some of my excitement, not realising that, some twenty six years later, I would be walking over these same bridges and sharing those wonderful sights with her; our daughter Celia having treated us to a tour of Italy for our Silver Wedding Anniversary. Such a wonderful daughter, she had, unknown to us, saved her pocket money for a whole year, denying herself dances and cinema visits to give us the holiday of a lifetime.

At the opposite end of St. Mark's piazza from the cathedral was a building that had been commandeered by the army and had been turned into a NAAFI. The buxom young blondes that enlivened the walls just as they did in NAAFI's all round Britain seemed to be out of place in this historic setting. This NAAFI was, as far as I was concerned, the one that outdid every NAAFI that I had seen up till now and there were no queues! It was a case of, find a table and a seat and, in no time at all, there was a waitress at your elbow. My two comrades and I had placed our orders (they actually had cakes and pastries as well as the customary 'wads') when a sergeant came in with a terrier on a lead. This was most unusual and my eyes couldn't help but follow him. The dog kept perfect pace as he walked along with a slack lead when a cat, sitting unnoticed on one of the bar stools, stretched down with one paw, claws extended, and raked the poor dog's nose. It spurted blood like it was coming from a syringe. Poor dog. He had not even seen the cat never mind objecting to its presence. It was yelps, curses, mop and bucket, cat flying from the scene and cries of 'Put that cat on a charge' from several quarters.

Prior to calling in at the NAAFI I had bought one of those little souvenirs that are popular at Christmas time; a glass dome with a tiny replica of St. Mark's cathedral filled with water holding tiny chips of sea shell or egg shell representing snow which swirls round when shaken. Why I bought it I cannot imagine as it would be the last thing I would trust to the post. The little waitress came with our orders on a tray and, when unloading them, she accidentally caught my snow scene with the tray and it fell crashing to the floor with the expected result. She was only about fifteen or sixteen years of age and very timid and immediately burst into floods of tears and many abject apologies. Maybe she had only just started to work there but she was desperate to make amends and offered to buy me another one as she feared she might lose her job. Despite my limited vocabulary I was able to convey to her that it was nothing and, with a smile, that I was not upset.

Christmas came and with it a certain something that is difficult to put into words. This was the first 'peaceful' Christmas following six that had been celebrated in a war time atmosphere. A kind of happiness pervaded the unit. We no longer had an enemy and our German prisoners celebrated much the same as we did. The threat of death or injury by bomb or bullet no longer existed. Our thoughts were very much with the folks back home, hoping that rationing would be easing, giving them a better fare than that which they had endured over the past Christmases.

Someone designed a twofold Christmas card which was depicting our building on the front and a seasonal message inside. This was run off in a two colour print on an offset lithography machine by the ATS girls. I do not recall whether they were bought or supplied free of charge (the cards, not the girls) but I do remember sending one to Josie and one to my family; thinking that it would give them a certain confidence in my being with a unit that could afford such extravagances.

Two incidents worthy of note happened on Christmas Eve but, before I relate them, I must picture for you the main characters. The first character was our frustrated RSM. He was frustrated because he had no square on which to drill and parade us and, I think, he was further frustrated because the discipline within the unit was excellent and therefore the complete lack of janker-wallahs must have given him sleepless nights. The only way he could exercise his authority over us was on the odd occasion he could arrange a parade complete with arms up and down the main street of the village. The villagers, especially the children, used to enjoy this much more than we did. We, to some extent, shared his frustration on the occasions because those of us who had been trained in infantry units were not too bad (albeit a little rusty) others had never heard of 'arms drill on the march' and as a result made quite a hash of it. We felt he was making us look a bit foolish in front of the locals. He was definitely not a popular man.

On Christmas Eve this RSM had indulged in more than just tasting the local brew and arrived at about eleven thirty back at the guard room. The guard asked him for the password. He couldn't remember it and remonstrated; 'But you know who I am!' and attempted to push past. The guard put his bayonet to the RSM's chest and said that he couldn't be allowed in without the password and added 'If I let you in you'll have me charged with dereliction of duty tomorrow morning' The RSM was frogmarched to the cells and locked up for the night. The joyous news was round the unit in no time.

The second character was a Major named Thelma Oxnervad who was in charge of the small contingent of ATS girls. Thelma was, to put it in a nutshell, (no pun intended) a cracker. She had a very curvaceous figure and the lads thought that she was the model used by the cartoonist that drew Jane in the Daily Mirror, the main difference being, Thelma was always properly dressed. She was liked by all the ATS girls and desired by most of the men. If the RSM was the most unpopular man at 02E then I can say with confidence that Thelma was the antithesis.

Well, the RSM was not the only senior NCO to honour Bacchus that Christmas Eve. Garth-Atkins, who I have explained before was our chief clerk, also partook heavily and retired to his billet to sleep it off. Thelma, probably well fortified herself, crept into the said billet and deftly, with the aid of scissors, removed a half of that famous moustache. We did not learn of this until we were back at our desks on the 27th. December when we all decided that now was most definitely the time to pay the utmost attention to our documents.

The noticeboard had proclaimed that there would be a football match at eleven hundred hours when the officers would be playing against the men and, not being chosen as one of the team, I decided to use my lungs on the touch line. (This on Christmas morning). Kick off time arrived and there were only ten officers in football strip and the word went round that it was the Colonel who was missing. The game started and guess who was refereeing. It was the RSM - released from clink and almost recovered from his overindulgence of the previous evening. He refereed the match on horse back, riding bare back and charging up and down the pitch creating havoc. After a little while he decided to dismount but he did so in the most unusual fashion by sliding down the horse's rear quarters. The horse did not like this move and stamped with one of its rear legs almost burying the RSM's foot in the ground. A great cheer went up as he limped off the pitch.

Another cheer went up when the Colonel turned up. He was in his football gear but he was also play acting. Why didn't I have my camera with me? I wonder if anyone had a camera? Here was our popular boss arriving on a horse drawn dray reclining on a heap of cushions and being fanned with one of those huge Egyptian fans by Thelma dressed in her pyjamas. I have never seen a better representation of Anthony and Cleopatra.

Fifty years on, at a 02E re-union, I have learned why the Colonel was late. He had been chivvying the prisoners to find some planks with which to board up the goal mouth as he was playing in goal.

The big event of Christmas Day was naturally the dinner when the officers traditionally waited upon the men. It really was a grand affair, the turkey dinner being followed by the Christmas pud complete with rum sauce, a mince pie and rounded off with a mug of coffee. I hoped that those back home were enjoying equally good fare

During the weeks following Christmas we were most diligent in our work, not daring to look up at Garth-Atkins in case we smiled and he misinterpreted it. We were all awaiting the moustache to reach its former proportions!

Most of the entries that I made on the officers' documents were in reference to them going on 'Python' or 'Lilop' leave (LILOP being leave in lieu of Python) and 'ceasing to be entitled to Mediterranean Allowance on en-training at Villach for the U.K.' For many this would be the first leave they had had for three years apart from a few snatched days in foreign parts. Each one of those one line entries on the documents was an unknown story. The majority, I hoped, would be going back to a happy reunion with a wife and family. Some would be going back to children who wouldn't recognise them. Some would be going back to an unfaithful wife or sweetheart. Some to see a child for the first time, conceived on their last leave. Some would go back to see the rubble that was once their home. They all had twenty one days, before rejoining their unit, in which to live it up or patch it up.

I had news that I was to be granted twenty one days leave at the end of January and I immediately wrote to tell Josie and my family the good news, asking Josie to arrange a week's holiday so that she could have a few days at my home in order to meet my parents and sister. It is impossible to find words to say how I felt about a week at home visiting my friends and relations; a week in Chester meeting Josie each day at the office when she had finished her tasks for the day; and a week when I would be introducing her to the Black Country and some of my many Aunts, Uncles and Cousins; all those pleasures welled up in my mind. The days wouldn't speed by quickly enough.

War Office issued an edict that all personnel going on leave were to withdraw all credits prior to setting out for the U.K. This order was following a devaluation of the lira. When I first entered Italy the rate of exchange was nine hundred to the pound sterling. Suddenly overnight it became nineteen hundred to the pound, a little less than half of its former value. Apparently the Government was worried by all the personnel abroad spending all of their money overseas - thousands of troops in Italy,

Germany, Holland, France, Belgium and in the Far East. We were told (years later) that the war had cost in excess of seven millions each day over five years so we must have been scraping the bottom of the barrel. Each squaddie's three bob a day times many thousands must make some difference to the Chancellor's sums.

On the day of the devaluation I was given an insight as to how the financial world works. Given no warning whatsoever we were told to present ourselves at the pay office with pay book and all of our money. The first two or three (always the same ones at the front of the queue) put down their money on the counter and it was counted, the smaller denominations being ignored. Whatever money was put on the counter was doubled and smiling faces showed appreciation. After the first two or three had been dealt with and the word passed down the queue as to what it was all about, chaps were leaving the queue to borrow a few thousand from those who had been unlucky enough to be eager. They were then getting their augmented sum doubled and were able to repay their debt plus a nominal 'interest' even before they got back to the office. It would be classified as insider dealing today.

At long last the great day arrived and I, along with a dozen others, all as eager as myself to get back to the U.K., presented ourselves at the pay office to collect three weeks wages in advance and all of our credits that we had saved. My total was about £40 which when translated into lira made me feel like a millionaire - approaching eighty thousand lira. Unfortunately when it came to my turn they had run out of thousand lira notes so I had to have over a hundred and fifty notes of five hundred lira values. Luckily the Army battle dress has a pocket on the front of the trouser leg designed to take an ordnance survey map and this was an ideal treasure chest in spite of it making me look somewhat deformed.

The journey by truck to Padua was uneventful but cold, it being late January. From Padua to Villach seemed to be taking up all of our leave as we had frequent stops apart from the one at the frontier where we had to change our lira into marks. At one of these stops we popped our heads out of the train windows to find that German prisoners and Italian labourers were loading snow into trucks to dump it elsewhere as the snow walls on either side of us were about eight feet deep. We hoped that the snowfall had been dealt with with a greater urgency across France.

At Villach we met with the usual efficiency and were given food, a night's rest and breakfast before setting off for Calais. Stopping at the Austrian/French border we once again changed our currency, this time into francs. Leaving the mountains behind it was exhilarating to see hundreds of miles of virgin snow with the occasional village or stretch of woodland to break the routine. We stopped at the transit camp and we obeyed the sign again to 'MARNJAY TOOT SWEET', setting off immediately afterwards towards Calais where once again we changed our currency, this time into sterling.

The Channel must have been as flat as a mill pond on that day because I am a poor sailor and I do not remember one minute of that crossing, or, indeed, a minute of the train journey to London and then on to Birmingham and ultimately to Cradley Heath. What I do remember was that Betty, my sister, was a leggy schoolgirl when I first went to receive the King's shilling and now she was a teenager and working for her living. She wasn't into high heels yet but the gym slip had been dispensed with and ankle socks were definitely out.

After two or three days at home I could contain my impatience to see Josie no longer and set off on the train to Chester. I took my suitcase to Mrs Edge's in White Friars where I had enjoyed her accommodation before and was pleased to find her without visitors and, I suppose, she would be pleased with a few extra shillings that my presence would bring. I had phoned the previous evening to say that I was coming so Josie wasn't surprised to see me waiting outside the office when she finished work. She told me that she had managed to book the following week off work and had cancelled her appointments at the Y.M.C.A. and the English Speaking Union where she did her voluntary work in the evening.

Until the weekend we spent each evening together, at her home, out walking or at the cinema. She placed orders with the grocer, the greengrocer and the butcher so that mum would be provided for during her absence and in those days all of these goods were delivered free on Friday evening. (I mean there was no charge for delivery!)

On Saturday we set out for my home town, Josie feeling nervous about meeting my folks for the first time and my Ma no doubt feeling nervous about meeting this young lady who had been educated at a public school and had never lived in a house that had an outside toilet and no bathroom. Introductions over, everybody got on well with everybody else. Ma soon won Josie over with her breakfasts. Although she had an electric cooker (one of the first in the street following the introduction of electricity) she used to grill the bacon in front of a coal fire and the fat used to shrivel up into a nice crispy texture that appealed to Josie. In fact she always maintained that Ma's grilled bacon couldn't be bettered. If Josie couldn't get along with Dad then nobody could because he had a very shy quiet temperament and couldn't fall out with anyone. I think he was a bit embarrassed coming along from his workshop for meals dressed in his 'gansy' (a Black Country word describing the thick homemade flannel shirt worn by chain makers designed for comfort and to absorb the perspiration caused by working so near to the furnace). With regards to Betty - well, she had to share her bedroom with Josie and I never heard any squabbles so I think they got on alright together.

A week in Winter in the heart of the Black Country is hardly first prize for any sort of competition but it was an outstanding week for Josie and myself. Early on in the week, having now really decided that we were meant for each other, we bought a tea service bearing a nice apple blossom pattern. At that time only plain china was available as all 'quality' things were being produced for export only and we considered ourselves lucky to be able to buy a complete tea service of 'seconds', the only faults being of a minor nature in the decorations. As I write, three surviving cups still sit on the pantry shelf fifty years later. (We never threw any of those at each other).

Midweek came and, as they said in those days, I popped the question. Josie didn't ask for time to consider, we went straight off to Peplow's in Stourbridge and she chose an engagement ring. Ma, never one to reveal her emotions, didn't say a lot; she was most likely thinking that the lad she had nursed through life threatening illnesses was swapping his allegiance to another woman. Dad said even less. I don't think he had realised that I had grown up until then, although I do remember a rather firm handshake when he came to New Street station to see me off when I was destined (prior to my injury) to go to serve in Burma.

The rest of the week flew by and it was time for Josie to go back to Chester. On the Saturday afternoon I went with her as far as Birmingham to see her safely on to her train, promising to ring her on Sunday evening. This I did but I cannot say that I was delighted with the message I got. Josie's mum was not at all thrilled with the news of our engagement. She said that we hardly knew each other and how dare I whisk off her daughter to go and buy a ring without so much as asking her permission. Looking back, I can understand her because Josie's eldest sister had, a couple of years before, entered into a marriage that turned out to be a difficult one, and here was her 'baby' committing herself to sharing her life with a fellow who had sent a deluge of mail from Italy but who could offer no future greater than that of a wife of a journeyman. Josie was content with the idea of being my wife whatever the future held in the way of employment - she was just as crazy about me as I was about her - so a truce was held between her and her mum.

I went back to 02E with mixed feelings: on the one hand, I was dejected at having to leave Josie, on the other hand, I was rejoicing in the knowledge that she had elected to share the future with me.

The route back (Medloc 'C') was uneventful; having a meal and a shower then collecting haversack rations at the transit camp; changing currency -francs, marks, lira; and an overnight stay at Villach. I found on my return that Alex Ferrans, a member of our office who was a special pal, had been unfortunate on his leave. He had left a couple of weeks before me and had really suffered from the weather. Because of the snow in the U.K. it had taken him forty eight hours to get from Dover to Glasgow. Two precious days of leave spent in a railway coach compartment and only snacks at stations on route. He would have been better off staying at 02E, at least they had had the central heating system repaired.

Back in the office I did not find my IN tray stacked high as my pals had shared out my work and completed it just as I helped to do their work when they in turn went on leave. One day I thought that I would have a look at my own records to see what the Army thought about me, so I wandered down to the appropriate records office, found a squaddie looking after the documents referring to 14899780 Pte. Ralph Homer and I was interested to find reference to that test I had been through at Villach. In fact I was not only interested but highly amused because here was I working in the biggest office complex in CMF and the findings of my test read; 'Not suitable for clerical duties'. How did we manage to win the war?

Having already paid visits to Venice by courtesy of our recce transport I thought I would try a visit to Padua one Saturday afternoon. My companion was a man with whom I had left Worcester and had been posted alongside from our infantry battalion. We went to the cathedral, the cupola of St. Anthony, and found it a most impressive building both from an architectural point of view and also from its ornate decorations. In the forecourt was a collection of piety stalls and from one of these I bought a set of Rosary beads for Josie and likewise for her mother and, just in case I did embrace the Catholic faith at any time in the future I bought a set for myself. The old lady at the stall was keen to assure me that they had all been blessed by the Pope. There was certainly a Roman connection because I found that the crucifix had a tiny hinged clasp that had a minute amount of soil with a strip of paper on which was printed, so small it was extremely difficult to read, the words 'Terra della catacombi'.

We left the cathedral and walked to the shopping centre to see what they had to offer compared with the paucity of wares shown in English shops. In the window display of a shop showing clothing for the tiniest child to the adult lady I spotted a tiny bolero style baby coat in pale pink simulated fur and thought that it wasn't too overpriced and that it would make a nice present for Josie's niece Kathleen. Going into the shop we were surprised to find that they already had potential British customers. There were two of the 02E ATS girls there and they were having a little embarrassed giggle brought about by language problems. The window display was of the type where the whole range of the shop's wares was on show and, as a result, hopelessly overcrowded. The customer had pointed to the article required. The assistant had wrongly interpreted the direction of the index finger and entering (shoeless) the window display had brought the wrong item back to the counter. This must have happened half a dozen times before we had entered because there was quite a small heap of attire on the counter and luckily the staff who were about the same ages as the ATS girls were thinking it was amusing also. Gallantly (or was it foolishly) I offered my services as an interpreter, not that my Italian was good but at least I could apologise for the inconvenience if nothing more. The article they wished to purchase was a dainty cotton nightdress in white. How the words entered my limited vocabulary I shall never know but 'camicia da notte' came tripping off my tongue as though Italian was my first language. A grateful 'Aaah' went up. In case you do not know the phrase 'camicia da notte', being literally translated, means 'shirt of the night'.

Sam and I popped into a quiet trattoria for a little light refreshment and ordered a cappuccino and a cake each. It turned out to be quieter than quiet - there was only one other customer, a very attractive girl about nineteen or twenty years of age. Sam said to me; 'Ask her if she would like to join us in a cappuccino'. (He never managed to get around the 'lingo' except for the word 'Te' (pronounced Tay) which is exactly how the word 'tea' is pronounced in the Black Country.) I found myself being a reluctant interpreter on Sam's behalf which lead to the question, you will have guessed, 'How much for the night?' I presented him with a barrage or reasons why he should not do this, including, how would he get into the building next morning?; how would he account for not signing back in at the guardroom?, how would he avoid the patrols in the grounds?. He had it all worked out. He would leave Padua at about five thirty in the morning, get a taxi and, knowing where there was a hole in the perimeter fence, he would say he had forgotten to sign in when he came back on Saturday night. All the time this conversation was going on the girl had taken a paper napkin from the holder on the table and was doing a charming little sketch of a gondola and gondolier - she was quite an artist. I played my trump card and asked Sam if he thought that his wife might be contemplating going out with a Yank for the night. He had no doubt about his wife's loyalty and agreed with me that cheating on her would be very wrong.

I felt truly sorry for the girl; not that she had just lost a customer, but that she had to resort to the oldest trade in the world to make a living, there being so much poverty.

It was said, and the evidence was all around, that twenty five per cent of the Italian population were starving. In fact, a middle aged woman could be seen at the entrance to the drive that led to our building on most evenings asking soldiers if they would like an evening with her daughter for the equivalent of two shillings. Only sheer desperation could have been the reason for most of these girls to earn their keep in this way. I remember one squaddie telling the tale of how he was surprised by what happened when he was spending the night with one of the village girls. He said that at six o'clock in the morning when the Angelus rang out at the nearby monastery the girl jumped out of bed, knelt down, crossed herself, said her morning prayers and then jumped back into bed again. I believe that this was not the act of an evil person.

My letters to Josie continued on a daily basis only now I was recording a serial number where normally the stamp would be affixed because I had, in one of Josie's replies, received the information that the deliveries in Chester were a little erratic and sometimes three or four of my letters would be delivered together with, as a consequence,, the envelopes being opened in incorrect sequence.

Paying a second visit to Padua I had a new experience. After visiting a few places of interest and doing a little window shopping I found that I needed to visit the toilet and I asked a passer-by the directions to the public convenience. I found it quite easily from his directions and discovered that it was an underground one. At the bottom of the steps I turned into a short tunnel with a kiosk and a teenage girl attendant. The tunnel opened into a rather splendid looking arcade where there were not only toilets but ladies and gents hairdressers, barbers and places where both sexes could enjoy manicures and facials. My trouble arose from the system. Everything was priced and it was necessary to buy a ticket for whichever service one required. Although I could converse to some degree the written word was still a mystery. I told the girl that I wished to go to the lavatory. She asked whether I would be standing up or would I require to sit down in which case paper would be supplied and that, of course, would be more expensive. There was no sign of embarrassment on her part; after all it's a perfectly normal bodily function and it was her daily job to issue tickets to enable people to carry out that function in a dignified way - with three pieces of toilet paper.

Why not have a haircut, I thought. The place was clinically clean and the whole barbers shop looked professionally kitted out. Yes, I would so I went back to the kiosk to buy the appropriate ticket. That wasn't too difficult. Yes, I just wanted a trim. No, I didn't want it burning at the ends afterwards. Yes, I'd be happy with just a plain trim, nothing more.

There were three or four chairs and one of them was unoccupied. I was indicated to it and presented the hairdresser with my ticket. A clean towel (not one the last fifty seven customers had used) was tucked in all round the shirt collar followed by the all enveloping robe. The hairdresser gave my hair a vigorous combing through followed by an even more vigorous finger tip massage. My scalp felt like it had done on that ride from Monfalcone to Duino in a jeep. Snipping away furiously, seventy five per cent of the snips in fresh air, he soon had me trimmed. The perimeter areas around the back and my ears were finished off with a super-honed open razor and I was dusted with a fragrant talc in those areas. 'Would I like some dressing on my hair?', he asked. 'Why not', I thought and said 'Yes please'. That will be extra he said and, since I was enveloped in that black bell tent he volunteered, if I could find my pocket, to go to the kiosk and get a further ticket. When he took a small bottle from the shelf I expected him to pour a little into the palms of his hands and then apply it to my hair, but no, he poured the whole bottle on to me and that which escaped his fingers and ran down past my ears he caught with tissues. There must have been a high spirit content because my scalp tingled more than ever. My head felt as though it was on fire.

I was very conscious of the strong perfume and felt that the whole population of Padua was turning round to view me as I walked along the streets. Getting back to the billet as fast as I could I was greeted by one of my room mates with: 'You pong like a Turkish brothel'. I said, 'Hands up all those who have been in a Turkish brothel?' No hands went up, including the speaker, and so I said, 'Once again you don't know what you're talking about'.

Life within 02E was running very smoothly with the rations now coming through regularly and plenty of local labour employed to serve it. We ate in the hall at little tables (with tablecloths!) in a civilised manner with butter dish placed centrally at tea-time; it was almost like being at home! Italian girls waited on us and accused us of 'always eating' because we not only had a cooked breakfast and two other cooked meals but we also had a coffee break mid morning. I had been told that the word 'carisima' was as near as one could get in translation to 'darling' and I used this word quite liberally with the girls when we required more bread, butter or jam etc.. (I cannot find this word in my dictionary so it could well be that it is a local one). I have said before that the Italians are quick to dish out the nick names and I was soon to be known as 'Carisimo' In the evenings and at weekends I was frequently waved to and hailed across the street in the village with 'Buona sera Carisimo' by the waitresses. If I replied 'Buona sera' and Wilf Sutton was with me he would whip out his handkerchief and wave it calling; 'Anky voy' which strictly speaking is spelt 'Anche voi' and means 'You also'.

Not only were we eating well and being waited on but we also had music to aid our digestion in the way of a small band made up of five or six musical German prisoners. The band up to late winter/early spring was led by a trumpeter who played an instrument that had probably been one of Monty's targets judging by the shape of it. The trumpeter was, I'm sure, the Spike Milligan of the German Army. He was built like Spike and played his type of music, the only trouble being that he couldn't take his foot off the loud pedal. Everything was fortissimo to the extent that the only other instrument to be heard was the drums played by a very young man genuinely named Fritz. Objections were eventually raised and Spike Krupps was restricted to playing in the German quarters, whilst the lead was taken over by a fat little violinist who favoured Strauss, Lehar and similar. Occasionally this little band gave us evening concerts and were really appreciated, the instrumentalists enjoying it as much as the listeners because they got well plied with the bottled stuff and had enough to take back to their quarters for the non-musical ones.

About this time, early spring, Garth-Atkins came to me one morning and asked me to open a special file on a Major Pye.

We had a file on each of the officers in Italy but he said that this was to be a special one and he considered that my Italian was, although very basic, the best in the office and that I should be given the privilege of looking after it. I was to get the major newspapers and take all the cuttings that I could find about Major Pye. The story was that early one morning two men walking alongside one of the smaller canals in Venice on their way to work had spotted an Army Officer apparently lying dead in the bottom of a barge. Those men had run to an Army post just off Saint Mark's square and raised the alarm. They then accompanied a couple of squaddies back to the barge to find that the officer was badly wounded to the head but was still alive. It seemed that he had attempted to commit suicide using his revolver. He was rushed to hospital at Mestre, but whether this was by boat or by stretcher over the many bridges and ultimately by ambulance, I do not know but for a few days his life was in the balance. The medical report said that he had blown about one seventh of his brain away and would be sent back to England as soon as it was considered safe to do so. The news hawks were camped outside the main gate at Mestre hospital asking anybody in khaki what they knew about the English officer who had shot himself. Had I been there I am sure I could have made a fortune with what I had found out.

Major Pye was essentially a family man. Posted to India he found that he couldn't manage life without his wife. He married an Indian woman not bothering to divorce the one he already had in England and by some means managed two marriage allowances. Major Pye was also an inventive man. Officers in India at that time were paid proportionately to the number of men under their command and he invented a few men. Essentially though he was a family man and when later he was posted to Italy he felt it only right and proper to have an Italian wife. Whether or not he had to relinquish one of his marriage allowances I didn't find out. Major Pye was, apart from being an inventive family man, was also a careless one because he was breaking about three hundred cups a week. At least that was what the NAAFI records said when he was in charge and that is what brought about the collapse of his house of cards.. He was eventually sneaked out of the rear entrance of the hospital and flown to England and I sent his file to the War Office. There was no more news on Major Pye.

Having worked over the Easter holiday, I was told by Garth-Atkins to avail myself of a truck and driver and treat myself to a holiday from Friday lunch time until midnight on Sunday, so I thought I would visit my old pals in the village of Paese. I went down to the P.O.W's quarters and was both surprised and pleased to see what excellent accommodation they had. I doubt whether they would ever have had it so good under Hitler. They seemed to have everything that we had except waitress service. They even had a dart board which we didn't. I told the officer there (a young and happy lieutenant) that I was going to Paese just outside Treviso for the weekend and I needed a driver. He had a word with the few men there and allotted me one by the name of Gottfried.

Friday came and Gottfried and I set off in a thirty hundredweight pick-up to Paese. Without any reference to a map he drove straight there and arrived mid afternoon; siesta time and everywhere quiet and deserted. I asked him to pull up at the mini trattoria in the village and we would have a refreshing drink. We hadn't spoken much on the journey, if anything at all, I spoke no German and he spoke no English. However his Italian, I found, was far superior to mine. Enjoying our ice cold drinks I asked him if he would prefer to doss down with his compatriots in the camp or would he like bed and breakfast accommodation in the village. I was surprised and shocked when he said that he had another assignment later that day and that I would have to make my own way back. Using public transport was something I hadn't reckoned on and was not looking forward to as I had not had any experience of it to date.

Gottfried set off for Battaglia Terme and I set off for the presbytery where I was sure that the priests would recommend some good soul who would give succour to a stray soldier. I rang the door bell and the door was opened by the same old dour lady that I had seen a few times before but who showed no sign of recognition. There was a sadness about her; maybe she had lost a husband or a son in the war, maybe the sight of a young man in uniform renewed her grief; who knows what thoughts made her the very opposite to the two jolly priests she cared for? They greeted me like a long lost brother and Don Luigi enthusiastically praised me for the improvement in my grasp of the language. Don Vittorio wouldn't hear of me staying anywhere in the village except with themselves. I enjoyed my brief stay in Paese, renewing my friendship with my old comrades, but strangely enough my outstanding memory is of when Don Vittorio was showing me the garden at the rear of his house he asked me if I would like a plum from the tree near where we stood. Thinking it might look a little churlish if I declined, I said 'Yes, please'. The fruit had a dark brown dull skin and was, for a plum, of very generous proportions. He pulled one from the tree for me and another for himself. Not knowing what kind of flavour to expect I bit into it and the juice ran down and dripped off my chin. It was without any doubt the most luscious fruit I have ever tasted. It was the type used for drying to produce prunes.

Not knowing what difficulties I might encounter on my journey back to O2E I set off from Paese mid afternoon getting a lift to Treviso in an Army truck, the driver of which, knowing his way around, dropped me off at the bus depot. At this depot there was a series of railed avenues each leading to a little window with a clerk behind each. There did not seem to be any information kiosk so I thought that I would join the shortest queue and ask advice at the window, but on getting there I could see that each window had a destination name over it. I decided that I would go to Venice where I would be able to get a lift in the 'recce' transport, so I joined that queue. The clerk explained to me that the bus and trailer would pull up in the yard behind and would have its destination on a board in the front window. The buses were not assigned any particular part of the yard and when one arrived the people waiting for that particular bus would rush across and scramble aboard. 'Survival of the fittest' is the phrase that springs to mind as queuing seems to be acceptable to an Italian only when it is forced hence the avenue rails leading to the booking offices.

I remember years later taking a bus from the beautiful railway station in Rome to Porta Pia (The Holy Gate). The system now was to pay the conductor on board and not buy a ticket in advance. Josie and I had boarded the bus along with half a dozen other people but had to wait about twenty minutes for departure time. The vehicle gradually filled up with passengers and all the seats were taken. There were plenty of leather straps for standing passengers to hold on to - a vital necessity when you appreciate how Roman drivers take corners. A weary old lady with two bursting shopping bags got on and I stood up and offered her my seat. She thanked me and sat down. She was not as weary as I had thought however. She proceeded to inform the whole bus load in a loud voice that I was most kind and gracious; that she had not been the recipient of such gentlemanly behaviour for many years; that the saints would surely bless me for my generosity and thoughtfulness. Passengers screwed their necks round to see what kind of foreign idiot (he just had to be foreign) had given up his seat. I almost wish that I hadn't shown my chivalry.

Part way along the journey to Venice the conductor, having collected his tickets from the occupants of the trailer, transferred, at one of the stops, his attention to the bus passengers. (I had not fancied travelling in the trailer - somehow it does not seem as safe as having a vehicle with a driver). When he got to me he started a conversation, telling me that he had been a prisoner of war and had been held in Scotland for a time but was recently repatriated. The mixture of Italian and Scotch accents was most difficult to follow and I found that my basic Italian seemed to be more easily understood. He seemed to be most interested in what I did for a living before becoming a soldier and wanted to know whether I would return to that or remain a soldier. On asking me what sort of wages I got as an engineer he got most upset when I told him that the last few weeks before being called up I had earned in excess of twenty pounds. He said it was impossible and became quite abusive. As a matter of fact it was way above the average but only because my partner and I had improved the method of manufacture of the components we were making and we were working twelve hour shifts. I suppose, converting my income into lira, my weekly income was something like he was getting for two or three months work and I guess I was a bit naive in telling him what was the exception. The fellow sitting immediately in front of me told the conductor to cool it - 'The soldier knows what he used to earn'. The conductor said that I was exaggerating. The temperature in the bus rose and the two of them almost came to blows and the language was flowing so fast that I couldn't understand it. It was very embarrassing and I was so glad to see Venice and cease to be the centre of attraction.

Making my way the few yards from the bus terminus towards the pick-up point for our 'recce' transport I was hailed by the driver of a jeep. He drew up alongside me and asked if I was going to 02E. When I replied in the affirmative he told me to jump aboard. As I did so I could see from his 'fried egg' that he was a warrant officer but I didn't recognise his face. If the devil had been chasing him I do not believe he could have driven any faster. After driving for a few miles he asked me to open the glove box (or whatever it is called in a jeep) where I would find a packet of cigarettes and a lighter. 'Light a cigarette for me' he said, obviously having to concentrate so much on his driving that he couldn't do it himself. 'Come on, Come on' he urged. I have never seen such addiction to the weed. I was not attending to his needs quickly enough. When I lit the cigarette I took a good draw to ensure that it was properly alight; after all, a jeep travelling at about eighty miles per hour can be very draughty; he said curtly, 'I asked you to light it for me , not smoke it'. I formed the opinion that the only reason he offered me a lift was to ensure that he could enjoy a smoke because there was no other conversation throughout the whole of the journey. All in all, I think I would rather have waited for the three tonner, at least there would have been conversation even if the journey took twice as long.

You can well imagine that, during our office hours, we had many directives from the War Office and one of those in particular was one that was dealing with demobilisation (demob). It seemed that there was concern about the number of officers who should have returned to the U.K. for discharge that were still on our strength. This applied especially to officers who had been called up at the outbreak of war who were either Territorial Army officers or had been regular officers called up during their reserve period. We all had to set to and comb through our documents to find these men who, for a variety of reasons, were not in civvy street. Some, having risen in the ranks, were better off financially than they had ever been; some thought the army couldn't manage without them; some were enjoying the sublime climate; some revelling in the Bacchanalian opportunities at very low cost; some couldn't resist the offers from ladies of easy virtue at an even lower cost. All of them received a letter from us together with a copy of the W.O. directive telling them in the politest terms to 'Go Away'. It was an R.S.V.P. letter and from one major I didn't get a reply. Having checked that he wasn't on leave and had not been posted to another unit I sent a copy after about a week presuming that my first missive had got lost in the post. After a second copy evoked no reply I assumed that he must have gone back to the U.K. and his adjutant had neglected to notify us.

Some six or seven weeks after receiving the W.O. instructions I was summoned to the office of our Colonel, (Benny) Goodman, who asked me for an explanation for this T.A. major still being on our strength and upsetting the W.O. by still being credited with pay at Cox and Kings, including a Med. allowance. I explained what action I had taken, all the time wondering what sort of punishment I would cop out for. He shared an office with his second in command a Major Bastard (pronounced Basstard) who had been listening to the conversation. (Contrary to what Spike Milligan says about him he doesn't live up to his unfortunate name, but is a most congenial fellow). Turning towards the said major, 'Benny' said, 'what shall we do with this man, Busty?' He then proceeded to tell me in a fatherly way that if I found myself in similar difficulties again not to fail to knock on his door and avail myself of his advice. No wonder he was a popular C.O.. Well, he was with me!

Only once in the twelve months I was with 02E was I placed on guard duty. There is an 'In' and an ''Out' drive to the building each running parallel, about a furlong in length, the guard room being the gate house at the 'In' drive. There was no ceremonial mounting of the guard which consisted of a dozen men plus a commander, in my case, a sergeant. It was small wonder that there was no ceremonial mounting of the guard when it consisted of fifty percent P.O.W's. What a complex situation we lived in. Germans, who months before we had been fighting, were here joining forces with us to repel Italian thieves intent on stealing whatever they could from us. The very same Italians who had been allies of Germany for about three years and who had switched their allegiance to us. The British members of the guard were issued with five rounds of ammunition for our rifles (we all still had our rifles, being essentially soldiers, even though our duties were all clerical) and the German lads were issued with a wooden club each, somewhat like a small baseball bat. It was the duty of the guard to attend to the main entrance - signing in and out personnel in the main, and patrolling the M.T. (Motor Transport) lines. In the early days of occupation of the premises the thieves had forced an entry beneath the wire mesh fencing and had jacked up several vehicles to remove their wheels for which there was a ready market, so in order to keep mobile (especially 'recce' transport) we had regular patrols.

My German partner for the M.T. patrol turned out to be Fritz, the drummer from the band. He must have been recruited from the Hitler Youth because he was then only about eighteen. His English was quite good but unfortunately centred on one theme. 'It's all propaganda' he said, 'that Hitler is dead. He didn't die in the bunker as all the allied newspapers proclaimed. He has gone into hiding and in a little while he will rise again with his followers and fan the embers of the Third Reich back into flames. Next time the Nazis will be the victors!'

Of all the Germans that I met, and I met many, he was the only self-proclaimed Nazi. I've wondered often since that day whether I should have reported my experience; had he been in possession of the rifle and me the club he might have felt disposed to start World War Three.

Garth-Atkins came across and had a quiet word with me early one morning. I was being transferred he told me to the Royal Army Service Corps but would be still doing exactly the same work. He must have seen the dismay on my face, (I felt a kind of allegiance to my old Regiment of Foot although I wasn't with them any longer) because he said, 'But there is an advantage. You are receiving two stripes'. I thanked him because it was most certainly his recommendation that brought about my promotion. The stripes not only gave me a boost in morale bringing me into line with the majority of my colleagues, who had all been in the job longer than me, but gave me a substantial rise in weekly pay. Just after lunch Garth-Atkins came to me again and said, 'Don't you want those stripes?' I said 'Yes, Sir', to which he replied ' It doesn't look like it; you haven't got them sewn on yet. Get along to the tailors right now and get them on'. I had had my head down attending to my job thinking it unwise to leave the office in view of the circumstances, but he apparently thought that my new status should be advertised.

I made a beeline for my billet to collect my spare K.D. shirt and my battle dress blouses and hurried to the tailors room. The tailor was a small Italian man of forty five or fifty who attended to uniform alterations (waist lines were getting bigger) and repairs, sewing on stripes and poached eggs etc.. He had an assistant, a young lad of about seventeen, who mostly did the ironing and pressing. The shirt that I was wearing was quickly removed for the stripes to be sewn on and the others promised for the next day. While the stripes were getting fixed I asked 'Tony' what his trouble was - he was looking so downcast. He had received a 'Dear John' letter. His girlfriend had given him the elbow and to prove it he showed me the letter. I said, 'You're kidding me. That letter hasn't got a crease in it. The paper is just as it comes off the writing pad'. 'I've been steam ironing it all morning' he said.

A gift shop was set up in one of the vacant rooms with a wide selection of things suitable to buy and send home to wives, sweethearts, children, grannies and so on and the young lady put in charge was the youngest daughter of the aforementioned tailor. She was a little smaller than average and was exceedingly pretty. Her features and skin were perfect and she looked like a large china doll with her long black tresses and dark brown eyes. I believe that lots of the fellows went there just to see her without any intention of buying anything. She turned a deaf ear to all the advances that were made by various men and told me, in confidence, that she wanted to become a nun but her father wouldn't hear of it. 'I will have to wait until he dies' she said. She had a soft sweet musical voice but spoke very little English apart from her numbers. Numbers, of course, were essential because she had to know the price of the goods and how to count out the change. It was quite entertaining to listen to her 'fiferty-five, fiferty seeex' and so on.

One of the ploys I used to advance my grasp of the language was to spend as much time as I could in the village and listen to the talk especially on a Saturday when the main road lost half of its width to an open market. Often I would hear a phrase and not have the faintest clue what it meant. The following Monday lunch time I would go to the gift shop and ask Emelia what the phrase meant and she would translate it into simple words that I already understood, or on the odd occasion she would say '*E non buono palare cosi*' (It's not good to say that) in which case I knew I had learned an oath or swear word.

I wonder if she still has that lovely soft voice? So many Italian women when they reach middle and old age develop a more strident tone. Is it developed by frequently chastising their lazy husbands? Perhaps 'lazy' is too harsh a word. By nature they mostly seem 'happy-go-lucky'. I always likened Italian men to grown up boys.

On one of my visits to the Saturday market I saw evidence of real poverty - an incident that has stayed fresh in my memory ever since. I had just seen two unusually quiet boys of about seven or eight years of age (most boys of that age were chasing each other in and out of the stalls) standing looking at a stall loaded with fruit and chatting away to each other. They both replied 'Yes' when I asked them if they liked apples, so I asked the stall-holder to give them a nice big one each. He weighed them individually on his hand held scales, told me the price which I paid. They bit into the apples as soon as they got them only to be chastised by the stall-holder for doing so before thanking me. 'Say 'thank you' to the soldier'. The adjacent stall was one that had about two dozen little boxes of different flavoured boiled sweets. A woman was taking a hard look at these, evidently trying to make up her mind whether to get some and if so which ones. She looked in her purse and was calculating what she could afford to spend here (she was the only customer around). After much deliberation and another look at the varieties she made up her mind. She would have one of those and one of those she pointed out. They were placed in the pan of the scales and the price was sung out. Two sweets (in a dunce's hat bag) and money changed hands and off she went. To my lasting shame I never offered to pay for her sweets or to buy a few extra ones. I ease my conscience by saying that she might have been too proud to accept an offer; she might have had a husband who might give her a hiding for accepting charity; she might have thought I was making improper advances; who knows what might have happened? No matter how I ease my conscience I always come to the same conclusion, that is, being put into the same circumstances again I would make some sort of offer and ask her if she would say an 'Ave' for me on her next visit to church.

Another manifestation of the endemic poverty arose only yards away from where the open market was held when I was in a bar one evening. A man came in with a girl of about thirteen years of age and while she took a seat at a vacant table he went to the bar. He came away with a bottle of beer and two glasses. She was his daughter judging by their looks and easy laughing conversation. Pouring a little into each glass he held up the bottle to the light and eked out a little more until it appeared that he was happy with the amount left in the bottle. He had asked for the bottle cap, which was of the crimped metal type, this he placed back on the bottle. When the time came for them to leave some thirty minutes later he took his half bottle of beer to the bar-tender and giving it to him said 'Sino a domani sera' (Until tomorrow evening). One bottle of beer between two people to last two evenings!

Italians excel in marquetry work and there were some nice examples of this in the gift shop. I thought that I might buy a jewel case in this fashion for my sister, Betty, and mentioned it in conversation in the office. Employed in the office was a young man (thirtyish) whose mother was French and his father a Tunisian Arab. He had come over from Tunis with 02E and was employed as a filing clerk, and very good at it too. His English was almost flawless and his Italian superior to mine. Overhearing my conversation he said that he was going to Venice the following day (Saturday) on the 'recce' transport and if I would like his assistance in buying some marquetry work there he knew some street vendors who would certainly be more reasonable than the gift shop and would have a wider choice. He advised me that cigarettes were a more acceptable currency than lira. I had plenty of cigarettes because I didn't smoke many what with having my pipe. Usually I sold the majority of my cigarettes to the Germans, knowing full well that they were taking them to the village and selling them on at a small profit (Our weekly ration was sixty free in a plain round tin and sixty duty-free in packets of twenty).

On the 'recce' truck I thought I would have a little conversation with this individual and get to know him a little better. Although he was as good as on the strength of our unit he didn't eat with us and I've no idea where he slept so I only saw him during office hours. Knowing that in some races the family name is used first I thought it appropriate to find out how he should be addressed as I had heard him being called 'Brignone' and also 'Salvatore'. So I said to him; 'I understand that your name is Brignone Salvatore. Which name is your Christian name?' The reply floored me; 'Neither. I'm a Moslem'.

Brignone took me right away to the street vendors area only a stones throw from the Bridge of Sighs and I was shown a selection of jewellery boxes. The one I selected was one with a lid that was depicting blue birds on the marquetry pattern. The box itself was made to look like a stack of small books with the top and bottom ones lying flat with five standing upright between them. Sliding the vertical ones forward permitted the spine of the centre one to be drawn down revealing a tiny key-hole. With the key the lid could be locked down, not that Betty had any gems worth locking away, but I knew that she would be pleased with the novelty of it. A bargain was struck. It is said that a bargain occurs when both vendor and vendee are pleased with the arrangement and that certainly happened on this occasion- the seller being pleased to accept forty John Player cigarettes and I being pleased with the lovely little box.

Brignone knew Venice better than I did and when I asked him if he knew any dressmakers, as I was thinking of buying Josie an evening dress - an impossible task in England with the rationing restrictions - he soon was introducing me to the Mike Baldwin of Venice. Having introduced me, he excused himself as he had his own business to attend to and left me with this man. We had met by chance outside his premises and standing there I explained that I had a fiancee for whom I wished to buy an evening dress and that Brignone had told me that he had the facilities to provide such a thing. 'Follow me', he said and sped off into his place of work. It turned out to be a little factory with about a dozen girls beavering away on their purring sewing machines. It was only a matter of seconds before we were exiting from the other end of the room - so fast that it never registered on my mind what garments they were working on. I followed along a few alleyways and we came out into a little piazza. The dominant building on this square was a large double-fronted shop displaying one elegant gown and a few et ceteras in each window. I presumed that Giorgio's factory did the sewing for this establishment. Going in it seemed that we were on a Hollywood set. There right opposite the entrance was a magnificent staircase at least ten feet wide with delicate wrought iron balusters topped with beautiful marble copings; at the top stood an imperious looking lady. It seemed that the room in which I was standing was merely the entrance hall as there was no sign of gowns on tailor's dummies or on racks or in cupboards or drawers or anywhere except a smartly cut one on 'Madame' at the top of the stairs. Whereas the man who had brought me here had sped along as though the Devil was on his heels, as well as me, this lady was in no hurry to meet me. It would be wrong to say that she drifted down because that would imply that she was not in full control of direction. Rather, she floated down with an elegance that matched the surroundings. Before she reached the bottom step I had formed the opinion that she was more used to dealing with the 'nobilta' (the contessas) than she was with the likes of a humble corporal from the British Army. I was definitely not in a C & A's or even Marks and Spencers. Following the statutory greetings my escort said, 'This man wishes to buy a dress for his fiancee. I will leave him with you' and withdrew completely, doubtless with the thought of commission or further trade in mind. I was asked, in very good English, what kind of dress I had in mind to which I replied that a simple evening gown was what I was looking for. Did I have any particular style in mind? No, I would leave that to her discretion. By this time I was beginning to realise that I would probably need a king's ransom to pay for a dress from this emporium and asked what sort of charge I could expect for supplying me with such a dress. (I had had to take all my savings back to the U.K. on my last leave). She said that she couldn't possibly give me any idea as to price until I had supplied her with all of Josie's measurements and a full length photograph. Needless to say Josie never did get an Italian evening dress! At least my idea was good!

Going back towards Saint Mark's piazza I was passing a shop that had a display of superior cakes, many of them decorated with segments of candied fruits. My mind wandered back to pre-war days when occasionally, especially around Christmas time, my mother would buy a small cardboard box full of mouthwatering sugary fruit with which to decorate her wonderful home-baked cakes. How lovely, I thought, if I could buy some of that stuff to send home - it had been completely unobtainable during the last five years. I went into the shop and asked one of the assistants if, by any chance, they sold the fruit separately. The reply was, 'Sorry, but no'. Pursuing the matter, I was asking whether she could advise me where I could obtain some when her boss came from a room at the rear of the shop and asked what the difficulty was. I explained my needs and he sympathised that we had been years without this luxury and straight away told the girl to go to the stock room and weigh out *mezzo kilo* for me and charged me a mere 200 lira (about two shillings for just over a pound in weight). Half was posted to Josie and half to my mum and was received with enthusiasm at both venues.

Going on again from the cake shop I came across another example of poverty. Turning the corner into one of the more popular routes through the city I was approached by an elderly man. He had surpassed his allotted three score and ten by, I estimated, at least five years and was wearing a broad-brimmed trilby hat and a long black coat. He was tall for an Italian but despite his age stood very erect as though he was an ex-military man. The coat fitted badly about the shoulders showing that at some previous time he had fitted it better. He asked me if I would like to buy some picture cards from him at the same time producing a small wad of them from his pocket. The pictures were biblical scenes reminding me of similar cards I had received at Sunday School as a little boy. I selected a few and asked him how much they were. Over the years the memory fades a little and I cannot remember the price but I hope that I was generous in my payment because it was so obvious that he was in need of money but was too proud to beg.

Those pictures grace Josie's prayer book.

Along with four of my colleagues I found myself entitled to a short local leave. I have an inkling that Fred (Johnny) Bull organised the accommodation and I was left to see to the transport. I had already had a satisfactory trip with Gottfried as my driver so I asked for him again and this was readily agreed. We had the use of a thirty hundred weight truck and a couple of jerry cans of petrol. Three double rooms were booked at an Albergo in the town of Simione on Lake Garda and I was elected to share one of these with Gottfried as he spoke no English and my Italian was the only means of conversation between him and the party. Knowing what Italian breakfasts were like we had taken the precaution to have words with the cookhouse before leaving and had come armed with two or three large cans of Canadian bacon.

Arriving late afternoon we quickly put our kit, such as it was, in the bedrooms and asked if there was a secure place for the truck. Yes, there was a yard at the side of the hotel that had double gates and a padlock. Having put the truck away until tomorrow we decided to waste no time and wandered down to the water's edge. There were rowing boats of a sturdy structure for hire and straight away Gottfried volunteered to take the oars if I fancied a trip. I willingly let him do the rowing, he was broad chested and had biceps twice the size of mine. He told me he had been a skiing instructor before being conscripted into the army. A hundred yards from the shore there were two radio masts of a sunken vessel projecting eight or nine feet in the air and he rowed towards them. The water was crystal clear and all the details of the boat down to the rivet heads could be clearly seen. It had been a ferry which had plied between the various towns from Riva in the north to Desenzano in the south.

What advantage either ourselves or the Germans could have gained by sinking this ferry I couldn't imagine but I thought that it was salvageable as it appeared, from the top view at least, to be in excellent repair. It could well be transporting holiday makers up and down the lake today. Gottfried turned his efforts to rowing back towards the shore at the northern end of the town where a rocky path ran along the lake's edge. An Italian family were having a picnic seated on some of the larger rocks. I am wrong in saying 'a family' because the men were missing - probably in a bar. There were three women and half a dozen children of various ages up to nine or ten.

I must tell you that the Italians do not have a word for picnic, after all we English pinched it from the French. The Italians say '*Scampagnata con refezione per cui ciascuno porta la sua parte di provvigioni*'. It takes longer to say it than to make the egg sandwiches!

Suddenly screams rang out, the children ran in all directions except the lake, the women jumped up on the larger rocks holding their skirts above their knees. Gottfried shouted out '*Eine wasser rat*!' There, more frightened than the women, was the biggest water rat I have ever seen. It was the size of a domestic cat and tore off along the path and then disappeared in the undergrowth. (This was the first time that I realised that quite a number of German words closely resemble our own). The picnic continued with lots of excited chatter from the party and we went gently back to the hotel to wash and change into our trousers ready for dinner.

We had all our meals including breakfast out on a paved patio that was surmounted by a timber framework that supported vines heavy with luscious grapes. It was much more civilised than the meals I had taken *al fresco* on the mountainside with my infantry pals.

After the meal we strolled around the tiny town and fell into conversation with three young ladies. Two of them spoke good English and told us that they were studying the language with the hopes of entering the tourist trade and their companion was

Aerial view of Lake Garda

Lake Garda

Gottfried and truck

studying French with the same object. Their friend could not roll her 'R's' - very necessary in Italian - so had taken the French course in preference. As they had been born and raised in a tiny town that is situated at the end of a long and narrow promontory with no room for expansion I could easily see why they wanted to widen their horizons and stretch their wings in the wider world. There would, most likely, be a shortage of eligible bachelors too with all the young fit men having been in the Italian army and they would have acquired a taste for a livelier lifestyle.

Saturday morning saw us up and ready for our English breakfast, but it was also the morning when we became quite irate when, having drunk our fruit juice the waitress promptly served us with a couple of fried eggs each. 'What's happened to the bacon?' someone asked. 'I gave the cans' he continued 'to the manager with the instructions that one was for Saturday breakfast and the other for Sunday'. The manager was sent for who immediately sent for the cook. The cook arrived wondering if he was for the firing squad. 'Where's the bacon?' he was asked. The manager translated. Slowly a smile spread over his face and he suggested, through the manager, that we turn our eggs over. He had chopped the bacon into tiny pieces, partially fried it and then dropped the eggs on top to fry them and completely fry the bacon beneath. We laughingly conceded that we had not been cheated; but it was easily understood that, having no English visitors for five years, our eating habits were somewhat of a challenge.

The only visitors staying at the hotel were an English family of four; father, mother and two school age children. They sat at a table nearest the water's edge and we had taken tables on the opposite side. Whether we chose our seating in such a way so as not to annoy them with our persistent jolly chatter or because it was nearer to the 'cookhouse' and our meals would be nice and hot, I do not know. What I do know is that when we greeted them with 'Good Morning' we did not get a reply. We knew that they were not deaf because they conversed with each other in somewhat affected tones. If father had instructed the family to stay aloof because we were soldiers and soldiers were boorish, drunken, loud-mouthed and a guffawing load of individuals then he was to be disappointed. The fact that we had sacrificed a few years of our lives to ensure that families such as his could travel with safety on the continent evidently counted for nothing. They were superior and that was an end to it. We did not bother them further.

It was agreed, without going to a vote, that we should devote the main part of the day to a leisurely trip right round the lake, so I asked Gottfried to get the truck from the yard. He came to me some minutes later to say that he had experienced trouble in starting the engine and on examination there was water in the carburettor so there would be some delay. Further examination revealed that the petrol had been drained from the tank and replaced with water so that the fuel gauge would give the same reading as before the theft. Whether Gottfried kept one in his kit or whether he had requested one from the hotel management (who might have one ready for such eventualities) I do not know, but he produced a small length of rubber tubing and proceeded to siphon off the contents of the petrol tank. Fortunately we had had the foresight to bring the jerry cans of fuel into the safer area of the hotel otherwise we would have been obliged to phone up our Headquarters with a request for supplies to be brought out to us. We reported the incident to the manager who was profuse with his apologies but we were a happy bunch and did not make an issue of it.

We eventually left, with full confidence in our driver, and we saw the three young ladies with whom we had been chatting the previous evening and asked them if they would like a ride around the lake. They laughingly shouted their '*Grazies*' but 'No'. We travelled up the eastern side of the lake, the road following the contours of the water's edge, passing through half a dozen little villages. At the northern extremity of the lake at the town of Riva (which means 'waterside') we stopped to stretch our legs and take a little liquid refreshment as the day was quite hot. This was the most imposing town on the lake and sported an important looking jetty where a ferry was sitting awaiting orders. Continuing our anticlockwise circuit we progressed along the western side, but this time although the road followed the contours of the water it was now elevated some thirty or forty feet with a sheer drop down to the lake. At intervals there were tunnels that had been cut through the rock. How villages had communicated with each other in the days before the tunnels were built (some of the tunnels being a couple of hundred yards in length) I cannot imagine as the terrain on that side of the lake is most inhospitable. Looking across the lake from this side the view is dominated by Mount Baldo, so called on account of its white crown of snow. As we approached the village of Campione di Garda (Champion of Garda) we were in for a surprise. Leaving a tunnel which had holes cut in the side so that the lake could still be seen intermittently, we were suddenly confronted by men leaping in front of the truck with long poles, barring our progress. Lemons were suspended along the poles and this was their way of advertising their wares. There was no sale I'm afraid because we did not have the means to convert them into the refreshing drink that they would certainly have made. Disappointed, they let us go and we eventually arrived back at the hotel.

I had neglected my duty of writing to Josie each day and so I went down to the few shops and bought some picture postcards to send to her in order to make amends. However, I could not post them until I got back to 02E unless I could find a tobacconists (which is where you bought stamps in those days) and determine the cost of the postage for a postcard to England and then somewhere to post it. I opted for the easy option of posting it, free of postage, at 02E.

Sirmione has a small castle complete with moat that was teeming with carp. One of the picture postcards was a photograph of this castle taken from either on or near the hotel patio. In a collection of Sir Winston Churchill's paintings I saw one of just the same view and recognised it instantly. Just think about it! I might have slept in the same room - or even the same bed - as Winnie! Then again, Winnie may have slept in the same bed as a German P.O.W!

We showered and changed and came down to dinner. The meal, like the one on the previous evening, proved to be a nice change being that it was in lovely surroundings and totally Italian in its content. The rest of the evening was taken up with chatting and smoking and, probably, complementing ourselves in organising such an idyllic holiday.

There was no reason to call for the manager at Sunday morning's breakfast; we knew where the bacon would be. After breakfast we went down to the lake and I, being the only non-swimmer, stayed at the edge sunning myself whilst the rest swam around. The water was, as I have said before, crystal clear and the bed of the lake could be seen in every detail. Long fissures, varying in length, ran along as though there had been an earthquake at some time. The manager had warned us about these cracks, telling us that a party of officers had taken rooms with them last Christmas and had gone for a midnight swim. One of their company had caught his foot in one of these cracks and had drowned.

I took off my shoes and socks and dangled my feet in the water and found that the top nine or ten inches were warm despite the early hours of the day. However, beneath ten inches it was icy cold. I sat there, watching my friends splashing about and thoroughly enjoying themselves when I felt a sharp pain in the big toe of my right foot. Thinking that it was the result of my feet being in that icy cold water I looked down to see a fish taking a bite! I thought that to be a bit rich, after all it was the other four soldiers that were disturbing his tranquil world!

When we were taking a last stroll around the town before departing we bumped into the , apparently inseparable, three young ladies. They expressed their surprise at seeing us as they thought we had left the previous day. They explained that, if they had known that we really meant it when we invited them to take a ride round the lake they would have joined us. They were afraid that we might have dropped them off somewhere for them to make their own way back home. We wished them well in their studies and said our 'Ariverderci's'. We settled our bills and made an uneventful journey back to Battaglia Terme.

In one of my letters to Josie I had explained that I had taken a great liking to Italy, especially its people and its climate, and that I quite relished the idea of taking my demobilisation there if she was willing to come out and join me. Those soldiers who had been called up long before me were now getting demobbed and naturally my thoughts turned to the future and especially my future with Josie. Couched in the gentlest terms I was told that a life in Italy would not be acceptable as her mother was so dependant on her for so many things and that she could only see a future for us living with her mother or nearby. If it meant happiness for Josie then I was willing to leave my friends and family in the Midlands and find my fortune in Chester. If I was to make my fortune in Chester; why not make a start to it now? On several occasions I had included a pair of silk stockings in with my daily letter and, more important than the value of the stockings, was the fact that clothing coupons could be used for other items. I therefore wrote to Josie telling her that I was going to give up smoking, sell my cigarettes to the prisoners and use the money to buy silk stockings. These I could send post free (Forces Mail) and she could sell them, at slightly below shop prices, to her friends, who would be pleased with their bargains. Josie opened an account (the S.S. account) at the post office and in the three months prior to demob we made £25 from my fags. This was something like a month's average wage in those days. What a pity I had not thought of it months before. Little did I know then but I was also improving my health.

To add to our list of luxuries the authorities installed a fruit shop on the ground floor and this was run by a man whose name I remember well because it is the same as mine but spelt backwards and dropping the 'H', Signore Remo. I soon became a frequent customer as I found the grapes and figs absolutely luscious . I would point out the fruit that I fancied and say for example, '*Duo etti, per favore*', which when translated meant 'Half a pound, please'. On one occasion I went along with grapes on my mind and found that the shop was bursting at the seams with Italian women waiting to get served. Although the hired staff were permitted to use the facility it was understood that we, the British, had priority and S. Remo, looking over the heads of the crowd, called to me, 'What do you want, Corporal?' From where I stood, behind at least a dozen people, I could not point to my requirements and when I said what I wanted the rogue pretended not to hear and asked me to shout up. I did and the whole shopfull fell about laughing. I had asked for half a pound of eggs. (The words for 'eggs' and 'grapes' sound quite similar).

Three of us hired cycles in the village and decided that we would go along to the next town on the road in the opposite direction to the one that we took to Padua and Venice. It is called Monselice and was famous for nothing that I had heard of except that it was, as was Battaglia, on the route of the Mille Miglia road race which we had watched passing through for the first post war event. The road was deserted as it was siesta time, the only traffic being about fifty sheep being led, not driven, by a shepherd on their way to the next bit of available pasture. This scene made me realise how primitive rural Italy was compared to the cities. Another thing that jogged my mind back to my history books at school, with vague memories of 'the three field system' and the 'hundred years war', was when I saw one of the monks in a chocolate brown habit leading an oxen-drawn dray with solid wooden wheels through the village. This was not an unusual sight as the monks had a tobacco drying plant and a quarry which employed quite a number of the villagers. Another substantial employer was the family Etti, who lived in a palatial villa just outside the village. I was told that the two brothers, both called Count Etti, ran the business of farming the surrounding land and ruled with a rod of iron, still maintaining a flogging post on their premises, which they were not averse to using.

Half way to Monselice we came to a wayside stall, rather like a market stall, with its bright striped awning except that it was more substantially built and was a permanent structure. It sported a row of brightly coloured liquids in glass bottles on a shelf and a table with a number of glass tankards. We came to a halt and asked the charge for a drink. (It's wise to ask first in case of argument about value afterwards). Finding the price acceptable we chose our colours and the proprietor went round to the back of the stall and came back dragging a heavily laden sack. Opening the sack he revealed a great chunk of ice and with an ice pick proceeded to hack off some small pieces. These pieces went into a device closely resembling the 'Spong's Mincer'' that my mum used to make the mincemeat for those lovely Christmas mince pies. The ice came out in even smaller pieces along with ice cold water into the tankards with a measure of the puree. Not altogether hygienic I suppose but Oh, so refreshing.

When we reached Monselice the effects of the liquid refreshment had worn off and we stopped at the first bar that we spotted eager for some more liquid. When we entered the bar all conversation ceased abruptly. Not one of the eight to ten men said a word, either to us or to each other. The only words the barmen said was the price as he served us with two beers and an orangeade. I can only describe the looks on the faces of the men as hostile. The atmosphere was bordering on evil and without saying more than a word or two to each other we drank up and were glad to get out into the open. It didn't take more than a couple of minutes to decide that if this was the reception committee of Monselice we didn't want to learn any more about that town and off we went back to Battaglia. Speaking to one of our waitresses a day or two later I recounted our experience at the bar in Monselice and asked if she could account for it. She said that it was a hot bed of Communist activity and that we had most likely entered the place whilst some political plot was being hatched.

The following Saturday, having enjoyed the ride to Monselice, if not the hospitality, we decided that we would repeat the exercise but travel in the opposite direction. Approaching the village of Mottegrotto Terme my rear tyre developed a puncture. The outskirts of the village were in sight so I thought it better to carry on, pushing the cycle, and get it repaired in the village rather than walk back the five or six miles to Battaglia. We arrived to find the village was enjoying a *'festa'*. Whereas Battaglia is a village divided territorially by a canal running right through its centre large enough to carry barges almost twice the width of out narrow boats and is crossed once by a road bridge at the northern end and by a footbridge at the southern end, Mottegrotto was more conventional with a piazza at its centre with roads radiating from it. This piazza was festooned with flags and bunting and had an impromptu stage with the village band playing with great gusto. Excited children chased each other between and around the stalls that buckled with the weight of all the good things there were to eat and drink. Young couples and mums and dads danced in the centre of the piazza to the music of the band. The older generation and the more staid members of the village stood in little groups chatting happily. What a contrast to our experience of the previous week.

    I asked a man where I could find a shop that did cycle repairs as my rear tyre was broken. (I didn't know the Italian word for puncture). He told me that the shop was closed, as indeed were most of them, on account of it being the village's Saint's day, but perhaps the man might help me if he could be found. Luckily for me he was in the square and right away offered to open up and repair my tyre. In the circumstances I was expecting, and willing, to pay a hefty fee but was most agreeably surprised when he said he couldn't charge me on this their Saint's day. He would not even allow me to buy him a drink and expressed his genuine pleasure in being able to help.

    If there is one thing the Italians know how to do it's to throw a party. Whereas we would have a street party to celebrate a Coronation or the end of a war, the Italians have at least one each year even in the dire circumstances and the poverty with which they are faced even in those days.

For the most part we made our own entertainment with games of cricket, football and rugby union in season, but we did get an occasional glimpse of other forms of amusement. On one occasion we had a visit from two men from the top of their kind in Italy, one being a violinist the other a pianist. Programmes of the works they were to perform were produced by our ATS girls, a grand piano hired and installed on the stage in the hall and an evening of classical music was thoroughly enjoyed.

A few weeks later music of a different kind and with a wider appeal came our way provided by Ivy Benson's All Girls Band. In preparation for this event the handymen amongst the prisoners had been put to work erecting wings on either side of the stage in order to give the girls the chance to apply their lipstick and titivate their hair in private. These wings were of rough timber construction covered with a hessian wall. When the girls retired to these wings after their first session, which was applauded loudly, members of the entertainment committee went up, ostensibly, to compliment them on their performance. Giving praise and thanks was not the only thing they had in mind as could be seen by the silhouettes on the hessian walls. Cries of, 'Put her down. You don't know where she's been' went up amongst other words of advice. I do not know whether the POW's had thought it out or whether it was by accident but the lighting was along the back wall and when the lighting in the hall was dimmed all was revealed.

I usually gave Gottfried first refusal when it came to selling my cigarettes and one evening on going down to the German quarters and asking for him I was told that he was in the calaboose. Naturally I asked what he had done to be locked up. He had been on a long journey, I was told, and he had got back after the evening dinner was finished but his meal had been put in the oven with a low light to keep it warm. After a quick wash he had gone to the oven and found it empty. On asking who had eaten his meal; Manfred, who seemed to be the only prisoner with a perpetual air of meanness and discontent, said that he had as he felt hungry. Gottfried struck him just one blow breaking his jaw. Manfred was now in hospital.

I believe that Gottfried was only under lock and key for one night and on going to see him a couple of days later I was invited to join the German lads in the village where they had planned a party to celebrate a birthday. There was no cake with candles but by jingo there was a lot of bottled beer and wine (and orangeade for me) and heaven knows by what means they raised the funds to pay for it as they didn't get any pay. They really put great effort into singing their popular songs; the only one I could join in was 'Lili Marlene'. I was the only Englishman there but I did not feel 'the odd one out' as they made me as welcome as if I was one of their own nation. It showed once again that the common denominator amongst ordinary men is respect for each other irrespective of race.

News was passed around that the Army Kinematograph Corps would be coming to give us a film show. To save the trouble of moving all the tables and chairs in the dining hall the show was held out of doors, which is what the Corps did in most cases anyway. The screen was slung from the two inner avenues of trees adjacent to the drives and the sound equipment set up alongside. Round about nine o'clock, as soon as it got dark, the programme started and we stood in little groups watching and listening. I don't recall the main film shown, but I remember the supporting one which was about the life of the man who composed 'Home Sweet Home', a man who was brought up in an orphanage. The man standing next to me, one of my office colleagues, had seen it so many times he knew every word of the narrative and was saying them in parallel with the sound track. The show finished with our National Anthem and we made our way back to our bedrooms.

A surprise awaited us when we got in. Whizzing round and round the room were about twenty bats. The windows had been left open to let out the heat gathered during the day; the poor creatures had found their way in but couldn't find their way out again. We tried adjusting the hinged windows at various angles to assist them with their echo sounding direction finding devices but all to no avail. Not one of them found his way out and they continued circling madly, twittering as they flew. There was no way we were going to be able to sleep with this frantic flapping going on so we decided that, unfortunately, they would have to be killed. A couple of us hoisted Pete Mortimer, the best batsman in our billet, in true assault course style, up on to the top of a wardrobe. Someone handed him his cricket bat and he struck out at them as they came around and around. It was not too difficult as they were all travelling in the same direction and at round about the same height. I was pleased that they all died quickly, none of them requiring a coup de grace. We gathered up the little furry bodies and put them in the waste bin just before 'lights out'.

Coming back from breakfast next morning we found Maria just about to enter our billet to sweep up whatever we might have dropped on the floor and the dust that had blown in. Maria was a pretty woman of some twenty one or two years of age with a bubbly captivating personality whose husband had been killed in North Africa. She was always dressed in black as widows in rural areas always did and was almost surely condemned to widowhood for the rest of her days. To me it seemed such a waste as she would have made a lovely wife and mother.

She gave me her usual greeting, laughing as she said *'Buon Giorno Brutto'* ('Good morning ugly one') and I replied *'Buon Giorno Brutta'*. Holding her rubbish sack in one hand she bent down and picked up the waste paper bin with the other. She glanced down at the contents which normally would have been empty fag packets and chocolate bar wrappers but she saw the little bodies, she dropped the bin and the sack, let out a scream and went flying along the corridor as though the Devil was chasing her. I caught up with her and assured her that they were all dead and that we would empty them into her sack. Coming back, somewhat reluctantly, she came and gave our room the speediest brushing out it had ever had. When she had finished she closed one of the double doors and as she pushed the door into the rebate a bat, that had come to rest on the top of the door (which had not been closed all night) fell at her feet. She repeated her scream and her flight from the room. Coaxed back yet again, with the assurance that there were no more, she took up her brush and sack, holding the sack between forefinger and thumb at arm's length, and went off to the next billet in a much more subdued manner than was usual.

Next morning saw a much quieter Maria coming in to tidy us up, peering nervously over the edge of the waste paper bin and looking up towards the top of the doors as though she was expecting a repeat performance of the previous day. I asked her why she was so fearful of such tiny animals and she explained to me that not only she but all the girls were afraid because if a bat flies on to a girls head those little hooks at the bottom of their wings get caught in their hair and as they flap around trying to get free they drive the girl mad. I could see from her serious attitude that this was a genuine belief.

The photographic club had been given a room to practice their hobby and was equipped with a dark room, enlarger and so on - all that was necessary to produce good results. One of its keenest members was Alex Ferrans an especially good pal of mine. A man with such capabilities was required at the British Embassy in Rome and Alex applied for and secured the position. His job was to be taking photographs of each individual soldier's grave to send to relatives, so his appointment was with the War Graves Commission. War Office had issued an edict to the effect that all properties in and south of Rome that we had requisitioned had to be returned to their rightful owners and that no military uniforms would be worn in those territories. After a couple of months in the job Alex came to pay us a visit. Just imagine the ribbing he got when he turned up in his new uniform - a pin-striped suit and bowler hat! He told us he had left his rolled umbrella in Rome.

I have, no doubt given the impression that our prisoners enjoyed a life of comparative freedom and this was indeed the truth. A lot of my old pals in the infantry battalion would gladly have changed places I'm sure. For instance, one of the drivers would go roaring through the village slipping the clutch and giving it lots of 'revs' to create consternation amongst the inhabitants with a plank tied across the radiator displaying the words printed in white paint 'Sempre Ubbriarco' (Always drunk). As far as we, the British, were concerned these Germans had only one rank - that of POW. Amongst themselves there was no rank except the solitary young Lieutenant who was, for the most part, 'one of the lads', but there was a kind of loose class structure. This consisted of the academics who, prior to being conscripted, had been the accountants, solicitors or the like and were highly educated with one or two speaking good English; the artificer types who were clever with vehicle driving and maintenance and basic joinery; and the labouring types the majority having come from rural backgrounds. It seemed inevitable that, human nature being what it is, that advantage would be taken of the relative freedom they had and that privileges would be abused. The academics were employed in the offices, some on occasions even conversing with War Office staff on the telephone and they seemed quite happy and applied themselves diligently to the job; the artificers seemed content with their lot, keeping busy, but not overworked, with maintaining our fleet of trucks and driving them as and where we wished; but those at the bottom of the scale had their grumbles. One of the tasks assigned to the 'labouring' types was keeping the external areas tidy and this proved to be an easy task until autumn arrived. Both drives, as I have already said, were lined with trees on both sides and there were lots of trees too between the two drives and from these trees fell literally truck loads of leaves. If left they became a slimy, slippery coating on the drives when the autumn showers arrived and were a hazard both on foot or in a vehicle. I never learned any details, even though I visited the German quarters on occasions, but the word spread like wild fire around 02E that the POW's had gone on strike and this news was met with both laughter and disbelief. Whether they were persuaded by threats (perhaps a posting to a unit without such privileges as those granted at 02E) or by promises (perhaps a few extra bottles of beer) I do not know but the strike was short lived and life went on as normal.

One of the cleaners that we employed was a woman in her mid thirties. She was a pleasant homely type and I had a few conversations with her which resulted in me taking a photograph of her baby son, Alberto. He was a chubby, happy smiling baby and the photograph, taken with him sitting on a gravestone of one of his ancestors in the local cemetery, turned out first class. I managed to eliminate all the nearby gravestones from the picture by careful siting and I was so pleased with it that I had it enlarged to postcard size. Taking it along to her house I arrived, unfortunately, at about eight in the evening, just as her husband was sitting down to his meal. I apologised but was immediately invited to join him in his repast. 'It was most kind of them' I said ' but I had only recently eaten'. 'But you must try some of these yams ' I was told. 'I don't think you grow them in your country'. Both husband and wife pressed me and I agreed that I would have just a tiny portion. The husband's plate was stacked with as many of these yams as you could get on it. It was a cone of these vegetables with no sign of meat or fish or any other kind of vegetable. He tucked in and I couldn't help but admire the way he started at the top with knife and fork and prodigiously worked his way to the bottom without one rolling off his plate, at intervals pausing to take a swig of milk from his glass. His wife took out his empty plate to the kitchen and returned a couple of minutes later with another load, not quite as large as the first, together with another glass of milk. She explained that her husband always had milk with his yams because they were so dry and somehow they do not slide down as well with wine. I too had been given a small amount of milk. The yams had a light floury texture and were very like a baked King Edward potato apart from the sweet taste - a very pleasant experience.

This type of hospitable behaviour I found typical amongst the poor Italians - it probably prevails amongst the poor of most, if not all, nations. What little they had they were willing to share and to do so with a smile.

Alfredo (They don't come any cuter!)

The poorest of the poor, that I saw, were a family of gypsies. Gypsies were not looked on favourably by the Italians because they paid no rates or taxes, they contributed nothing to the country's welfare, they did not earn any wages and they had to steal their food and clothing; so they were treated with complete mistrust whenever they were seen. The family that I now saw at close quarters as I strolled down a country lane had a caravan with a canvas top shaped like the ones I remembered in those old Western films, the canvas being stretched over three or four timber hoops. The painfully thin horse was not between the shafts but was foraging amongst the roadside scorched grass for something worth chewing. Dressed in rags and looking as though their next wash would be the first in a long time the children were a pitiful sight. Where Italian children would be dashing around in play the two little gypsy boys stood still and watched my progress along the road together with their parents; all wearing a downtrodden expression. When I passed their home I looked in at the open door and was shocked to see the stringent conditions in which they lived. The room was bare apart from a few cooking utensils hanging from one wall; there were no bunks to sleep in; a light scattering of straw covered the floor, so light, in fact, that the floorboards could be easily seen between the strands of straw; there were no pillows or blankets. How they had survived the last winter, when I had seen the sea frozen over at Venice, I cannot imagine. Perhaps these were the survivors if the two little boys, with the expressions of adults, had had siblings last year. Poor people; not only did they have the vagaries of the weather and the hostile attitude of their host nation to contend with but it must have between even worse during the German occupation because they, under Hitler, had been indoctrinated with the belief that, if there was anyone more despicable than a Jew, it was a gypsy and many thousands of them had found that out in the labour camps and death chambers. It is no wonder that they looked miserable. It is said that we cannot live without hope. Hope lies in improving our own lives or in easing or encouraging the lives of our children, if we are lucky enough to be granted them, but these gypsies could look to no greater future than to be able to snare a hare for their cooking pot and stealing some vegetables from some sleepy unsuspecting farmer, probably during siesta time and when their allotted time had run its course would they, who were passed all hope, have to occupy a cairn on a mountainside as they did not have any tools with which to dig a grave or would they be granted a little unmarked plot in some cemetery amongst all the grand mausoleums with their marble angels and cherubim? Are the gypsies not also the children of God?

I have already stated that Battaglia Terme is a village divided by a canal and, as a result, has two roads running parallel one on either side of the water. The eastern road is the main road and, as such, is well made whilst the western one has a poor surface and does not have a pavement and it is this one which leads to 02E and then on, with a surface little better than a cart track, into the countryside. Each of these roads boasted a bar, the bar on the main road being the much larger of the two with the luxury (?) of a juke box. This is the same bar in which I saw a man and his daughter sharing half a bottle of beer and saving the other half for the next day. I only visited this bar on a few occasion, I was not a drinker, but I favoured and preferred the homely atmosphere of the smaller bar since I invariably met the same bunch of soldiers, in the larger bar, drinking to the health of a certain private who invited anyone in khaki to join him at his expense. One morning I saw the landlord of the larger bar in the corridor leading to the Colonel's office and I mentioned this to a colleague who said that it was not the first visit he had made and that he was most likely calling to see if he could get the bill of private 'X' paid following his bursts of generosity. I had no idea that this soldier had an account at the bar and possibly this applied to some of his 'friends' also. In fact, I had been led to believe, and I felt that there was a certain amount of truth in it, that he came from a well heeled family, his mother living in a castle or mansion house. He had the correct accent and the air of confidence that comes with higher education and he did not deny himself any pleasures because he bought himself skis and a saddle. It was also said that he had the right connections, having recently diverted a cargo of coffee destined for a southern port, probably, Naples, to a German port where the price was much higher, the Germans having been drinking ersatz coffee since before the war. Whether genuine talent came into the equation or whether the Colonel's forecast of less frequent visit from the aforementioned landlord was part of it, I do not know, but what I do know is that within a few days of the visit Private 'X' became Corporal 'X'. The smaller bar was run by a woman in her mid forties who was known as Elisa to her own generation and to her elders but as Mamma to the youngsters. She was helped in the bar by her daughter Aldina aged about seventeen and another barmaid a year or so younger called Anna.

Elisa was built like the typical Italian mamma, who evidently enjoyed her pasta and had as classical a Roman nose as any I had seen in Italy. She stood no nonsense from any youngsters who showed any signs of being boisterous. Aldina was slim and quite pretty and I could not imagine her growing up to be like her mum in appearance but she was like her in nature and it was easy to see that, despite a strict discipline, there was a strong bond between them. Anna, not long out of school, enjoyed her job and I often saw her and Aldina having a quiet giggle together no doubt discussing the attributes of the various young men or soldiers seated around the room. Being teetotal I only drank orangeade and on one occasion I was privileged to be taken down into the cellar by Elisa to be shown the stock of my favourite 'poison'. After that visit, whenever they were busy, I was told, 'You know where it is - go down and get your own'.

Talking to Aldina one evening I was puzzled with her pronunciation of a word that contained a double 'L'. I cannot remember the word but for argument's sake let us say that it was 'Ballo' and she pronounced it 'Bay-o'. Always willing to learn a little more of her language I asked her. 'When do you

Aldina, Elisa and Anna
Bar staff at Battaglia Terme

Wilf Sutton and Author "It's a hold up"

Wilf Sutton at 02E
If only he could drive

pronounce double 'l' as a 'y' or an 'i'? Her mother heard this and came into the conversation which followed with her giving her daughter a verbal hiding in front of me. 'How dare she employ this lazy city-style way of saying things?' In future she should speak to everyone in the manner in which she had been taught!' Just as many people today use the glottal 't', saying 'Go' i' for 'got it', so the young Italians fifty years ago were getting lazy in their speech. Don Vittorio had once apologetically explained to me in my first Italian lesson. Mussolini had westernised the language by forbidding the use of the words 'Thee' and 'thou' and other words considered archaic. However, the nation was not entirely subordinate and retained the 'thee' and 'thou' for addressing family and close friends.

Another experience I had with the language was when I called at the village hairdressers (still called 'barbers') just a few doors from my favourite bar. I went in and found myself in a passageway with half a dozen chairs, three of them occupied. The solitary barber's chair was in a room partitioned off (almost like a doctor's surgery) with access through a door-less opening at the end of the passage. Since I gathered from the pitch of the voices behind the partition that there was one of either sex and, as it was a gents hairdressers, then the one wielding the scissors must be a woman. This was the only gents hairdressers in the village and, as I had not seen any freakish hairdos around, I felt confident enough to take my turn in the queue and so I sat down. I found myself next to an Italian man who I recognised as one of the locals we employed at 02E. After sitting a little while in silence I said to this neighbour 'I don't want to appear nosy, but I have not understood one word of what they are saying over there'. He said, 'I haven't either - I think they are talking in Neapolitan dialect'.

Someone in the office, probably Fred Bull because he was very keen on classical music, arranged a visit to the opera in Verona. I jumped at the chance of hearing some serious music little knowing, when adding my name to the list, that I would be experiencing the most wonderful musical event of my lifetime.

Dudley Opera House was the only place that I had been to in my teens to see operas and they had all been well presented by Sadlers Wells Opera Company (with their orchestra augmented each time by Vincent Foley and his wife and their cellos; Vincent being the proprietor of the only music shop in Cradley Heath) and I had enjoyed everyone. Now, here I was in the very birthplace of opera - Italy with its plethora of natural singers and dancers and I felt it in my bones that it would be good.

It was the first week in August and although it was still hot during the afternoons the evenings were beginning to draw in and it was getting twilight at around eight thirty and, naturally, it was getting just that little bit cooler. Anticipating a late return from Verona, before we set out from O2E, we swapped our shorts for long K.D's, not just to thwart the mosquitoes but to be that much more presentable to the opera going public. The journey, courtesy of our three tonner 'recce' truck, was uneventful and we arrived in Verona with a good half hour to spare before the opera was due to start. We pulled up adjacent to the arena and I didn't know until the moment we jumped out of the back of the truck that the opera was to be in that arena.

Having, of necessity, quenched our thirsts at one of the trattorias with tables on the pavements we made our way to the entrances of the arena. We crossed the road and, as we did so, we passed a man of about thirty immaculately dressed with a young lady on each arm, each one apparently trying to outdo the other in dress and jewellery. I could not resist wagging a finger at him and calling out; '*Una per volta*' ('One at a time'). After all it is an operatic line -from The Barber of Seville if my memory serves me well. His chin went up and he looked down his nose at me with sheer contempt and disdain and anything else like that. I still do not believe they were his sisters!

I bought a programme as we went in. I have previously enthused about how Italians know how to throw a party. Another thing I found they excelled at was producing a programme. On checking (yes, I still have it) I find that it has eighty four pages of which only seventeen are of advertisements.

Admittedly it covered the three different operas that were being performed during that week and the following week but it gave details about musical directors, principal artists etc. not only for the operas being performed at this time but also going back to 1913 when the idea was first conceived. Reading it some years later I found that I had missed, by one day, seeing the famous Maria Callas in *La Gioconde*; mind you, she was a mere girl in those days and had not yet reached her ascendancy. It was interesting to see that one of the singers in the opera we were to see was an English tenor by the name of A. Tucker.

Much has been written about the building of the pyramids and rightly so but I have yet to see a word on how the many arenas were built. They are not so huge but they appear much more complex in their design as I was to find as I made my way to the centre ground. All but fourteen of the entrances had been cordoned off for the occasion and we made our way through one of these. A short passageway built wide enough to take comfortably a chariot led to a circular interior road that ran entirely round the whole structure. This road was a little wider although I doubt whether it could take two chariots - in any case the Romans were into one-way road systems. Electric lighting had been installed where originally it would have been lit by oil lamps and rush flambeaux. A few little shops had been introduced to sell souvenirs which I thought was a shame as it detracted from the atmosphere of antiquity. Crossing the circular road we came into a continuation of the primary passageway which was a little smaller in dimension and which led into the centre of the arena. Branching off this passageway were other minor passageways with steps leading to exits at various heights around the steps of the arena. I was amazed at the complexity of the architecture. As we progressed along the passageway which exited at ground level, much the same as the tunnels do in today's football stadia, we passed a number of rooms, some of them with apertures or windows all of which were fitted with very substantial iron bars. Were these the rooms where our early Christian martyrs were herded together to say their last tearful prayers before being thrust into the arena with the lions for the amusement of the local populace? I would have liked more time in this environment and the services of a knowledgeable guide but we had come to see another kind of entertainment and it was soon due to start, so I pressed on.

Fred (I feel confident in saying it was Fred although sadly he is no longer with us to confirm it) had chosen our seats well. We were near the front (I think it was the third row of seats) centre stage and sitting on 'director' style canvas chairs. When I saw the distance we were from the orchestra pit (about half a football pitch) I wondered what the sound would be like but I had no need to worry because the acoustics were (at least where we were) superb. The stage stretched right across the arena and had that gentle slope towards us that permitted us at ground level to appreciate the choreography. It had a considerable depth and was surmounted with scenery of gigantic proportions, some of it being higher than a typical modern semi. Initially it was difficult to see these details as a battery of spot lights was aimed at the audience which occupied not just half of the arena floor but up the terraces to the highest level. The object of this was that as it grew dark and the time arrived for the opera to commence so the entrance of the cast could not be seen. Dozens of attendants scampered up and down the terraces hiring out cushions. (I think a high percentage of arena -going enthusiasts must have suffered from piles in those far off Roman days). Other attendants were armed with cardboard boxes full of little candles which were to be lit during the intervals between acts and these were given to every man, woman and child.

As the last rays of sunshine disappeared the orchestra struck up the overture and all the chattering ceased immediately. Verdi's music is always entertaining but on this night, with no breeze to waft it away and no electronic devices to distort it, and with one hundred and forty instrumentalists playing as if their lives depended on it, it was magical. With the final notes of the overture dying away two hefty men, one at each end of the wooden structure that held the battery of lights, took hold of a contraption that looked like a ship's wheel and turned it, which, through a system of gears, rotated the lights that had been facing us to their new position now facing the cast already assembled on the stage. After a few seconds pause the orchestra swung into life and the opera had begun. The first act took place in front of that magnificent scenery, the actors being dwarfed by its size.

Whether the perfect acoustics were consciously woven into the design of the saucer shaped arena by the Roman architects or whether it just happened I do not know, but the voices came over as clear as a bell without the aid of microphones and amplifiers.

At the close of Act One the spot lights were swung back to face the audience and the scene shifters got to work preparing the stage for the next Act. Candles were lit at the end of the rows of seats and the flames passed on from candle to candle until the thousands of tiny lights gave a soft glow over the occupied half of the arena

Was that noise the sound of the percussion section playing their part in the Anvil Chorus from *Il Travatore*? No, it was the stage carpenters demolishing the hall of the Governor of Boston's house in preparation to erect a number of trees ready for Act Two which takes place in a field. I never for a moment thought that such a transformation could take place between acts and, thinking about it since, I marvel at the organisation that must have taken place considering that there were three different operas each requiring three (in one case four) changes of scenery that week.

Act Two came to an end and the procedure with the spot lights and candles went on as before whilst the stage carpenters uprooted the trees to replace them with a room in the residence of Renato - not quite so grand as the hall at the Governor's mansion.

We had been advised that it was the custom for Italian audiences to shout '*Bis*' if they particularly liked the rendering of an aria or duet etc. and we were not to be confused because when a few thousand people all cry '*Bis*' together it can sound like hissing and we must not misconstrue the meaning to be that the piece was badly performed. When the tenor (A. Tucker) sang the aria '*Eri tu che macchiani*' he was applauded and bombarded with these cries of '*Bis*'. When the applause died down after his acknowledgement to the audience and the orchestra conductor, he proceeded to give us another rendering of it. This brought about an even greater amount of applause and the opera was not allowed to continue until he had acceded to sing it once more. I was just about to write 'Poor fellow' when I thought: oh, no. How his adrenaline must have been flowing; he, an Englishman, being extolled to this degree by an Italian audience.

What I have failed to mention is the chorus which numbered two hundred. They were so trained both in their singing and dancing that their movements on the stage seemed quite natural and it felt as if you were one of the guests at the ball. I was so thrilled with it all that I just do not remember a thing about our return journey to 02E.

Why do some of today's so called song writers have to change their names to something 'ear-catching'? Giuseppe Verdi, born to a little village's shopkeeper was quite content with his name of 'Joe Green'.

Things must have been fairly desperate because I was picked to play in our office football team and I was more of a snooker man. Joe Dixon, I seem to remember, was captain because it was he who gave me the dressing room instructions. I have two memories of that game; the first being that from my half back position I managed to lob the ball over into the enemy's goal mouth giving our centre forward the opportunity to score and the second is of overreaching to prevent a ball from going out of play and pulling a muscle in my thigh as a result. This had disastrous consequences as I found a couple of days later that it was too painful to climb into the back of our three tonner which was scheduled to take all those interested to an opera in Venice. Really I should have taken advantage of the services offered at the medicinal baths at the rear of our building where the sulphuric mud packs had been found to be very beneficial by our rugby players. Incidentally, baths could be taken at this establishment by booking one or two days in advance and I found that these soakings were indeed a pleasure. The bathroom was vast, being about twenty feet square, and the bath itself, made of marble, was sunk into a tiled floor. There were no taps, the water being controlled both in temperature and quantity by an attendant outside in the corridor with the water coming up through an orifice in the base of the bath. The proportions of the bath were generous and the bather could bathe seated Roman style or stretch right out, with the three or four steps so situated that they didn't interfere with either position. Having completed one's ablutions a signal to the attendant caused him to turn one of his valves and the water disappeared down the hole through which it had arrived initially. What a contrast to the primitive contraption we had enjoyed at Duino!

With September came the news that the first batch of Germans were to be repatriated and I thought, 'Well, it can't be long now before I too will be making a homeward journey'. How the decision was reached as to which prisoners should go first I have no idea. There were so many ways of looking at it. Did they have age and service groups as we had? Did the date of their capture play a part in it? Did their one and only officer dictate? Did they draw lots? Did their usefulness at 02E have any bearing? Who knows? A mild excitement pervaded the German quarters. Some of them, especially the few younger ones, spoke excitedly of getting back home to their families. Some, knowing that they would be going back to depleted families, were going with mixed feelings. Some, having elected to go back to the Russian zone because their families were there (and Gottfried was one of them) knew they would be leaving a life that was easy and giving them three good meals a day to a life of penury. One of them, Karl Kiebel, had elected to take his freedom in the American zone as he had lost all his family except a sister whose whereabouts he did not know. He said that he hoped to get a job working for the American Army of occupation as he had a good command of the English language. I went down from the office to see this party leave and to say my farewells to Gottfried whose company I had enjoyed on a number of occasions and to Karl who had traded with me cigarette-wise for some time. I gave my home address to them both and suggested that they wrote to me in a few months time. (which they both did).

On the Presbytery steps at Paese

In the Vendramin's garden saying goodbye to Bice and Enrico

Chapter Seven
The Discharge

Shortly after the first batch of prisoners had been dispatched to their elected zones we had notification of the dates on which certain 'Age and Service' groups were to be demobilised. We, being GHQ, automatically got these dates first and sent the news on to all the many units still in the country. We set about drawing our individual demob calendars on pieces of card to figure prominently on our desks so that we could strike out each day as we completed it. Mine was one of the smallest calendars because I had not been conscripted until I was twenty-one and had served a longer period than most of my pals, whilst most of them were two or three years my junior. One poor chap said, with wry smile, that he couldn't find a piece of card big enough for his calendar as he had, on being conscripted, been coerced into signing on for seven years.

Our chief clerk, Garth-Atkins, took me aside a day or two after our demob dates were announced and told me that the whole theatre was soon to be evacuated with the exception of a small contingent that would be left in the Trieste area to keep the peace between the Italians and the Yugoslavs who were still bitterly arguing their case for ownership. It would be necessary to set up an HQ there and he thought that I might be the man to run Officers Records department. I could 'G.A' for three or six months and I would have immediate promotion to sergeant with the strong possibility of becoming a Warrant Officer shortly afterwards. (G.A. stands for Gentleman's Agreement - whereby one's service could be extended beyond demob date by incremental periods of three months). The briefest mental glimpse of thousands of extra lira to be gained from a sergeant's pay and even more from a W.O's was soon overshadowed by my memory of my last visit to Trieste when hand grenades were being tossed around and, more importantly, I thought of that lovely girl in Chester who was eagerly awaiting my return, just as I was longing to hold her in my arms again. I thanked him for the offer and declined.

Life went on as much as usual apart from crossing off the square daily. An irrigation ditch ran along the left hand side of the 'Out' drive and this was the domain of dozens, if not, hundreds of bullfrogs that croaked loudly and continually; but far more interesting was the scene that lay on the right hand side which, as I have said before, was virtually a copse that was planted between the drives. Here we could see the antics of the fireflies. As they flew along between the trees their tiny furry little back ends would light up intermittently like an aircraft's navigation lights. They must have very poor night sight because frequently one would fly into a tree and his rear light could be seen dropping to the ground and, after a few seconds recovery, would gain his previous height and set off again in the same direction. One night coming back from the village we decided that we would have a closer look at one of these insects so we caught one after it had collided with a tree and put it in a match box to carry it to the billet. Someone's cruel streak must have been in the ascendancy because he tied a strand of cotton to one of its tiny legs and the other end to the bottom rail of his bed. The fly sat a little while to compose itself then flew slowly upwards struggling with the weight of the cotton until it had reached the full extent of its tether. It struggled for a few seconds trying to lift the bed off the floor and then fell exhausted on to the bed rail. After repeating this exercise a few times we agreed that it was a plucky little thing and deserved its freedom so, releasing it from its harness, we took it to the window and set it free.

A fine Sunday afternoon and nothing much to do, so, Peter Mortimer, Wilf Sutton and I set out on a country walk. We had covered a fair distance in both directions along the main road by bicycle in the past so we decided to take the lane that led into the countryside. There was nothing very exciting to see other than a dog chasing a hare up the hillside. The dog didn't stand an earthly chance of catching it, in fact, the hare stopped from time to time to watch the dog's progress! The hill which was not very big or very steep tempted us and we climbed it to get a vantage view of the country that lay around us which was largely flat. We came across a wall about seven feet high built from the local stone rather like our dry stone walls except that it had a coping of concrete about a foot deep. It seemed strange that such a formidable wall was built miles from anywhere and we could only assume that it was the boundary mark to one of the local feudal baron's land. Through this wall was the evidence of war - a gaping hole about five feet in diameter. Pete photographed Wilf and me standing in this hole pretending to hold the upper part intact. We walked on not gaining any more height and saw a collection of cottages which could, I suppose, be called a hamlet although on closer examination we found there were only five or six built in a terrace style. There was no bar, church, shop or any other kind of building around. Descending the hill towards the houses we saw the womenfolk chatting together in the road. (There was no footpath and no traffic). When we approached they stopped talking and from the way they eyed us up and down it was obvious that strangers were a rarity in this place. They responded to our 'Buon Giorno' rather frigidly and seemed to be somewhat apprehensive. One of them was holding a tiny baby of only days or weeks old and I asked her permission to take a photograph of them. This move had the effect of easing the atmosphere and the other women fell to chatting again as I took a snapshot. We turned towards the setting sun and made our way 'homewards'.

When, a few days later, I collected my last batch of prints from the little photographic shop in the village I found myself well pleased with the one I had taken of the mother and baby on the previous Sunday and suggested that we went along to the hamlet and give it to the mother. Wilf decided to come with me and we set off one evening armed with a bag of fruit and nuts as we felt we couldn't arrive with just a photograph. We walked by road, such as it was, and not over the hill and by the time we arrived it was quite dark. Going to the cottage that I thought the woman lived in I, being more conversant with the language than Wilf, knocked on the door. An adult male voice called out '*Avanti*' ('Come in'). Thinking that the occupants presumed a neighbour was knocking and that it would be an effrontery to just walk in, I knocked again. The same voice called out '*Chi a lei*' ('Who are you?') I called out in reply '*Sono soldati*' ('We are soldiers'). There were sounds of commotion within the house and the light that had been creeping through the chinks in the poor old shutters disappeared. Half a face of a teenage girl peered round the edge of the door and the question was asked 'What do you want?' 'Does your mother have a new baby?' I asked. Fearfully she said, 'Yes, Why?' 'Well, I took a photograph of her and the baby and I've brought it along for her' I said. '*Momento*' she said and shut the door and I heard the heavy catch drop into place. A minute or so later when the chinks in the shutters were again showing streaks of light the door was opened and the girl invited us in. The passage was lit only by the light that came from the one and only room that lay to the left and the door to which was open. Going along the little passage, the girl, about thirteen or fourteen years of age, invited us into their living room and, indicating the lady of the house said '*Ecco Mamma*'. ('Here's Mum'). Taking the photo from my pocket I gave it to her and she expressed her delight. In all probability it was the only photograph they ever had as their abject poverty could be seen at a glance. The floor was the very antithesis of that which we enjoyed a few miles away along the road - where we had marble - they had mother earth. The walls had been whitened many years ago and were adorned only with a few pans near to the fire. The hearth was built of house bricks in a rectangular shape about two feet high and there was no chimney, the smoke going through an aperture in the ceiling. I can only presume that it was ducted by some means through the bedroom and out beyond the roof. Access to the room upstairs was by an almost vertical ladder. The furnishings consisted of a rough wooden table, three or four chairs and a cupboard which housed, I guess, their china and cutlery. Light was from an oil lamp suspended from the ceiling whilst the fire was a few thin branches from trees (which would be superseded no doubt by logs in the winter months).

Mysteriously there appeared a man in the doorway. I say mysteriously because I hadn't heard the door opening or his approach. He was obviously the man of the house and was dressed, as were the mother and daughter, in coarse drab clothes. He greeted us civilly and showed an interest in the photograph and then went on to explain why there had been some confusion about inviting us in. 'When you said that you were soldiers I thought maybe you were Germans. You see I was one of the local partisans who harassed them. A party of us had a fight one night and I was knifed and left for dead, but I survived and lived in a cave on the mountainside over there'. He indicated by pointing in the direction of his lair. He pulled up his shirt and dropped his trousers as far as decency would permit in the presence of his teenage daughter to show us a terrible scar across his abdomen - an untidy scar because the skin had never been stitched. 'My little girl used to sneak up to the cave to bring me food and drink until I was fit enough to creep back to the house one night' he said, 'And when you said you were soldiers I thought that my old enemies had caught up with me. So when my daughter opened the door to let you in I was behind the door with this'. Here he produced a rough piece of timber from the passage. It was about three inches in diameter and a yard long and could have caused some trouble had our uniforms been grey instead of khaki. Wilf and I laughed with him about our lucky escape.

We were invited to join him in a glass of wine, but I explained that I didn't drink alcoholic drinks. 'Well, what about a coffee?' he asked, to which we acceded willingly asking if we could have milk in it. He murmured something quickly to his daughter who left the house to come back some minutes later with milk in a little bowl, probably begged or borrowed from a neighbour. His wife in the meantime had stirred up the few sticks in the hearth and put on a pan of water with which to make the coffee. When he suggested that we should all tuck into the fruit we had brought we said that we had brought it for them but on his insistence we did, to save appearing churlish, indulge in a few walnuts. Italian walnuts have a shell that is not quite as hard and brittle as the ones we get in this country and we found that by placing them on the edge of the table and standing up to grip them by clenching the fingers under the table with the palm on top of the nut it was not difficult to crack them. When I had cracked a couple and eaten the kernels I rose from my chair and using my left hand as a crumb tray swept the broken bits of shell with my right hand on to it. I then walked round the table and threw the shells on to the fire. 'Don't bother doing that' we were told, 'Throw them on the floor - the wife will sweep them up'. The term 'Chauvinist pig' had not been concocted in those days, but the attitude was prevalent. I thought, 'Poor woman, - her life must be a tough one living in these conditions - why add work unnecessarily?'.

I sometimes wonder what happened to that pretty teenage daughter. Did some 'Prince Charming' come along and bless her with all those wondrous things like a tiled floor, a radio, electric light, running water? She's in her sixties as I write this and if she is still with us does she wonder what happened to the soldiers that took the photograph of her little baby brother in her mother's arms one autumn afternoon soon after the war had finished?.

With the winding down of the theatre and many officers getting demobbed I found my binders containing the documents listing the history of the officers getting thinner which meant that business was not quite so pressing and life was made even easier by the fact that the War Office had put out a memo to the effect that replies to their queries would be accepted written in pencil instead of being typed. (I had passed the necessary speed test in typing but the written word was still quicker in my case). This easing up permitted me a little time to browse through the files that we kept on each officer and some of these made interesting reading. The facts that were recorded in some of the Courts Martial were the absorbing ones. One in particular that I remember was an instance of bare - faced fraud. A certain hotel in the South of the country had been commandeered for use as quarters for some of the troops. As the Army had advanced slowly Northwards so such sequestered property was handed back to the rightful owners with some compensation for their loss of trade and profit etc.. This particular officer whose Court Martial I was reading had, instead of handing back the hotel, sold off the cutlery and linen separately and then sold the hotel and furnishings. He ended up getting cashiered, losing all pension rights and a two years sentence to complete in the U.K.

Three or four of us coming back to the billet one night opened the door to a strange sight. Sitting cross-legged, tailor like, on the top of one of the wardrobes was one of our colleagues. He was a strange chap who had little to do with anyone else - a veritable loner, was tall and skinny and wore thick lensed glasses. Definitely not forces material, but like so many others he had had to conform and take the king's shilling. As I said he was sitting there and until we entered he was sitting in the dark except that he was striking matches one after the another and dropping them, still alight, onto the marble floor beneath. How long he had been doing this I have no idea but there was more than a couple of boxes of England's Glory remains on the floor. That he was a pyromaniac of the first order there was no doubt because he never even acknowledged our entrance but sat entranced by the little flames, his face having an expression like a child seeing a Christmas tree for the first time. We coaxed him down and got him to bed and put his debris in the waste bin. Next morning no-one referred to his antics and we went about our duties as normal. Looking back I realise that one of us should have reported the incident because a few days later there was a sequel to the story. In a small room a little way along the corridor where I had been instructed to put a notice on the door in bold letters '*Vietato Entrare*' ('You are forbidden to enter'). It was here that we stacked the documents of the officers who had left the theatre, ready for despatch to the War Office. The reason for excluding the Italian personnel from this room was because the documents had been sorted into Regiments and Corps etc. and we didn't want the cleaners to 'tidy them up' for us. There is no prize for guessing who set fire to the pile of documents. Within a couple of days he had been posted .

Answering a call to the surgery I was invited to have a smallpox inoculation and I said to the M.O. that I would not accept his invitation. He was surprised as my records showed that I had received all previous inoculations and injections. I explained that when I entered the Army I had received a smallpox jab at that time and I was told that it would give me five years immunity. (Actually the scar was so tiny that it could hardly be seen, showing that my childhood inoculation was still giving me immunity). I asked whether the War Office had discovered that the vaccine dispensed in 1944 was not up to scratch (no pun intended), or what other reason had they for saying that a further inoculation was necessary. I was warned that having refused treatment, if I fell ill, the Army was justified in denying me further treatment and, what is more, he added , by way of subtle(?) persuasion, 'There's an outbreak of smallpox in Padua'. I said, 'I'm going home in three weeks time. I'll avoid going to Padua before then'. My pay-book was duly marked up in red ink to show that I was a naughty boy!

A travelling fair came to the village and was set up on some common land not far from my favourite bar. It was a poor affair with no rides apart from a little round -about for the kiddies that was powered by a man. There were no 'Roll your penny' stalls because all the currency was paper money. The lighting was third rate, the electricity being provided by a generator driven by a diesel engine. There were coconut shies and a rifle range and a number of side shows. I thought that I would see what entertainment they could offer in one of these shows. On the hoardings outside it proclaimed that for a few lira (I forget how many) you could see the most marvellous of spiders. It had a body that resembled a human head and it carried electric power just like an electric ray (the fish) and this would be proven to all who came to see it. The tent containing this 'insect' was about ten feet wide by fifteen feet long, about five feet of this being occupied by a board the full width of the tent raised to about three foot off the ground and sloping at some ten or twelve degrees upward to meet the rear wall of the tent. On this board was stretched a conventional spider's web made of thin rope (about the same thickness as a washing line) and on this web sat this most marvellous of spiders. It is no wonder that its body was described on the hoarding outside as resembling a human head because that is just what it was. The head was wearing a kind of wig that started out as a fur collar and ended in furry legs that were positioned on the strands of the web. The face was heavily made up with brown greasepaint except for the nose which was red at the tip. It had an intelligence too because, on command, it would close its eyes - a feat that brought lots of 'Ahs' and 'Oohs' from the audience; however, what brought the crowd to life was when the proprietor came to the front of the crowd with a pole some four foot in length with a red electric light bulb on the end and announced that this was the moment they had been waiting to see. Elevating the end with the bulb so that all could see it, he pressed the other end against the spider's nose and the bulb lit up!

Apart from a few modern contrivances such as electricity, photography, a metalled main road with an infrequent 'bus service and radios, this was, as I have said, a mediaeval setting with drays drawn by oxen, a whipping post in the grounds of one of the employers, a primitive sewerage system all of which had been further impoverished by years of war, but, despite all this, I found it difficult to believe that a large percentage of the audience in that tent were expressing their amazement at what they had just witnessed. That they could have been taken in by what could have been presented by a couple of junior schoolboys was beyond my comprehension.

About a week before I was to depart for demob in the U.K. I gave my news to Elisa, the owner of my favourite bar. She decided to make it publicly known, and, demanding '*Attenzione*' she told the customers assembled there that 'The Corporal was going back to England next week to become a civilian once again'. Many of them came over to me to shake me by the hand and wish me well. What I remember most easily about that evening was when 'Seppe, who I knew from past acquaintance to be the village postman, came to say his farewell. 'Seppe was the type who got emotional when he had had a few and he had certainly indulged before I had arrived. He came to me and gave me the embrace of a long lost brother and with tears freely flowing down his face wished me so many good things, some of which I couldn't decipher on account of his voice being so broken with emotion. Amongst the things he wished for me were a good job as a civilian, a happy life with my wife to be and a good demob suit. Dear old 'Seppe.

On the 27th. October 1947 I received my Release Book complete with glowing testimonial (of which I am proud) together with all the necessary paperwork to get me to a demob centre in the U.K. I said my farewells to my colleagues with whom I had spent just a few days in excess of a year and whose company I had enjoyed. I exchanged home addresses with a few knowing that they, in the main, would be following in my footsteps in the course of the next few months.

Next morning I was on my way to Padua by truck and then on to Villach by train. There was no one else in the same Age and Service Group as myself from Officers Records department so I was virtually travelling alone; the only other one I recognised was the fellow who I have described before as coming from a well-to-do background. I steered clear of him because every time we had to get aboard a train, truck or ship he was shouting for assistance with all his luggage. He had three bulging suitcases apart from his kitbag plus a saddle and a pair of skis. Why I took such an interest I cannot explain but I counted fourteen pairs of shoes dangling from his suitcases.

At Villach we found that we would be staying overnight and departing for the U.K. in the morning. I got my customary two blankets after dinner and went to my allotted hut. My hut was not what it used to be. The roof was intact but the walls were almost non-existent and even as I approached I could see squaddies tearing off planks of tongue and groove cladding breaking them up to feed the cast-iron stoves. All of the men that I spoke to that evening were going back to England for demob and the general excitement was such that sleep was out of the question so we sat around that stove with blankets draped around our shoulders sharing our experiences with emphasis on the funny ones.

There was little point in writing to Josie at this juncture as even if I posted it immediately any letter could not reach her before I had the opportunity to contact her by phone on reaching England, but I was happy that I had managed to maintain my daily missive with the exception of when I had had my three weeks leave nine months before. She had written frequently, though not as often as I had, the main reason being that she did not have the variety of incidents to write about as I had encountered in the fifteen months in Italy. I had kept all her letters and they constituted quite a volume and weight in my kitbag.

Next morning we washed, shaved and breakfasted before getting aboard the train for the next stage of our journey, collecting our haversack rations as we left. We had, of course, changed our currency at the border, not that it was to be of any use to us because we had no time at all to call anywhere in Austria to spend it. All we wanted was full steam ahead for that troopship.

Our next stop was at Salzburg where our currency was changed again into German marks. This again seemed to be a formality as we had no intention of spending any time in Germany other than travelling time. However, I was wrong. There were opportunities to spend money (and cigarettes) on route because we stopped at a station which could have been Stuttgart, Mannheim or Frankfurt,- I do not know which as no name was displayed on the platforms, and here there were dozens of men in the long grey greatcoats of the German Army selling all sorts of things from the multitude of pockets they had sewn to the inside lining. The engine was uncoupled and went off to get replenished with water and it was obvious that this was a routine event because all these vendors were here waiting when the train arrived. They had cigarette lighters, wrist watches, pocket watches, black forest carved animals and a variety of bric-a-brac and the squaddies were hanging out of the coach windows doing a brisk trade. It seemed that for some reason this trading was illegal because, as two policemen walked leisurely along the platform, the salesmen moved away from the coaches and quickly fell to bargaining again when the police were a few yards away. No one, to my knowledge, was arrested or even cautioned - it was a case of live and let live. What was selling best was a cheap little cigarette lighter, going for twenty fags. It had a hinged lid and a flame guard and was made of tin plate with a gold coloured trigger mechanism. The cardboard box it came in was of poor quality and not printed with any words or devices, but had a little cut-out revealing the corrugated gold coloured trigger. One of the fellows in our compartment, having been given a demonstration of how 'they light every time' decided he would have two -one for himself and one for 'our kid'. Shortly after resuming our journey he decided to try out his purchases and was thoroughly miffed to find that the second lighter was nothing more than a piece of wood carved with a few grooves along one edge with a bit of gold foil (probably from a cigarette packet from some previous exchange) pressed hard into these grooves simulating the trigger. He was all for starting the war with such rogues all over again.

    For my part I was tempted to buy some of the lovely wooden carvings but wondered how they would survive the journey knowing how kitbags are tossed into trucks, so I decided I could spare twenty cigarettes for a pocket watch. As an investment it turned out to be little better than the lighter. It had a healthy tick - in fact, it sounded more like the old fashioned tin-plate alarm clock. Sometime about half way through my demob leave it stopped working so I opened up the back to find the roughest set of gears I have ever seen. It seemed nothing short of a miracle that it had worked at all. The gears were of poor quality steel with huge burrs on the teeth showing that the press tools making them had long ago passed their valid production run. The watch was consigned to the bin.

As you will have gathered from some of my previous words I am not averse to a little musical entertainment and it was my fortune, and that of my travelling companions, that we had a couple of Scots aboard the train who saw to it that we would not be neglected in that direction. They paraded up and down the train with their instruments tirelessly giving it all that they could. I am not qualified to assert whether music has been composed for a duet by harmonica and bass drum, but that is what we were privileged to listen to for most of that journey. Whilst the tempo of the drum beat couldn't be faulted, the volume was not at all consistent since the only time a full blow of the drum stick could be delivered was when the beat coincided with it being delivered by an open compartment door, other blows being restricted by virtue of the narrowness of the corridor. The exponent of the mouth organ was evidently a military man because all his renderings were marches and those he knew well, going from the last bar of one to the first bar of the next without pause. Under normal circumstances I think that these musicians would have been prevailed to 'put a sock in it' after a while, but such was the good humour of the lads, all going home at last, that they condoned the over-enthusiasm. I personally was grateful that it wasn't a trio incorporating a bagpiper.

I had realised that we were not travelling along the conventional route of 'Medloc C' and wondered where we would be getting aboard a ship and where we would be docking, but before that we were due (I hoped) another meal, so would we be calling at a transit camp and would it be another overnight stay on the continent? Having secured a corner seat in the compartment I managed to tuck my head into the corner and partook of a little sleep interrupted from time to time by the aforementioned military band and some hours later we pulled into a station. The platforms and tracks were in good repair but there was no roof and all the necessary offices and related buildings were of a temporary nature. (This was unlike the border stop that we had made on the Medloc 'C' route where the roof-supporting stanchions and superstructure had been transformed into steel Gordian knots at the Strasbourg station) This place was Cologne, easily recognised by the twin spires of the Cathedral, which was quite near.

We were instructed over the Tannoy system to parade outside our compartments with knife, fork, spoon and pot and to follow the guides to a place where a meal had been arranged and to be back on board the train in two hours time. A nice hot meal was dished up in what I imagine was a typical German beer garden and musical entertainment was provided by a typical German Oompah band, playing popular music of the day. Following the meal one or two of us decided that in the hour left we would stretch our legs and do a little walkabout. We walked along a road which ran parallel to the railway track at about three hundred yards distance. On either side of the road were heaps of rubble, the remains of houses that had suffered bombing worse than any I had seen in England. The pavements were covered by the bricks and masonry that had been bulldozed to give access to any road vehicles, of which there seemed very few. At intervals paths had been made through the rubble and we were intrigued to see people going along them and quite suddenly disappearing from sight, or, just as suddenly appearing from nowhere and then walking along the path to the road. Our observations brought us to the conclusion that these people were living in the cellars of what had been very desirable residences (as Estate Agents put it), and this was a year and a half after the war had ended. Deciding that it was not prudent to continue walking here - the people could hardly be expected to wish us well - we turned about and made our way back to the station as there would not be enough time left to visit the Cathedral which had miraculously survived the bombing almost unscathed.

We were all impatient to get back to the U.K. and the wait aboard the train following the two hour ultimatum seemed endless giving rise to many choruses of 'Why are we waiting?' This from about six hundred (untrained) voices must have been heard all around the old city. When eventually the train did set off it was to six hundred cheers even louder than the choruses and on we went to Rotterdam and the Hook of Holland without any further stops.

I wasn't looking forward to the next stage of our journey because I am a poor sailor. I've never been seasick, but I've been very near to it and have felt, to put it mildly, most unwell. Lord Nelson, I have read, was sick every time he went to sea. All I can say is that, if he felt like I did, I couldn't understand him going to sea a second time and that would have altered the whole course of history.

At Rotterdam we changed our currency for the last time, swapping our German marks for good old L.S.D, as we had not changed into guilders at the Dutch border. Then we boarded the troopship with the knowledge that we were bound for Harwich, and by now it was dark. Long after the last of the troops were aboard the ship stayed quietly in port. I, and I guess many others, wondered about the delay - we were just longing to get going. Were we waiting for a favourable tide (I don't know about such matters)? Were we waiting so that the tide would be favourable for docking at Harwich? Was the pilot drunk and had they had to send for a stand-in? (I know the water is very shallow around this area and I didn't want to get beached.) Had the captain had a bad hand of cards playing poker at his favourite bar and was he staying on to recoup his losses? I cannot list all the possible reasons for this delay that ran through my mind. I even wondered if the dog had fallen overboard, which meant that a dogwatch couldn't be raised!

At last - at long last - we cast off. (I am tempted to say that we 'weighed anchor' except that I feel confident enough to bet that the anchor hadn't been weighed since it left the foundry. I could also venture the thought that we 'set sail' except that I am given to believe that the only canvas kept aboard these days is a remnant or two in case there has to be a burial at sea.

These naval terms are so confusing - I'm glad I was called up for the Army. We were on our way and it promised to be a sleepless night again with all the excitement. The sea was very calm, so unlike that first trip of mine from Dover when the ship seemed alternately on top of a wave crest or in a trough so deep I wondered whether it would ever make it. After a wash and shave (and a visit to the 'heads' - another naval term I find hard to get my brain to accept) I went up on deck and found dawn just breaking. I could hardly believe my good fortune. The sea was absolutely flat - not even a ripple. It was as smooth as the boating pool in Mary Steven's Park at Stourbridge where I had learned to row, and I wasn't feeling the slightest bit queasy. In fact I went to join the queue for breakfast, which consisted of a couple of hefty slices of bread with a filling of bacon or pork sausages. The breakfast was being prepared by two or three matelots on what was, to my eyes, a field kitchen set up on the foredeck. These jolly tars were on a good number because they were trying to dissuade us from having breakfast by relating all sorts of things to make us feel a little sickly which could have worked with me had the sea been the slightest bit choppy. It was their obvious intent to save as many sausages as possible to take ashore to their families and friends, but that day the weather was not in their favour because of the lack of wind and waves.

We seemed to be making headway at a very leisurely pace - there was no danger of rivets popping out from the vibrations caused by over-exertion of the engine - and I was standing at the rail forward looking to see if I could spot any land when a sight came into view that had I been walking would have stopped me in my tracks. Ahead and slightly to starboard was the biggest ship I had ever seen. Even with my limited knowledge of naval matters I recognised this as a battleship and as we neared it I could see another one a little way ahead with yet another creeping into sight. In all there were four in line astern lying at anchor. I was amazed at the sheer size of them. It seemed impossible that so many thousands of tons of steel riveted together could float and not just float but carry, I don't know how many crew with all their necessities, plus guns larger than any in the Army. They were the dinosaurs of weaponry. There was no sign of life on board - no smoke issuing from the huge funnels - it seemed as thought they were at rest following their years of frantic and dangerous activity. I suppose there were skeleton crews aboard to keep things ticking over, if only to keep the men on their toes. Among the duties I imagined a number of bilge pumps would be operating (perhaps even day and night) because I couldn't see all those riveted joints being watertight especially after being in action and suffering damage from shells or bombs, or, for that matter, near misses. Generators too would have to be running to maintain electricity supplies to the thousands of light bulbs (since there is no daylight below decks), to the telephones, to the ovens (if they cooked with electricity), to the refrigerators and I'm sure many other things of which I am ignorant. The more I thought about it the more I realised that a skeleton crew on board this floating fortress must number at least a couple of infantry companies.

One thing about these ships attracted my attention more than any other aspect. Those massive anchor chains. I am reasonably sure that they were made within a couple of miles of my home. No way could it be reckoned that I am an expert on handmade chains but I do know quite a bit because my earliest memories are of sitting on an upturned apple box (yes, apples came from the Southern counties in wooden boxes in those days) at the side of my Dad's furnace watching him making a living by converting rods of iron into links of chain. My Dad worked on the premises with his two brothers, all three making the same size chain, my Dad being the only one of the three qualified to make chains to Admiralty specification. Each of the links he made had to be gauged for girth and length and each yard in length had to fit a steel profiled gauge. He was proud of his test piece - a length of chain that had been given the ultimate test at Lloyd's and had failed to break even when the links had bitten into each other rendering the chain as rigid as a walking stick.

Next door to us was the firm of Woodhouse Bros. which employed about two dozen chain makers making chains in various sizes from three eighths (chain sizes are designated by the diameter of the iron from which they are made) up to one and a half inch. Some of the largest chains had a stud in each link which made it an anchor chain and would be used for the smaller vessels. However when it came to making chains for the huge ships like the ones I was looking at now a different technique was used in manufacture. No one man could forge an iron link of these proportions and it was usual for the chain-maker to employ three strikers. The chain-maker was paid (37/6d a link. I remember printing the price on a price list when I was an apprentice in the printing trade) and he paid his strikers what he thought they were worth. The object of having three strikers was that on drawing the iron from the furnace as many blows as possible could be rained on the white-hot metal to forge it into the required shape before it needed reheating for the next onslaught of blows. Real precision was called for from these strikers not just in placing the fourteen pound hammer in the right spot from an overhead swing but in timing the swing so that it didn't interfere with the swing and blow of either of the other strikers, in the meantime the chain-maker manoeuvred the link into the right attitude to receive the blows. In order that they should not be working during the heat of the day it was common for those teams to start their work at about half past four or five in the morning and to consider it a days work when two links were 'shut', so in order to see these men at work it was necessary to go to the side of the 'cut' (canal) before lunch. This was the only place (Noah Hingley's of Netherton) where it was possible to watch the whole process of the forging of these massive chains without entering the premises of such firms as Ernest Woodhouse and Sons who were in the adjoining street to my home.

    At the lower end of the chain which had caught my attention was, of course, the anchor and this was another component which, as a boy, I had watched being forged. An anchor for a capital ship is a huge size and a complex shape so it took days to manufacture. I cannot claim that I have seen an anchor made but from what bits I did see I feel that I was privileged to witness the skills of those men who appeared so ordinary when you met them in the street. What weight these anchors were I have no idea but I remember as a youth watching one finished article being lowered by a manually operated crane into a narrowboat on the canal. As the anchor was lowered into the centre of the barge we watched as the vessel sank lower in the water, the slings only going slack when the barge was within two inches of sinking. The bargee in charge of that load must have had a few sleepless nights getting to his destination which had to be on the coast at least a hundred miles away. I don't suppose his horse worried one jot!

Chain-making was an essential part of my life as a boy. My best friend, George Walker, is the son of a man who worked in the rolling mills of Noah Hingley where they converted iron ore into rods of iron of many various sizes and sections. In my first week at school I so impressed the teacher with my plasticine chain that she brought it to the attention of Miss Shearer (all lady teachers were 'Miss' in those days), the Head Mistress, who presented me with two boiled sweets as a reward and an incentive to 'do my best' always. The local ironmonger, Harry Case, kept a range of hammers from the smallest used by women chain-makers to the sledgehammers used by the strikers, and, of course, stales to fit them all. In the market there was a stall that dealt in woven flannel material from which chain-makers wives would make those peculiar floppy vests. Another stall dealt in a kind of light canvas from which the same wives would fashion aprons which prevented sparks doing too much damage to vests and trousers. However, by far the best trade was done by the public houses who, with their own home brew, slaked the thirst of these men who spent so many hours by their furnaces. Chain-making ran in families - my grandfather, son of a chain-maker was one of four sons, George, Will, Charlie and Alf all of whom were in the trade, my grandfather George being the only one blessed with sons to carry on the business. The Woodhouses, who slightly outnumbered the Homers at Graingers Lane Methodist Church, were a family of 'bosses' and I doubt whether any one of them could weld a link although they employed more 'workers' than any other family. I remember one of the elders of our Church, Harold Harbache, who got a mention in the local press when he was awarded the contract for making the davit chains for the lifeboats of the Queen Mary. His daughter, Margaret, sang solos in the Church choir of which my sister Betty was a member. At the expense of a horrible pun - it was chains that linked us all together all those years ago.

As we passed the last of these four ocean-ranging monsters I couldn't help but wonder whether any or, indeed, all of them might have some of my Dad's work aboard. After all, he must have made miles of chain in those years between the wars and during the years of this last war and much of it to Admiralty specification.

Could someone of naval persuasion explain to me, a true landlubber, how those four huge vessels stayed in a line all facing in a due South direction? Why didn't they swing about their anchor chains, driven by the tides, currents and winds? It all looked too tidy to be true.

Soon after leaving the four huge ships behind we came into Harwich harbour. Only a few miles away was Colchester where three years before I had taken the King's shilling and signed on for the 'Duration of Hostilities' and watched the doodlebugs come put-put-putting across the night skies to destroy lives and property. Disembarking, we found ourselves shepherded into the Customs sheds. Unlike many, I had elected to declare anything that I had that was liable to 'duty' and was willing to pay the price rather than have it confiscated. On inspection of my worldly goods it appeared that the only things I was bringing into the country that were liable to duty was a 'cocktail' wrist watch (very popular at the time) for Josie, a pocket watch for my Dad and a cute little 'travelling' clock for my Mother. The Customs Officer was a considerate one who said that although the regulations only permitted two timepieces to be brought into the country (apart from one worn by the traveller) he would let me go uncharged as the clock was not an expensive one. I think that the tales and rumours of what happened at the Customs sheds had influenced a lot of the lads and they had indulged in all sorts of subterfuges to get their souvenirs and gifts through without being charged. I had seen toothpaste tubes squeezed dry to make way for wristwatches and forearms with as many as six watches strapped to them and on the other hand (excuse the pun) one fellow panicked long before we got to Harwich and threw a bag into the sea that contained seven German revolvers.

The three timepieces that I brought back had been purchased from an unassuming little shop in one of the offbeat alleys in Venice. The alley led to nowhere except to humble little dwellings - the opposite to the gorgeous palaces which lined the Grand Canal not many yards away. Had the shop been a grocers, newsagents, greengrocers or the like supplying every day needs I could have accepted it but for a watchmakers to be the only shop along there seemed quite odd. Passing trade would be the locals who lived around and the odd stranger like myself just idling around. Perhaps he did repairs taken in by the grand jewellers around St. Mark's Piazza to keep the wolf from the door. It was only when I looked at his selection of ladies and gents wristwatches that it dawned on me that this would be a nice kind of souvenir to take home, so I looked with greater interest. As you can imagine, the window lighting was not brilliant, in fact it was barely adequate, but I thought that I would go in and have a closer look at the goods and enquire about prices. Not surprisingly I found on entering that I was the only prospective customer and received a cautious greeting from the old gentleman who came through a door-way behind the counter a few seconds after my entry. He was of Jewish persuasion and about seventy years of age. I say that he was a Jew without any reservation because he had the right nose, the right hair, in fact he could well have been a direct descendant of Shylock, from

The Merchant of Venice. He could have played the part without the need of make-up. His demeanour, however, was not that of Shylock - he had a soft gentle voice and an attitude that almost implied perpetual apology. Maybe he had been treated with indifference over the years because for a number of years the Italians had been allies of the Germans and we all know how they hated the Jews. Perhaps his subservience was a direct result of this. Maybe worse than indifference - had he been attacked and robbed by someone like me in uniform either German grey or Allied khaki? Who knows? I hoped that he looked upon me as no threat and my behaviour, that of a genuine customer, seemed to give him confidence and he appeared to warm towards me. I soon made my choice of wrist watch for Josie and a little travelling clock that hinged and slid into a little metal case for Ma. There was a wider choice of pocket watches and I hesitated a little, but he didn't attempt to influence me at all or to hurry me. Knowing nothing about watches I made my choice on appearances only and hoped that it would please Dad. The little shopkeeper complimented me on my choice and said that it was a jewelled movement and he would show me the mechanism. Taking a small roll of green baize he put it in the centre of the counter and with his penknife removed the back of the watch which he placed face down so that the works were exposed. No wonder he had said that I had made a good choice for he proceeded to tell me that he had built it himself and that it had no less than seventeen rubies for bearings. 'I will point out the rubies to you' he said as he picked up a small wooden pointer. I told him that it was not necessary as I believed him but he insisted and started pointing to them as he said slowly and distinctly '*Uno rubino; due rubini; tre rubini*'. I leaned forward to get a proper look at the tiny jewels he was pointing to. As he got to about number five or six and he gently but firmly put his hands on my shoulders and pressed me back with the admonition 'Please. Not to breathe over the mechanism'. He then started all over again with his pointing and counting and proudly proclaiming again what a good choice

I had made. I felt that he was almost sorry to part with it. When it came to price I didn't attempt to beat him down as I would have done with the street traders or in the souvenir shops, as I felt the prices seemed fair ones and he didn't appear to be a 'sharp' trader.

As we went from the Customs sheds to the railway platform it dawned on me why we had had such a long wait after boarding the ship at the Hook - it was to fit into the timetable of LNER (London & North Eastern Railway) and so that a few hundred soldiers would not be cluttering up the station for a few hours. The train journey to York was uneventful and the convoy of trucks to take us to the demob centre was the biggest I have seen. Arriving at the barracks not far from the City we filed into drill sheds full of desks with a soldier behind each ready to complete our 'documentation' which was little more than date-stamping the Release Books we had brought from our Units and issuing us with a travel warrant to get back home. Next came a meal followed by getting kitted out with that promised demob suit. There was a choice of materials and I selected a light grey with a chalk stripe. They were two piece suits such as could be bought at the thirty shilling tailors and were marked with the 'Utility' sign. We were allowed to try on these articles to ensure that they fitted. I might add that the place was like one huge fitting room - after all we were all used to dressing and undressing with complete lack of privacy. When satisfied with our selection regarding material and size the suit was deftly wrapped up in brown paper and tied with string by some poor squaddie who had probably had to learn how to do it by numbers whilst dreaming about capturing enemy machine gun nests and other soldierly activities. We were given the choice of keeping our greatcoats or handing them in and receiving a ten-bob note (half a weeks pay for a private). As mine was in excellent condition without bloodstains (mine or anybody else's) and mud-stains I had always managed to clean off, I elected to keep it thinking that it would make an excellent winter coat to go to work in.

The Army had by now released thousands of men and the whole system was running like clockwork. A huge noticeboard listed at what time trucks would be available to take demobbed men to the station to catch trains to the many destinations. My departure time was to be in the evening and I realised that I wouldn't be seeing home until the next day. The journey to Birmingham was without any event worth a mention, punctuated by a few stops on route to allow people to get rail or road connections to their ultimate destinations. New Street station at Birmingham was the end of the journey as far as this train was concerned and all those left on board detrained (without instructions over the Tannoy system). There was no parting with friends - we hadn't had the opportunity to make friends as we had frequently swapped companions as we had travelled by train, by boat, by train again and had eaten each time with strangers. What I hadn't anticipated on getting off the train was being mobbed by 'spivs'. We had heard of them dealing in black market goods, clothing and petrol coupons and the like but here we were with dozens of them with only two things in mind - they either wanted to buy our demob suits or ferry us to our home address. My new suit was not exactly Saville Row or even made to measure by Montague Burton but to me it seemed worth more than the price they were offering so 'No Sale' was recorded. However getting home by car did interest me - until I was quoted a ridiculous price. I thanked the driver for his offer and said that I would 'hump' my kit to Snow Hill station (only a few streets away and no problem to a chap who had been trained in the Infantry) and wait in the waiting room for the first train to my home town, the time now being about 2 a.m. He disappeared in search of more profitable fry, but just as I was shouldering my kitbag he came back and said that he had another passenger for Blackheath and we settled for a little less than half of the original quotation. The driver was not familiar with this side of the city and since my fellow passenger and myself knew even less, and the road signs hadn't yet been replaced since removing them to confuse any enemy parachutists, we made slow progress until we got to within striking distance of Blackheath. Here it was easy for the 'local' to navigate but not quite so easy for the driver to get back to the main road afterwards. Back on the main road I was able to guide the driver as I had worked in this town for a few years prior to being conscripted into the Army. When we reached the 'Four Ways' at Cradley Heath I elected to pay the man and walk the two or three hundred yards rather than he be committed to a three-point turn on a narrow steeply inclined road thereby waking up the neighbours.

With the neighbours sleep still in mind I thought that the only way I could wake Ma and Pa was to throw gravel chippings from the gutter against their bedroom window. Three or four attempts had the desired effect and Dad signalled that he would come down and let me in by the back door. He was soon dressed followed by Ma and Betty. There were big smiles all round despite the fact that it was well before dawn. As I have said before, we were a loving caring family, but like the majority of working folk in those days we were not given to revealing our emotions. Dad beamed as though he had won the football pools. Ma stood with a little tear glistening in her eyes and a look of thankfulness on her face that I was back home almost unscathed. Ma, who had nursed me back to health on two occasions when my life had been despaired of, who had beaten cancer herself and suffered with stomach ulcers and who hadn't been able to find the strength to come to see me off when I was destined to join the unlucky ones who were posted to that far away war in Burma. One of my regrets in life (and we all have some) is that I didn't break the code and give her a hug. Betty was showing signs of emotion, not surprising considering that she was at that vital age of fourteen, just having left school and in her first job. She whispered tearfully, 'I can't speak'. I can't remember it happening but I guess that that is when the kettle went on for a cup of tea!

All this happened in what we erroneously called the 'veranda' which was really a large glass covered passage from the kitchen to the dining room. This was strangely the largest room in the house and yet had no furnishings, being but a means of cover from any bad weather when carrying meals from the kitchen to the dining room. I am not being entirely truthful when I say 'no furnishings' because there was one item that was new to me and that was a washing machine, a far cry from today's devices, for with this one the hot water had to be poured in from kettles and pans along with soap flakes, the washing then added, the lid closed and the whole lot agitated by a crank on the top. The opportunity to indulge in one of these modern devices had occurred when the family moved from next door (No 34) where there was nowhere to house one practically - this move taking place following the death of dear old Grandpa which happened during my stay in Italy. Not only was this house a cosier one but it also housed the main switches and fuse boxes for the workshop, so the move was more or less obligatory. When I had arrived on my previous leave some nine months before, the move from No 34 to No 33 had recently taken place and forgetting the information that Dad had sent me I had gone boldly into the living room of No 34 with my kitbag on my shoulder before realising that this was not our furniture unless there had been changes for the worse. (People didn't bother about locking their premises except on retiring for the night in those trustful days). Luckily, there was no one in and I made a hasty exit to next door.

 That first evening home I went out to a public telephone and rang Josie to tell her of my safe arrival and to make arrangements for seeing her at the weekend. Josie's eldest sister Marie had been a midwife and district nurse prior to her marriage so there was a 'phone at No 23. Accommodation was booked at Mrs Edge's in White Friars by Josie. Although there was ample space - two spare bedrooms - at No 23, the thought of me sleeping there before getting married never entered our heads - things were done properly then. The days wouldn't pass quickly enough until the weekend when I could hold her in my arms again. Those few days I spent visiting old friends and relatives and, in some cases, the parents of friends not yet demobbed. I found it a nice change also to read newspapers - a thing I hadn't indulged in for three years. (During my training I had paraded on a regular basis to sessions held by ABCA (Army Bureau of Current Affairs) which, as the name implies, informed us of how the war was progressing and how Civvy Street was coping etc., but, of course, not giving us everyday news and pictures that were available to the press. This service was no longer available at the end of our training so we learned little about what was going on in the world).

Knowing what a good seamstress Ma was I asked her if she would alter the style of my greatcoat by removing the half belt at the back and removing the box pleat that ran the full length of the coat. (Incidentally, I had sent her a length of material from Italy for her birthday and she had made a lovely dress from it). She said that I couldn't do better than put it in the hands of Auntie Beat (Beatrice) who had worked in a supervisory position for the Swallow Raincoat Company in Birmingham. An excellent job was made of it and it was dyed navy blue with buttons to match, replacing those polished brass ones (a collectors item now). It was an unmilitary garment when it was finished and pressed and saw me through many winters riding my bike to work.

Josie's Mum

CHAPTER EIGHT
THE WEDDING

These few days did eventually pass and I met Josie at her office when she finished work on Friday evening. Kissing in the street was frowned upon then - an arm round a trim waist was as far as I dare go. However, Josie didn't seem quite at ease. She had something serious to discuss with me she said - something she couldn't put in her letters to me or approach in our telephone conversation of a few days ago. My heart fell into my boots - was she going to call it all off? I was pleased that she didn't keep me on tenter-hooks but told me the reason for her attitude right away. It seems that there was more than one reason why her mum hadn't expressed great delight at our getting engaged. Josie at that time was not acquainted with her family history and her mum felt that it was time that she knew and also realise that it could mean that I might want to withdraw my promise when I was told. When Josie was a babe-in-arms her father had a successful garage business but had suffered a rebuttal by the bank when he wished to expand. He had taken this badly and had turned to the bottle for consolation. His friends, and he would have many as he was quite wealthy and was educated at a public school, soon helped him to deplete his fortune to the extent that he was selling his wife's jewellery to augment his binges. He had unfortunately become an alcoholic and his wife, Josie's dear mum, had had to take out a court order to restrain him from selling the furniture and anything else that might raise funds. She had also fled their lovely home in Liverpool and come to live in Chester where her husband was not given her address. Josie, the baby of the family, had been protected from this knowledge and had always presumed that her father had died when she was still a baby. She had always felt disadvantaged as a school girl with no father to turn up at school functions and she certainly found it hard going as a teenager being responsible for the garden, with both her sisters away nursing and a brother who wasn't interested in gardening, and also doing most of the shopping due to her mum's poor health; and now, was this the final twist of the knife - the giving up of the one she had grown to love so deeply?

Josie's mum had prompted her, I feel sure, into revealing this previously unknown side of the family with the knowledge that I was a Methodist and therefore biased (if, indeed, not bigoted) against anything alcoholic. As I was to find out in the years that followed, she was a wise woman, and no doubt saw that this dark patch in Josie's history could be brought to light in any family squabbles that might develop. Only Heaven knows what she herself must have suffered as a result of excessive alcohol abuse and it was only natural that she would want to protect her 'baby' from anything associated with it. She had come from a privileged family that employed servants; whose daughters had nothing more arduous to do than attend art classes and music lessons; whose sons were put into professions; and here she was now, having married a brilliant motor engineer who came from a wealthy family of antique dealers that sported the Royal Cipher over their shop doorway in York, living in what she called her 'doll's house', and having barely enough money on which to exist. As if fate was not satisfied with reducing her standard of living so drastically, it also cursed her with poor health, she had a heart condition and serious problems with her kidneys (the latter turning out to be hereditary in nature as Tom, Josie's brother, Marie her eldest sister and Josie herself all died of this curse).

I listened without interrupting the story of Josie's father's downfall and she concluded by saying plaintively, 'I don't suppose you'll want to marry me now?' My immediate reaction was to assure her that what she had told me would not influence my feelings for her - it was she I wanted to marry and misdemeanours by any of her family, past, present or to come would not alter those feelings. She gripped my hand a little tighter and I could almost see the burden lift from her shoulders. I think it made her even more happy and secure when I told her that my family had a similar disaster except that it was generations before. My great-grandfather, by all accounts, was a brilliant engineer too and had fallen in the way of drinking far too heavily. His brilliance could be assessed by the fact that his income (and I saw a record of this some years ago) averaged about £7.00 per week at the turn of the century, whilst I, signing on as an apprentice in 1939 hoped to command the sum of £3.50 when I had finished my time in 1944 and this was one of the highest skilled wages of the day. My great-grandmother and her four sons all suffered physical abuse and my grandfather, if not the others, was frequently kept off school to work in great-grandfather's workshop from the age of seven. This unhappiness culminated in the four sons all vowing that their families would not suffer the same hardships and indignities and decided that the only sure way was to become teetotal. This they did and the next generation followed suit with me, the only great-grandson bearing the name of Homer following in their footsteps.

I have pondered longer over this paragraph before writing it than I have over any previous one because I cannot think of a way of wording it without appearing full of self-esteem or even conceit. Josie's previous serious boy friend, Graham, had a mother who thought that, not only was Josie not good enough for him (he was an only child) but she was also a Catholic. As Graham had all but proposed to her, Josie was most upset to the extent of having to take a week off work. She was brokenhearted. Now, here she was with the circumstances almost reversed - she felt unworthy of me because of an erring father and once again religion also reared its ugly head. Was she going to be brokenhearted again? As I said before, I didn't care a jot what the father's behaviour was like although I couldn't make any promises regarding faith. I would give it (Catholicism) a fair hearing and we, if necessary, could always go to our separate churches. I was sincere in what I said and I won her heart and we both could see a very rosy future stretching ahead.

What turmoil her emotions must have been in during that time between learning the truth about her father and the time when I said that the skeleton in her family cupboard was no greater than the one in mine! If she needed more conviction regarding my feelings about alcohol I told her that I had always paid my round even though I was the only one on orange juice and that I had helped drunks back to their billets and even put them to bed. I do not think that I could be classified as a bigoted teetotaller.

At this stage, with the reader's indulgence, I would like to write a few words about my grandfather although it is not strictly within the bounds of my story. I would have loved Josie to have met him (he died a few months prior to her first visit to the Black Country) just as she would have loved me to have met her Aunt Agnes, a nun, (after whom she took her second name) who, it was said, radiated a happiness, a serenity and a holiness that was never forgotten once you had met her.

My grandfather was, in stature, slightly shorter than average height but had a well proportioned figure. His features showed happiness and contentment and his voice was gentle and I never heard him give vent to anger or a bad word. Despite his harsh upbringing he did not harbour any rancour or bitterness, looking upon life as an adventure and showing genuine interest in modern inventions such as the radio, the gramophone, the aeroplane etc.. Few men had the strength and stamina to work in the chain industry beyond their middle fifties, such were the physical demands, and I don't even remember 'Granfer' working. When he had worked it must have been with enthusiasm and diligence because he raised sufficient money to buy two houses - one to live in and the other to rent. The house was furnished with good solid furniture which included an American reed organ which was frequently used to play popular hymns on a Sunday evening. With the aid of a 'tutor' of some forty pages he had taught himself to read and play music and in addition to his ability to play the organ he was quite an accomplished flautist. In addition to raising a family of three sons and a daughter he had also managed to raise enough money to see himself happily provided for in his old age, except that he couldn't anticipate that the bulk of his savings would be lost when two officers of the local building society absconded with the funds leaving the poor innocent secretary (who had unknowingly signed for the release of the money) to serve a jail sentence. (Horace Hackett; the unfortunate secretary of the building society was also secretary of the Sunday School belonging to the church I attended, who resumed office after serving about two years 'inside'. His younger sister, Lilly, was one of my able assistants when I was in charge of the team of Life-boys - the Boys Brigade the equivalent of the Cubs.)

''Granfer's tales of his childhood and youth enthralled me and I think I learned far more about local recent history from him than I ever did from my teachers or history books.

One incident he recounted was about when the 'jungle telegraph' told the family that the 'school inspector' was on his way down the street searching for truants. George was hastened from the workshop to the house and there thrust beneath the table. In those days it was customary to cover the table with a heavy cloth that hung down almost to the floor, usually with a decorative fringe around the edge. His father threatened him that if he so much as murmured when the inspector was there he would be for a thrashing later on. When the dreaded man did put in an appearance a kick to the one hidden was a reminder of the consequences of moving or making the slightest sound, and promises were made that George would be sure to attend in future because he would suffer the hiding of a lifetime when he did eventually come home.

Long before he became, what we would classify as school-leaving age, he was taught to make chain and had the misfortune to drop a link that had had its first bend introduced. It was red hot and unluckily fell into the top of his boot. (No doubt his boots were a sloppy fit to allow him to 'grow into them'). He yelled out with the pain and his father quickly tore off the boot and plunged the injured limb into the 'bosh' of cold water. (The bosh was a cast iron box filled with water for the purpose of cooling the various tools). The burn did not invoke any sympathy from his father but rather the opposite. He was made to carry on working, standing on one leg, with his injured foot resting on a stool. He carried his 'brand mark' to his grave.

These two little yarns I told to the children of Cherry Grove School when I was privileged to give a talk on 'Chains' and the boys especially were very taken with the tale about truancy - I think one or two of them had ideas of hiding under the table instead of doing their sums.

Of all the stories that I heard from Granfer the one that I cherish in my memory above all others is one that he told me of his days of courtship. (I must admit that I am a bit of a romantic). He had fallen in love with a servant girl and she with him. The family she worked for, for reasons unknown to me, moved from the Black Country to Liverpool and took their retinue of servants with them. After a while he felt that he must see her again and so, having saved a little money, he set out to hitch-hike to Liverpool. I love to imagine that journey. There were no cars or lorries - the fastest means of transport being on horseback. In prosperous towns and cities the roads would be paved with cobblestones but between towns the roads would be, for the main part, mother earth with ruts and pot-holes, with streams and small rivers to ford where today we have bridges, with lots and lots of woodland, with turnpikes at intervals that received tolls to pay the road-menders who hammered rocks into the worst of the pot-holes. That journey started off with lifts from various waggoners until, luckily, he chanced upon a man with a horse and dray who was taking a load to Liverpool docks and he stayed in his company for the next sixty or seventy miles. I suppose that, in total, the journey would have taken three or four days, so nightly accommodation would be sought at the hostelries on route where a meal of cold meat and bread could be obtained for a few coppers and a bed of straw provided for a penny (or tuppence if the landlord was greedy). Mostly sitting alongside the waggoner or sometimes walking alongside the horse, especially when he was hauling the heavy load up a hill, he made his way to see his loved one. Arriving at Liverpool he thanked the waggoner for the ride and cheerful company and put a shilling in his hand. The man was almost overcome by this gesture and sprang down from the cart to hand down my grandfather as though he was of the highest rank. He was profuse with his thanks and wished Granfer all that he could possibly wish upon himself, bowing and scraping until he was out of sight.

Granfer must have been just as crazy about Annie, his sweetheart, as I was about Josie to have made such a journey and I bless his memory for the example he set me.

I have transgressed long enough and must get back to my real story - what happened when I came back to England.

Following the revelation of our separate, but similar, family histories the rest of the week was wonderful with meeting Josie from the office each evening and escorting her home, where I got to know her mother better. We talked earnestly about our future together. Josie did not like the Black Country and could not envisage living there but she had said that Quinton, which she had only seen from a Midland Red bus did have some appeal, so I said, 'Should I start by looking for a little house in that area ? It is not too far from where I worked, prior to becoming a soldier, and to which I would be returning.' It was not going to be as easy as that! Josie's mother was to be the main consideration - she had a daughter in Chester, a son and another daughter in Manchester and did not want to be involved in moving about seventy miles away. She was not fit enough to live alone and whilst she would be made welcome to live with any of her children, they all had young offspring and, perhaps, that aspect might be too wearing for her, although she loved them all dearly. We therefore came to the obvious conclusion - I would have to find work in Chester and live with Josie in her mum's house.

On my return home following that heavenly week, I broke the news regarding our plans and it put my mum's stoicism to the test. She had just got me back after three year's absence and here I was proposing to leave for good, and not just to leave the family home to get married, but to go to live some seventy miles away. When I was a five year old I had gone to school holding hands with Mary Bennett and it was her mother's wish that we should hold hands for a lifetime! Since Mary lived only three doors away both our mums saw each other quite a lot and I think that had it been the custom for arranged marriages then the die would have been cast and I would have married and lived locally. My mum was not against that idea. Many questions were raised. Was I sure she was right for me? What sort of job could I secure as good as my existing one, which was being held for me? How did I fancy living under my mother-in-law's roof?, and many more. There is a saying that love is blind and I could see nothing but a happy future. Dad accepted the inevitable.

My length of service had qualified me for twelve weeks paid leave following demob but after a week in Chester and a couple of weeks of kicking my heels I felt that it was time to put on the harness and get properly back into civilian life, so I went along to Blackheath to see how things stood at B.T.H. (The British Thomson Houston Co.) where I had been working until I was conscripted. (Talking of conscription brings to mind the vagaries of war). In December 1941 I had volunteered for air crew duties in the RAF and following a successful medical and three days of written examinations at Edgbaston I had been accepted as a potential officer and observer. The following month, the manager of the machine shop where I worked sent for me to tell me that he would not release me from vital war work. Almost three years later, when to my mind my work seemed even more vital - turning out generators for Lancaster bombers - I was released with no option but to enter the Army. Cannon fodder, at that time, was paramount.

At B.T.H. the personnel officer, Alf Cannon, welcomed me back and said that I could start work again as a turret lathe setter-operator in the machine shop. He was also pleased to inform me that there had been no more than half a dozen fatalities from all those who had conscripted for the forces.

So, off I went to work and found that I was allotted the very machine that I had worked on for a couple of years in my pre-

Army days, and what is more, most of the chaps I had worked with were already back there as they had preceded me by a month or two. It doesn't take a great imagination to think how we all enjoyed swapping tales of our adventures in various parts of the world - that is, all except Ray (I forget his surname) who had been conscripted as a Bevin Boy and had had to spend three years working down a mine in the Welsh valleys. (Once again it defies belief that the 'authorities' could take a mineworker and put him in the forces so that he could be replaced by a man who had no knowledge of working in a pit and who was doing a vital job in armaments!). Poor Ray tried valiantly to outdo some of the North African campaigners with his stories of runaway coal trucks and canaries falling off their perches.

    I had not forgotten my promise that I would put my mind to finding out what the Catholic faith was all about, so I went to see the parish priest at Old Hill as there is no Catholic church in Cradley Heath. The church is a tiny one constructed with corrugated iron sheets on the outside and sparsely furnished (as Catholic churches go) on the inside, with a capacity of approximately seventy. The priest, who I had met on a couple of occasions when Josie had been to visit us, was a Father Rose. He was a very devout man who had obviously taken his vows with sincerity as could be seen by his down at heel shoes and the rectangular patches in the knees of his trousers. He was not a secular priest but was on loan from a friary at Leamington Spa and said Mass at two other tiny churches each Sunday, using an old Austin Seven for transport. Having told him the purpose of my visit and a brief resume leading up to it he assigned me one evening each week to instructing me in all things Catholic. I was not exactly virgin soil for him to plant out as I had been steeped in Methodism from the age of four and had collected three or four prizes for examinations passed in Scriptural knowledge set by the Birmingham diocese (Non-conformist) during my teenage years. As the weeks went by I found myself getting more and more interested in the spiritual aspects presented and I was finding gaps filled in that I didn't realise existed. Where the Methodist Church is austere in the extreme as regards statues, candles, clerical attire etc. the Catholic Church revels in its panoply of regalia, its multitude of Saints (not that all Saints are Catholics nor all Catholics Saints) and its devotion to candles whose flames and smoke reach for the sky as surely as the prayers hasten to heaven. The differences and the reasons for those differences were all pointed out to me in a logical and methodical way by that learned and holy man.

At B.T.H. I settled down to the old routine in a matter of days. The basic pay had been raised a little sometime during my three year absence but the bonus system remained the same indicating that, overall, our wages were a little behind those of nearby industries. The bonus system that was used was known as the 'Debt System' to the employees and worked as follows. A weekly target was given for each man (or woman) to achieve, each job being given a price for setting up the machine and a price per article, or a price per hundred articles if tiny ones. The target might be, for instance, £3.15.0 and, if achieved, would be added, along with any over or above that target, to the basic wage. However, if a person underachieved, which was more often than not, then, if the total of £2.15.0 had been raised, then the person owed the firm £1.0.0 which would be deducted from any excess made above the target the following week. After a few successive weeks of underachieving the person would be summoned to the manager's office to be told that he was going to, generously, cancel his debt to the firm and that he had to put in a better effort in order to try to achieve a bonus and thereby support his family in a better style. When I tell you that setting up a turret lathe would be rewarded with a sum, varying from 3.4 pence to 14 pence, you might realise how hopeless it was to make a good wage - indeed, the time taken in collecting the various gauges and tools from the stores would take up to the time to equate to that value. It was quite customary to withhold a few piecework dockets from the wages department each week so that following the week in which a person was discharged from his 'debt' to the firm, he could submit these and claim a 'bumper' week's wages that might give him a few extra shillings.

The machine shop in which I worked was a vast one and I was told that it housed one thousand machines (although I never checked the accuracy of that statement) and the section that I worked on comprised centre lathes, capstan lathes and turret lathes. In this section some sixty per cent of the operators had been conscripted and of these only one did not come back to his old job. It was only natural that the ex-soldiers should get together (and we accepted two Bevin Boys) and we discussed seriously the fact that the firm was taking us for a ride. The work that we did was the most varied and most demanding of all the work in the machine shop and, on investigation, we found that our wages were the lowest. We had all grown in confidence following our army experiences and decided that we should approach the management with a view to getting a fairer deal. The gentlemanly approach did not work. We were told that the jobs had been timed by stopwatch and that it had been agreed at the time that it was a fair time. What they did not concede was that most of these prices had been set and agreed prior to the onset of war. There was no alternative left to us but to give the management notice that we were so incensed with their attitude that we felt inclined to withdraw our labour. Our manager, Charlie Morris, did not believe us so we had no alternative but to walk out of the factory gates in the middle of the morning (this was about three weeks after returning to work).

We gathered in a group outside the main gate and chatted about the situation, most of us feeling somewhat apprehensive as we had no union backing or the support of our fellow workers. In less than half an hour Alf Cannon, the personnel officer, whose office adjoined the gate, came along and asked us to elect a couple of spokesmen as a meeting had been convened with Mr. Broughton, the General Manager, Charlie Morris, the Machine Shop Manager, Ken Hamblett, representing the rate-fixers and our two representatives, plus Alf himself. Within the hour a message was brought to us that, if we returned to work, the case would be received favourably and we would be given a 'waiting time' chit for the time that we had been absent so that we would suffer no financial loss. At lunch time we all gathered together again to hear what our representatives had to tell us and we were not surprised to learn that Charlie had advocated 'sacking' two or three as an example to the rest. However, Mr. Broughton, who was a gentleman, (a fact confirmed by my cousin Minnie who was his chauffeuse) told Charlie, in no uncertain manner, that those days were over and went on to lecture him on the fact that 'these lads had been fighting for the pitiful sum of three bob a day for a few years with the very object of getting rid of such dictatorial attitudes'. The rate-fixing department was instructed to re-time any job that we felt to be unfair; time was to be allowed for re-grinding of cutting tools and, best of all, a sensible time was to be allowed for setting up the machine. It had been a very short sharp battle but we had won it and found ourselves receiving something like a pound more each week and never 'in debt' to the firm.

A practice known as 'the Saturday morning inquest' was a thing that most of us found not only embarrassing and repugnant but also time wasting (thereby reducing our earning capacity). Each Saturday morning at eleven o'clock the whole workforce of the machine shop had to gather round the front of Charlie Morris's office which was a timber one elevated on four great angle-iron legs with access gained by a steel staircase and having a balcony running along its front face. It was from this balcony that Charlie would take great delight in informing us of any scrap components that had been produced during the past week; who had produced them; how many there were; at what cost to the firm (some scrap can be produced after several operations have been paid for); and the promise that, if it happened again, then that man or woman could look for alternative employment without a reference from him. I am sure that no-one knowingly or willingly produced scrap because, if a component did not pass inspection and fit all the gauges, then they did not receive the wages due for it - this was just Charlie's ego trip. With the end of the war working hours had been reduced and Saturday morning work became overtime and therefore attendance was no longer obligatory. This had, as a result, brought to an end the Saturday morning ritual and about three quarters of an hour's embarrassment..

Saturday was not, therefore, a day when I was forced to work so this meant that I could travel by train to Chester on a Friday evening to go to visit my loved one. This I did on alternate weekends, as funds would not allow a weekly visit taking into account that I had to pay my fare but also my accommodation expenses at Mrs Edge's. My Saturday morning on these weekends was used in searching for employment in the Chester area. The local press did not seem to include advertisements for vacancies for which I felt qualified and, as a result, I had to resort to 'knocking on doors'.

What did I have to offer any future employer beyond the testimonial that was written into my Army release document and which I am bold enough to quote:- 'Cpl Homer has been employed in this headquarters since October 1946. He has at all times done well and worked hard displaying intelligence and initiative. Sober in habits and trustworthy and punctual. He should prove an asset to any civilian employer. Quiet disposition'; signed by the Camp Commandant GHQ 2nd Echelon C.M.F.?

Firstly, I had foregone my lessons in languages, music and art to concentrate my efforts on a handicrafts course which had been introduced to the school for the first time. The course was almost exclusively to do with cabinet making; from the drawing stage (we produced our own blue prints - from a light box that we made ourselves) through to making, inlaying, staining and French polishing. God had blessed me with fingers (and brain) attuned to this kind of work and at the end of my first year I took the exam along with apprentices and found myself, not only with a first class pass, but the only one to gain a distinction.

Secondly, I had been apprenticed to the printing trade but the war brought this to an untimely end after three years. Thirdly, I had worked at B.T.H., machining almost every kind of metal except the precious ones (gold, silver and platinum) for almost four years. Fourthly, I had not only proved myself a marksman with the rifle and light machine gun (the Bren) thereby gaining myself a few extra coppers each week - an ability that was useless in civvy street - but I had on being transferred to the RASC passed the test and qualified as a clerk/typist, a trade which I fancied only as a last resort.

In those days there were no 'Yellow Pages' or 'Local Directories' to point me to the targets I wished to aim at (not with a light machine gun) namely cabinet makers, printers and engineers, so I applied myself to scrutinising the two local newspapers to see who in those particular fields was advertising their wares if they were not advertising for labour. The Observer and The Chronicle threw up no information on cabinet making and on thinking about it I realised that furniture was being mass-produced in factories and my experience was more related to the methods used by Chippendale and Sheraton. Printing, however, was another matter and I found several printers within the city walls. Approaching what appeared to be the largest of these, namely Evans and Co., I was granted an interview on the spot as they had just lost a 'machine minder' - whether he had retired, died, left for a better job, I was not privileged to find out. In answer to the boss's questions I told him that I had done well at the job and after some eighteen months had been put in charge of setting two hand-fed machines (the Arab - well known to all small printers and the German, Schnellpressen fabric) and one automatic, the Heidleberg. Although I was familiar with a couple of 'cylinder' presses I confessed that I had not been in charge of them. Another 'platen' machine I knew well was the British 'Falcon'. A further feather in my cap was that I was used to half-tone work and four-colour printing. I told him too that as an apprentice I had attended Dudley School of Arts and Crafts one evening each week to learn the other side of the trade - compositing - and the technical side of coloured inks etc.. The range of work had varied widely - from the simplest of raffle tickets to multi-paged full colour catalogues for Raleigh cycles -from ledgers to hessian sacks for car skid-chains, from 'stills ' that were posted outside the cinemas declaring the 'Coming Attractions' to relief printing of those 'posh' letter headings where the shiny ink stands up proud of the paper. I had not taken part in, but I had witnessed, bookbinding (including embossing with gold leaf), folding, stapling, ruling (those coloured lines on writing pads and in ledgers are not printed but are made on 'ruling machines') and perforating - in all I had been lucky enough to be an apprentice where every aspect of letterpress printing was practised.

The boss seemed impressed with what I told him and said that it sounded as if I was just the man they were looking for. He told me to step across the yard to the factory and ask for Mr 'X' who was the shop steward and foreman who would give me a further interview, then to come back to discuss hours of work and salary. Going across the yard and entering the premises I couldn't help but notice how tiny it was compared with Cradley Printing Co. - it was less than a quarter of the size and didn't seem to be laid out with any semblance of order. The first person I saw, I asked for Mr 'X' only to be told that I was speaking to him. I told him the purpose of my visit and that the boss thought that I could fill the vacancy. His first question was to ask me where I was working at present and I thought it might not be such a good thing to say that I was working in engineering. I said that I had recently come home after three years in the Army to which he immediately said; 'Oh, you've been out of the trade too long - you will have lost your touch. You'll be no good to me' If he thought I was going to grovel and ask for a months trial he thought wrong. I went back and reported to the boss and he said with a resigned air; 'I'm afraid there's nothing I can do'. I had forgotten that the printers union was, at that time, the strongest in the country and that there would be lots of little Hitlers scattered around the country.

Leaving the premises with feelings of disappointment, frustration, rejection and anger all rolled into one I realised that if this was the attitude adopted universally throughout the printing world I stood no chance except with a 'one horse' outfit and the likelihood of a vacancy there was next to nil.

With one of my options virtually cancelled I had to concentrate my efforts on looking for work in the engineering field or failing that see whether my Army qualifications as a clerk/typist could secure me a place in the Town Hall, a Bank or similar institution. Engineering in Chester was almost as foreign as farming is in the Black Country and I almost despaired of finding an outlet for my skills. Job Centres had not been dreamt of in those days and the Labour Exchange which in some areas had lists of local 'situations vacant' was not open on Saturday mornings, so I continued to scan the newspapers on my fortnightly visits. Apart from motor engineering, of which there seemed plenty, there seemed to be only two engineering firms worthy of note, namely Chester Hydraulic Engineering Co., which had an excellent reputation for apprenticeships and the factory at Broughton a few miles into North Wales. The Hydraulic Co. had no vacancies and had a reserve list of people trained by their good selves to call upon, so that was a dead duck from day one, whilst the factory at Broughton that had been turning out Wellington bombers by the hundred during the war had turned to producing prefab houses to temporarily replace the thousands that had been destroyed by the German Air Force, V1s, V2s and doodle bugs.

Learning that the prefab production was coming to an end and that the de Havilland Aircraft Co. were contemplating taking over the factory, I wrote to the Head Office at Hatfield asking if it was true and if so could I be considered for a position with them as a machinist, preferably as a turner. Their reply was that what I had heard was true and that as soon as the factory was opened in their name I should apply through the usual local channels, but not to assume that this would be immediate. There was no indication to suggest that the delay would be weeks or months so although I felt reasonably confident in getting a job,

I thought that it would be wise to continue scanning the local press.

This turned out to be a sensible move because I spotted a vacancy for a turner at St. David's Manufacturing Co. in Saltney and submitted my written application, stating that I was available for interview on Saturday mornings. An interview was arranged for the following Saturday and I turned up not knowing what this firm manufactured only that they needed a turner. I was interviewed by two men, one with an educated accent and the other with a strong foreign accent, with them sharing the questions more or less equally. They seemed to be happy with the replies they received and I was asked by the Englishman if I would care to look at the machine that I would be expected to operate, to which I readily agreed. He took me to the workshop and there stood a gap-bed centre lathe of generous proportions, brand new and complete with face-plate, 4-jaw chuck, 3-jaw self-centring chuck and a range of cutting tools. A quick glance showed me that the only other machines were a pedestal drill, a small milling machine and a surface grinder, with a couple of work-benches with engineers vices and a marking off table completed the contents. Whatever St. Davids manufactured it was obviously not from this room, this being more like a mini tool-room or maintenance department. The boss volunteered to show me the firm's production in process and took me through into an adjoining room. I was surprised to see about a dozen girls sitting down at benches each having a powerful gas burner before them and each blowing glass bubbles as they twisted the glass round and round in order to retain its spherical shape. Others put a liquid into these spheres using a small syringe and shook the contents around as they played it around the flame, this giving a silver coating to the inside. One girl was taking a percentage of the silver spheres to dip them in various brightly coloured dyes, twiddling them round to ensure that they had an even coating and placing them in a rack so that any excess dye ran down the stem. Yes - St. David's manufactured Christmas tree baubles.

We went back to the office where we agreed a starting date, wages, hours and conditions of employment. At this stage I must admit that I couldn't see where a centre lathe turner fitted into the picture, but who am I to argue if that is what the bosses wanted. The wages were not as good as the sum I was earning in the Midlands but I was looking on the job as a stepping stone or a stopgap until de Havilland's came up with something better. Josie was as delighted as I was with the successful outcome of the interview as it was an important stage towards our aim of getting married as soon as it was practical.

The next stage was for me to give in my notice at B.T.H. and to get 'digs' in Chester. Regarding the latter, Josie volunteered to find something a little more palatial than Mrs Edge's in Whitefriars (where there was no bathroom) and I had the easy task of handing in my notice. The day after giving in my notice I was requested to put in an appearance at the manager's office, this being the first time I had ascended that staircase without the knowledge that I was in debt to the company! Charlie was wearing his 'diplomat' hat that day - well, at least for that meeting - because he asked, in an unusual tone for him, why I was considering leaving the company that had only very recently awarded me concessions that amounted to a substantial rise in pay. He thought that maybe I had found somewhere where my skills would bring in higher wages (and that he could offer inducements to reverse my decision) or then again quite a number of men had come back to civilian life to find it not so satisfying or as exciting as life in the Forces and were going back to rejoin their units. I explained to him that my reason for leaving was that I had secured a position in Chester where it was my intention to get married and settle down. The decision was irreversible he realised, so he offered me his hand, wishing me 'all the best' and I was pleased to hear his parting words, 'If things don't work out in Chester you know you will be welcome back here'.

Suitable accommodation was arranged very quickly thanks to a fortuitous meeting of Josie's mum with one of her neighbours. She had by now accepted the inevitable and was telling Mrs

Jones, who lived three houses along the road from herself, what (little) she knew about me and how I was looking for somewhere to live until Josie and I got married. Mrs Jones was a widow who shared her house with her younger brother Bob, a bachelor in his fifties, and who offered bravely to put me up, feed me, wash for me and tend to all my needs. I say bravely because she had never seen me and Josie's mum couldn't tell her a lot other than I was responsible for the postman getting his shoes repaired more frequently during the last couple of years, and Mrs Jones had never taken in a lodger before.

My leaving home would be most traumatic for Mum as she would, like all good mums, worry in case my underwear wasn't aired properly (not realising that I'd often slept under hedgerows in the pouring rain); would worry that I was being fed adequately (not realising how short I had been on rations on occasions and still remained fit and healthy); would worry in case I hadn't enough blankets on the bed (not realising that two blankets was enough in the Army, no matter how cold the weather); would worry most of all in case Josie and I didn't have as happy a marriage as she shared with Dad. Dad, not that he didn't care, would not worry so much - he was more philosophical and would accept that it was the natural order of things that I should want to set up home with my loved one. After all I was twenty five - two or three years older than he was when he got married. Also Betty - she had been without my company for three years, and the years before and during the war had been all work and sleep for me; so we didn't really know each other, the ten year gap between our birthdays was such a disparity.

I could not visualise a better arrangement than what had been negotiated on my behalf by Josie's mum and Mrs. Jones. I was treated like one of the family by Mrs Jones, even to sitting down to Sunday dinner and tea with them when her son and daughter-in-law came on a visit. She was a lovely old lady and I doubt whether I adequately expressed my gratitude for the extraordinary way she saw to my needs. Bob was a robust character both physically and in his general approach to life, being always in possession of a wide smile. Some forty seven years later (give or take a couple of weeks) I learned from Josie that Bob had met her Mum in the street and passed the following remark; 'You've no need to worry about your future son-in-law, Mrs Greenwood. A nicer lad never walked this earth' (This was when I had been living with them for only two or three weeks). Untrue, I know, as I have no pretensions to being worthy of a halo, but how nice and how typical of him to ease any anxieties she might have had concerning me. I sometimes wonder why Josie left it all those years before telling me, long after her Mum had died and after Bob had been killed in a road accident.

Bob Gregory, we were to find out later, had another connection apart from being the brother of my landlady. In the First World War he and Syd Millward, with several other Christleton village lads, had volunteered to serve in a Liverpool Regiment. Syd Millward was the father of Josie's best school friend Elsie (a friendship that lasted from kindergarten, unbroken, to Josie's death). During a battle Syd was wounded and lay in 'no mans land'. Bob didn't hesitate to go out to rescue him and to carry him back to the comparative safety of the trenches. No explanation from me is necessary to state the relationship which ensued.

One of the first things I attended to on coming to live in Chester was to keep my promise to look into the Catholic way of life. I went to the presbytery attached to the Church dedicated to St. Werburgh and I was met by Canon Welch who listened attentively to my story of my anticipated marriage and how I had progressed in my knowledge of his faith in the little village in Italy and in the heart of the Black Country. He introduced me to a young curate by the name of James Fraser and said that he would continue with my instruction. 'Receiving instruction' was a phrase that irked me somewhat - it smacked of the Army to my mind, and even now, some fifty years on, I feel that a better choice of words must be available. The dictionary defines the word 'instruct' as 'to prepare: to inform: to teach: to direct: to give guidance.: and all of these suit the case, but it also states:- 'to order: to command': and these I think are more commonly accepted interpretations.

Father Fraser, a person little older than myself, fair-haired and fresh-faced, had a retiring or unassuming personality and I took to him right away. We agreed on a regular weekly meeting to continue with my studies. On my first attendance I was introduced to Father Kevin Byrne who asked if I minded if he sat in on these sessions and I saw no reason to argue with this arrangement as I found his manner equally acceptable. He was a little taller and dark haired and had a more studious appearance, being of much the same age as his fellow curate. They asked if I minded starting off with the teaching that was given to the children in school and build up from there. I thought it a good idea as I could then compare their teaching with that which I had received at Sunday School twenty years before. The subject or essence was obviously similar, but I found that the Catholic way was so much more methodical and organised. The 'Penny Catechism' didn't have an equivalent in the Methodist Church, but it played such an important part in laying down the foundations of the Faith in a Catholic child. We went on discussing issues from time to time, with me having to give way to superior knowledge and conviction most often. The 'Credo' was taken apart word by word as was the 'Pater Noster', every word being subjected to the minutest analysis. I was given reasons for the disciplines of the Church - obligations - fasting and abstinence -venial and cardinal sins - confession and absolution -intentions - vestments - vocations - Holy Orders - the priest's daily office - indulgences and purgatory - vigils - the Church's calendar - votive candles - statues - shrines - miracles - mysteries - why the Mass was celebrated in Latin - why Rome was the centre of the Catholic Church - the implications of the fourteen stations of the Way of the Cross - baptism and confirmation - all culminating in an explanation of the real meaning of the Mass celebrated on a daily basis (with the exception of that one awful day each year).

At work I soon found, as I had half suspected, that operating the lathe was not to be the entirety of my labours. The first job I had to do was to make half a dozen burners for the extra girls that were going to be employed and since the body of these burners was basically copper I had to anneal the metal before I could form it by roller on the lathe. There was no temperature controlled oven in which to conduct any heat treatment so it was a case of using an oxyacetylene torch and a bucket of water to achieve the necessary result, depending on the colour of the metal to gauge the temperature. This method also applied to hardening tool steels except that whale oil was used instead of water and tempering was done in air. Two other men shared this tool-room, Nev Hughes and Don Hampson who also put me wise on various aspects of the job (such as tea breaks, and how to alter the clock when clocking in if one happened to be late!). The foreign boss, Mr Gratzer was of Czech origin and had brought his knowledge of glass to England, where, with the English boss he had set up this factory to make Christmas tree decorations. Mr. Waters, the English boss, had presumably helped with the initial financing of the venture and, being a local councillor, aided in securing a suitable building and negotiating the setting up of the business as his partner's English was not very good. Apart from the girls employed on production and our three selves in the tool-room there were only three other employees; a truck driver, odd job man and a young married woman who was secretary, wages clerk and general office factotum. The tiny spring-steel clips from which the decorative balls hang were made by workers who took home a spool of steel and a tiny hand operated bench press. These clips were paid for by weight and precious little they got for the time it must have taken to make them. Whilst we in the tool-room saw very little of Mr. Waters, we saw Mr, Gratzer at least once each day as he passed through our room to get to see the girls on production. When I had been working there a few days he came across to us, called us together, and said that he wished to automate some of the operations and would we put our heads together and design and make a machine that would dispense

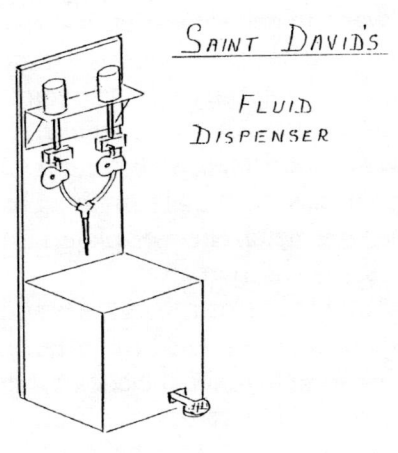

Saint David's Fluid Dispenser

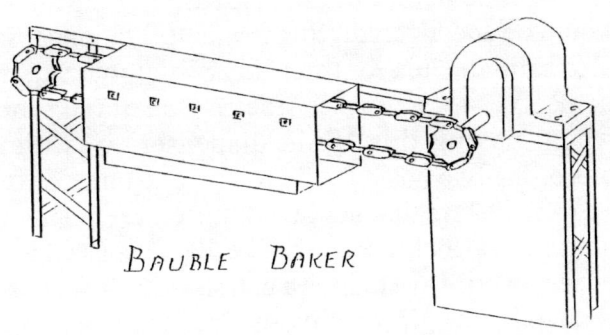

Bauble Baker

the fluid into the glass spheres that made them silver. Nev, Don and myself had been used to working to detailed engineering drawings, so an abstract kind of request of this nature could only be looked upon as a challenge. It turned out to be more than a simple challenge because, as far as possible, the machine was to be made from material we could glean from a pile of scrap metal that was situated some eighty yards along the road. This scrap metal was to be the nucleus of our metal stock for all future ventures, deviating only when special things like the copper tubing for burners, or silver steel for shafts etc. was required, and was comprised of bits and pieces of every description - angle iron, sheet metal (anything but flat of course) gear wheels, expanded metal, chequer-plate, castings of all sorts of shapes and most of it fairly rusty.

When I had studied physics it was the branch of chemistry where my light shone dimmest and I can offer no excuse for not remembering what went to make the cocktail that was fed into the glass bottles. All that I do remember is that in one fluid was water and sugar and in the other an acid (possibly nitric) and some other commodity. The two could not be mixed for any great length of time before being dispensed or the silvering process would be endangered. (Sugar was still rationed, so the girls used to bring the tea for their 'brew' without sugar and helped themselves to the firm's stock). One of the problem arising when making this 'fluid dispenser' was that the proportions of the two basic fluids was two to one, so we had to devise a cam system that achieved this end. This machine was duly finished and looked vaguely like the chocolate machines we used to see on railway stations a couple of generations ago. It was operated by the girl placing the feed pipe - a tiny glass extension from the rubber tubing - into the glass bubble's neck (which was about four inches long at this stage) and depressing a pedal with her foot. The pedal activated a switch that engaged the tiny motors controlling the two cams, which, in turn, opened the valves allowing the two fluids through at the correct proportions.

That was the first stage of automation working satisfactorily - and it wasn't long before the next stage was requested. Mr. Gratzer wanted a machine that could shake the ball around so as to evenly distribute the fluid inside and, at the same time, to bake it. It was decided that the best way to heat the oven would be by electricity, controlled, as is the domestic oven by a rheostat, as this would mean that we could experiment with the mechanism without having to do plumbing (for gas) which would have to be rearranged when the machine was completed and installed in the production workshop. A chain was purchased with two sprockets to suit, looking rather like the tracks of a military tank without all the intermediate bogie wheels. The links of the chain were about five inches long and were joined by hollow rivets. We made a number of devices that were secured loosely through the hollow rivets and these would carry the glass balls through the sheet-metal oven, each device having a lever that would foul against pins within the oven causing the glass balls to swing vigorously. The chain was driven by an electric motor with a reduction gearbox and the glass balls were clipped on with a wooden clothes peg (part of the swinging device) at the 'feed' end and unclipped by a second operator at the 'exit' end. Teething problems were remarkably few and we were glad to get rid of the machine with its interminable 'clacking' as the balls bounced about inside the oven.

Whilst all this was going on Josie was busy in her dinner hours making arrangements for our wedding and seeking a suitable venue for the reception. Having fixed the dates at the Church and the hotel and informed the registrar she then applied herself to getting the invitations printed. (I wonder if it was the printer's firm that had given me the elbow a few weeks before?). She had to choose, with her Mum's help, a suitable dress and to ask my sister and an old school friend, Margaret Slack, if they would be bridesmaids. A colour scheme was devised for the bridesmaids comprising blue and white to go with bouquets of delphiniums. How the girls managed to attend 'fittings' I cannot imagine as Betty lived seventy-odd miles away and

Margaret was, I believe, at college in Manchester studying to become a physiotherapist, but they both looked very nice on the day. I, of course, had the easy bit - all I had to do was to ask my friend of twenty years, George Walker, to be my best man and to arrange to hire morning suits for the allotted day. George was at college too, studying to become a teacher, but Moss Bros had, as we all know, suits that fitted everybody and both George and I had standard measurements. Josie's Mum had limited means but she was generous to a fault and showed it by saying that she would invite forty guests from my end of the world (people she had never met) and Josie and I set to in the evenings compiling a list of friends and relatives to whom we could send RSVP invitations. From the way in which Josie applied herself, so methodically and diligently, getting all these things running as smoothly as clockwork, you would think she had been trained to the task.

Mid-May arrived and with it the end of my sessions with Father Fraser and Father Byrne, and I was asked whether I thought the Catholic Faith was for me. I thought seriously about it, feeling twinges of conscience and pangs of deserting some of my old friends - some would not ever view me again in the light that they had done before; but I decided that the truths that I had learned were paramount and that I would ignore them at my peril. Having voiced my acceptance I felt a kind of happiness that has pervaded the whole of my life since then and, of course, Josie (who had prayed so hard for my conversion) was 'over the moon'.

My conversion was not like the lightening strike that Paul experienced on the road to Damascus - it was more like watching the sun come up at dawn - a gradual process brought about by reasoning and logic. It was the acceptance of a Faith that was to sustain and support me in the tough times that were to come.

In case I hadn't been 'done' properly in the first instance I was given a 'conditional baptism' and welcomed into the Church. Arrangements were made for me to receive Holy Communion for the first time next morning, followed by breakfast in the presbytery before going on to my days work. Seven o'clock Mass saw me there promptly and I engaged in the celebration fully for the first time. Breakfast followed, cooked and served up by a slip of a girl called Joan. (we all know that many of our family names have been arrived at in the distant past by the association of a person's trade, profession or some characteristic - Barber, Smith, Cutler, Baker, Merchant, Purser, Sharp, Proud, Rich, Heath and many many more, but of all these inherited names surely the one of which a person could be most proud is Christian. Just think of being known as a member of the village and being identified as belonging to the Christian family.) Well, Joan Christian gave me my first 'Catholic breakfast' - a proper full English breakfast - Joan, who was to marry later on a Mr. Wells, who was to foster well over a hundred children and be acclaimed for her wonderful work on the B.B.C. television programme 'This is your life'. My claim to fame is that I've had a breakfast cooked and served by Joan Christian.

Whether or not there were chip shops in Czechoslovakia before the war I have no idea, but often at lunchtime Mr. Gratzer could be seen going to the workshop to ask the girls 'Eees anyone goin' for cheeps?' We had no canteen other than a tiny room in which to make a pot of tea, so it was either sandwiches, or a packet of chips that were invariably almost cold as the shop was a good half mile away. I think that he ate well in the evening because he was quite a portly gentleman, the steering wheel of his car chafing his waistcoat as he drove. His driving! That was something else! Acknowledging that they drive on the wrong side of the road over there, there was little excuse for his erratic behaviour behind the wheel. Only once was I his passenger and I cannot forget it. Apart from hogging the centre of the road his main fault was that, on approaching a corner, he would begin to turn about fifty yards before getting there, and so have to correct his steering about five or six times before actually reaching the corner. Another of his eccentricities was drawing something on the palm of his hand whilst explaining in his poor English what kind of new gas burner or some other object he wanted making. It was quite frustrating at times because there was nothing to refer to in the way of a drawing and if they didn't work he expressed his annoyance.

One afternoon Mr, Gratzer came into the tool-room and called us together and said; 'I vont you to make a machine to make zeees' and showed us in the palm of his hand, not a drawing this time, but a small glass ampoule. It was about twelve millimetres in diameter and shaped like a bottle except for having a semi-spherical base. Its purpose was, we found out later, to hold an analgesic gas in liquid form. The ampoule would be filled and then sealed by applying a small flame to the tiny neck thereby melting the glass. The filled ampoule would be inserted into a canister resembling a big torch with a face mask attached. The appliance would be used by midwives to alleviate the pains of childbirth by striking the base which would break the ampoule thereby releasing the gas. (Most confinements took place at home in those days). Following his request, Mr. Gratzer added, as though he was doing us a great favour, 'I haf bought for you an electric motor to drive the machine' I'm glad that he had, otherwise we would have been devising pedal power or using the flow of the river Dee that was only thirty paces away.

We went into a huddle to discuss the principles we would have to employ to build such a machine. The glass tube from which the ampoules would be made would have to be held in a vertical stance and would have to rotate so that gas flames would play uniformly where required. It would have to be held by some contrivance that would hold or release its grip and that was capable of moving in a vertical mode as it rotated in order to form the neck of the ampoule. The gas flames would have to be controlled as regards direction - one to form the semi-spherical end - one to form the neck as the tube rotated and stretched - and one to part off the completed article. Don advocated a system of levers culminating in a scissor motion for stretching the glass when softened by the flame at the neck portion, but I argued that a cam action was less demanding on the motor and could be contained within the framework we had envisaged whereas his levers would extend some two feet beyond the back of the machine. I won this little argument on the condition that I would have to plot the profile of the cam. Don did not feel aggrieved when I readily agreed to his idea of rotating the three flames as opposed to turning the gas high or low as a low flame could always blow out in a draught, and Nev busied himself initially with sketching the skeletal framework of the machine, which looked something like a cooker with no door and no side and back panels. We agreed, without division, that the speed of rotation should be around one revolution per second (not that any of us had any experience!).

The heap of scrap was raided to see what could be found in the way of gear-wheels, plummer-blocks, strips of steel suitable for the many levers required and angle iron for the frame-work. I was delighted to find not only a gear-wheel with forty teeth but a piece of bronze from which I could make a two-start worm gear to mesh with it thereby transferring the motion from the horizontal motor to the vertical drive necessary and producing an acceptable spindle sped (71 r.p.m.) at one fell swoop. Now I was in my element. I ground a tool to form the teeth to match the gear-wheel and worked out the necessary gear train on the lathe to produce a matching two-start worm gear. When the worm gear was about seventy-five per cent finished Mr. Gratzer came in to ask what decisions we had come to and how work was progressing and saw me putting in the form tool to make the second groove. He asked; 'Unt vot is that?', and I explained. 'I am not having that in my machine' he said, ' I haf seen such things wearing out'. He may have been an expert in glass ware but although he was twice my age he exhibited his profound ignorance in engineering because a cast iron gear in mesh with a bronze worm was just about as good as you can get in these days. From past experience we knew that there was no point in offering an argument so had to be content with saying that it would be difficult to achieve the necessary ratios by other means and that other than an expensive train of gears including very expensive bevel gears the only other alternative was chains and sprockets. Magnanimously, we were told that we could have just as many cycle chains and sprockets as we needed to do the job. Three types of gearing were available in those days (mountain bikes hadn't been invented) the fixed gear ratio; the Sturmey-Archer; or the derailleur, so from this range of sprockets we worked out a suitable train involving six wheels. My luck was in once more because I found a matching pair of bevel gears in that pile of scrap.

In was about this time in the proceedings that I suffered what could have been a serious accident. Approaching Don, who was working on the surface grinder, I was unfortunate enough to arrive when he was dressing the wheel with a diamond in a holder on a magnetic chuck. Whether he had forgotten to switch on the magnet or whether he had positioned the diamond incorrectly I do not know, but just as I arrived at his side the diamond heeled over and the wheel burst asunder with a fragment hitting me in the eye. Nev took a look to see whether a bit of the grit remained in the eye (which I felt it did each time I blinked - which was often, as the tears were flooding) but could see nothing except that the eye was very bloodshot. Don was taking a look when who should walk into the tool-room on one of his very infrequent visits but Willowby Waters, as we called him. He wanted to know what the trouble was and on being told, sent for Jack Iball the truck driver and sent me off to the Royal Infirmary, but not before delivering a sermon about how he had attended to all sorts of medical emergencies in the jungle but had always fought shy of attending to eye problems as the eye is a very delicate organ. I walked to the truck half listening to the tale of how he had even attended to the confinement of a native woman, but he wouldn't have taken a foreign body from her eye. Apart from his sermon I was pleased with his timely arrival and action because on being attended to at the casualty department of the Infirmary I was told that a fragment of the grinding wheel had pierced the iris of my eye and was still inside. The eye specialist was luckily available and after 'freezing' my eye with cocaine cut out the offending fragment. With him was a nursing sister who was, he told me, going out to a mission in Africa and would be interested to see the minor operation. I remember him telling me to fix my eye on a spot in the ceiling and not to move that focal point a fraction even when it disappeared as his head intervened, otherwise the knife could remove a bit of my eye. I consider I was very lucky because after a couple of days with a Nelson eye-patch I was back to normal.

We fitted plummer-blocks and made bearing housings to suit the layout of the sprockets within the frame-work of the machine, but because the gear train was running horizontally the chains would fly off the sprockets from time to time. This problem was overcome by the purchase of three more sprockets (Mr. Gratzer did say we could have as many as we wanted!), and fitting them to spring loaded bearing housings to take up any slack as the chains stretched with use. Nev or Don found a self-centring two jaw chuck which was ideal in principal for the device we needed to hold the glass tube (about a metre in length) but unfortunately it would not close down sufficiently in diameter. It was mounted on a steel tube with another tube inside effecting the opening and closing of the jaws. Using the chuck as a pattern, each part was sketched and dimensions calculated to produce a smaller replica. As the majority of the work to be done on the chucks was to be on the lathe, I opted to make the two identical chucks whilst Nev and Don designed and fashioned two pillars that carried the necessary gas jets complete with levers that swung the flames on and off the glass at the appropriate times.

I had asked for and been granted a week's holiday pending my marriage and it duly arrived. The girls in the factory organised a 'whip-round' with which they bought Josie and me a set of table mats. It was most kind and considerate of them as I had only known them a matter of weeks and once again revealed how the underprivileged share each others pleasures (as well as their sorrows). Invitations had long since been sent out and replies received, mostly favouring witnessing our union. George, my best man, had been briefed as regards my new 'digs' as Mrs. Jones had taken a holiday and I had to move to another house (not very far away). Leaving the factory on the Friday afternoon I felt no twinge of conscience at handing over my share of the responsibility of dealing with all the teething troubles that surely must come with putting the ampoule-making machine into operation - my thoughts were with Josie and her concern for her big day because it had rained every single day of that week and the forecast for the weekend was not exciting. Friday night was not my 'stag' night as such events were not really in fashion then plus the fact that I hadn't had time to make friends in Chester and in any case I was teetotaller, so a little time was spent with Josie and her Mum introducing them to George and finalising any details for the next day.

In defiance of the weather forecast the dawn erupted in brilliant sunshine which thankfully lasted the whole of the day. (The previous week's rain proved to be quite expensive as the flowers -not many were imported in those early post-war days - were costly, the red roses, of which there were a dozen in Josie's bouquet, had cost the florist half a crown each he told us, and the delphiniums in good condition for the bridesmaid's sheaves had been difficult to find). That Saturday morning, June 12th 1948 was for me a strange one because, usually having something positive to do, I found myself with nothing to occupy myself apart from seeing to my ablutions with particular attention being paid to having a close shave and trimming the moustache, followed by getting into my morning suit. (No doubt a dab of Brylcream was applied in case of a breeze spring up to ruin my coiffure). George and I reminisced about our schoolboy days but strangely we did not talk about our Forces experiences - he had spent three years on a French corvette mostly in the Med - and I am still waiting to hear of his adventures! During this period of inactivity on my part in other parts of the city there were scenes of feverish exercises. Custom forbade me calling at Woodville (now No.23) and I don't suppose for a second that I could have eased any problems there had I called.

George, my best man

Josie's dad and mum

Dad, Josie, Mum and author

Coming from Manchester was Tom, Josie's brother, accompanied by his wife Hilda - on his way to give Josie away; and in another car from the same city was Marie, Josie's eldest sister, her husband Harry, nursing the bottom tier of the Wedding Cake on his lap. (Heaven knows where he found someone who could find the ingredients to make a three tier wedding cake in those days of stringent rationing, and someone who hadn't lost the art of sugar icing decoration). The couple with the shortest distance to travel was Hilda, Josie's youngest sister (ten years her senior) and her husband George, who had but to put on their finery and park their two children. They lived in Chester. Some lived in the Wirral and others in the outer reaches of Liverpool, one of whom was Vincent - a cousin of Josie. Vincent had been enrolled to act as an usher at the Church and performed this role dressed in a morning suit as were the rest of the male principles in this ceremony. He was soon to change this 'uniform' for that of Holy Orders for he became a Jesuit Brother later that year, his brother Peter becoming a Jesuit Priest a little later on. In all the years that followed, whenever Vincent's name was brought into conversation, Josie very rarely failed to bring to memory how he not only excelled in his duties at the Church but displayed remarkable initiative in putting the gifts on display so that guests could see them all to advantage after the reception. He managed this virtually single handed despite the confusion that must have been taking place - the frequent interruption of kindly neighbours leaving gifts for Josie (and the man of her choice) who they had seen growing up from childhood - the setting out of cups and saucers for the countless cups of tea that would have been dispensed to callers.

Whilst he was attending to this I can well imagine Josie's Mum (who from that day on I always addressed as 'Ma') with interminable questions like, 'Do you think we've got enough milk and sugar? Has anyone put a new tablet of soap in the bathroom? Is there a spare toilet roll in the lavatory?'

As the people from Manchester, Liverpool and the Wirral made their way to Chester others from the Black Country had gathered in force and (unbeknown to the Mayor and Aldermen of this good city) were already putting into effect the plans for their invasion in no uncertain fashion. My Mum and Dad had arranged (without my knowledge) to hire a charabanc (they are called coaches today) to bring relatives and friends from Cradley Heath. Some on foot and some with the aid of the Midland Red Bus Company made their way to the appointed venue at Cradley Heath, coming from Old Hill, Cradley, Stourbridge, Quarry Bank and Dudley Wood, all intent on blessing one of their own with their company on the occasion of his wedding. The chara' stopped outside Woodville to allow Mum and Dad and Betty to alight, Mum and Dad to meet Josie's Mum for the first time and Betty to change into her bridesmaids' dress. On went the chara' to the Church (St. Werburgh's) and parked outside, (there were no double yellow lines in those days and as the one way system had not yet been devised the road to the Church was a side road and carried little traffic) where the travellers alighted and no doubt took advantage of the aesthetic pleasures offered by Grosvenor Park, the entrance to which is less than fifty yards away.

 The sunshine was brilliant as it should be in June and as the guests were bringing to an end their saunter in the park or that stroll along the Rows, George and I set out by taxi to the long awaited appointment. There were no external signs of activity as we passed Woodville and we arrived with ten minutes to spare. It seemed to be a long ten minutes and I was delighted that Josie was prompt although it seems almost obligatory that the bride is a little late (Punctuality is the sign of princes). She stepped confidently along the aisle on her brother's arm looking absolutely ravishing. What a pity that we didn't have weddings that lasted three days like the Indians do - it seemed such a shame that she would be in that finery for just a few hours. Father Fraser, who had been pacing back and forth across the altar for a few minutes prior to Josie's arrival took command and proceeded with the wedding ceremony, admitting to us at a later date that this was his first wedding and that he had probably felt more nervous than either of us.

When I was receiving instructions I had been told that accepting the married state meant accepting that the altar was an area out of bounds - in fact out of bounds to all the laity except for men or boys when serving Mass or for the ladies attending to the replenishment of altar cloths and polishing of candlesticks etc., the one exception being when invited to enter that area during the wedding ceremony. How things have now changed. Nowadays men and women dispense the Eucharist and children are invited to read out mini-homilies from the altar.

Josie and I stepped into that sanctum to take our vows, to take them and mean them, knowing in our hearts that this really was a marriage made in heaven. There were no hitches - nothing at all went wrong - George had the ring safely in his waistcoat pocket - neither Josie or I hesitated, stammered, mumbled or made a display of ourselves by fainting, weeping or laughing. After Father Fraser had pronounced us 'man and wife' we followed him to the vestry to sign and have witnessed the document that declared the fact that we were now one. This gave the congregation the opportunity to look around and admire the magnificence of the Church; the beautiful stained glass windows, the magnificent crucifix, the bas-relief of the Stations of the Cross, the delicately sculpted marble pulpit (presented by Pat Collins, the fairground owner).

Looking back I see no justification in feeling nervous as we walked up the central aisle, as Josie in her finery would be the centre of attraction. However, I did feel nervous and I remember the photographer, taking our pictures on the steps of the Church saying, 'Come on, let's have a smile' to which I replied 'This is a serious occasion'. I am pleased to say that the happiness of the occasion eventually pervaded my thoughts and I did manage to come up with some smiles.

The reception at the Queen Hotel went according to plan, the clergy being well represented as Josie's Mum had kindly invited both Father Fraser and Father Byrne as well as the budding Jesuit Brother, Vincent.

What happened after the reception apart from our departure for our honeymoon in Devon I can only quote from hearsay.

Betty, Author, Josie, George and Margaret
(Tom and Marie in the background)

'Ma' was put into a bit of a fluster when the coach pulled up outside Woodville and the Black Country guests came to take a peek at the presents (and a look at my future abode) and was heard to say 'All these people coming here and I don't know a single one of them!'. Following their visit to see the gifts, they all got aboard the chara' and off they went to the Groves, that pleasant little area alongside the river and to a man embarked on a trip up the river on one of the 'steamers'. Altogether they all seemed to have enjoyed the outing and at a date much later I was so pleased to hear my Uncle Wilf, when describing Josie's Mum, say 'She was just like a queen'.

They all returned safely to the midlands having witnessed the end of my courtship - and that is where I must end my story.

And to think; it all started with me taking a couple of aspirin tablets and a mug of tea instead of going to the cinema!